SCREENWRITING
for Narrative Film and Television

SCREENWRITING for Narrative Film and Television

WILLIAM MILLER

VIRGIN

This edition published in 1991 by
Virgin Publishing
338 Ladbroke Grove
London W10 5AH

First published in Great Britain in 1988 by
Columbus Books Limited

British Library Cataloguing in Publication Data
Miller, William Charles.
Screenwriting for narrative film and television.
1. Cinema films. Television programmes. Scripts. Composition
I. Title.
808'.066

ISBN 0-86287-419-X

Printed and bound by
Mackays of Chatham Limited

Contents

Introduction

Give me a good script and I'll be a hundred times better as a director.[1]

—George Cukor

I HAVE A FAIR NUMBER of screenplays on my bookshelves: published copies by Fellini, Antonioni, Bergman, a copy of *Citizen Kane,* some Marx Brothers filmscripts, teleplays for *All in the Family, Maude,* scripts for *Barney Miller, CBS reports, The Birds, Five Easy Pieces, The Sting* and others. Each resulted in a finished film or program which was appreciated by millions of viewers. Each was conceived and developed by a screenwriter. So I find it puzzling that the screenwriter is so often the forgotten man in filmmaking. In the sumptuous panoply of contemporary film criticism, the writer has been shunted to the side much as a slightly embarrassing distant relative at a formal reunion, while the director has been enshrined as the august *auteur.* The writer's situation is no better in television, which matches the neglect by theorists and critics with its disconcerting approach to production. In television, as often as not, producers, directors, network executives, and standards and practices censors each hack at the writer's script until the result is some strange and often unrecognizable bastardization. Maybe this is why so many writers have the reputation of indulging in a drink or two . . . or three. Still, the pay is rather decent, and I suspect that most console themselves with frequent trips to

[1] George Cukor as quoted in Pauline Kael, "Circles and Squares," *I Lost it at the Movies* (New York: Bantam Books, 1965) p. 275.

the bank and wistful dreams of better worlds. And occasionally one will cleverly retort, as when Robert Riskin handed director Frank Capra a sheaf of blank paper bound as if it were a script and challenged, "Here, give *that* the Capra touch."[2]

I think this situation is changing and that we will soon have a critical reevaluation of the screenwriter and his contribution to the completed film. The narrative story is an intrinsic part of the feature film as we know it. Behind narrative screenwriting lies centuries of dramatic theory and tradition plus newer techniques intrinsic to the film and television media. Some critics seem to have the notion that the writer's work is more literary and less cinematic (whatever that may mean). They don't understand that a screenwriter works primarily with images, not words, and that the film appears first—to some degree or another—in the writer's imagination. We need now to recognize the importance of the writer's vision and his contribution—in story and structure, in character and its development, in theme and tone and style. In the real world of film and television production, there has never been any question of the value of a good script.

Screenwriting is tremendously exciting. The excitement is in working in film, as lively and stimulating a contemporary art as there is, and in the pervasive and promising medium of television. A friend who writes television shows expressed this feeling one evening when he said, with a sense of wonderment, how staggering it is to realize that something he created was being seen and enjoyed by twenty to thirty *million* people!

I'm always amused when I hear it authoritatively declared that "you can't teach writing," as though it is some esoteric mystery more appropriate to the archives of a Tibetan monastery or the Rosicrucians. Not so. Writing is a craft with appropriate techniques and guidelines that can be studied and mastered. True, it does require a certain basic competence. You need a minimum intelligence of some sort, and the acquired skill of presenting ideas, characters and story in an interesting and meaningful fashion. I like to think that you need to know how to write a coherent sentence, although this ability seems to be increasingly waning among students. Most importantly, you need an imaginative perception of people and the world. If you've got this, you'll learn from what I've written here.

There's a limitation to this book, which bothers me. While narrative—storytelling—film and television dominates what we see on the screens, other voices are challenging this dominance. Marxist, feminist, and third-world critics and filmmakers are calling for a reevaluation of the traditional "Hollywood" product and demanding a new, revolutionary cinema to replace it, they call for a cinema that is less captive not only to capitalistic, bourgeois methods of production and distribution, but also to the way that dominant ideology is

[2] Screenwriter David Giler relates this anecdote in William Froug, *The Screenwriter Looks at the Screenwriter* (New York: Delta/Dell, 1972), p. 222. But I've also read it about two people other than Riskin and Capra. This may well be just one of those Hollywood stories.

presently expressed—through formal filmic principles of audience identification with characters and immersion in a dramatic, fiction narrative. I recognize the commendable impulse motivating their concern as well as some measure of validity in their argument (but only some). Nevertheless, I don't see an immediate viable alternative to narrative cinema and television. At least there is nothing that can immediately replace our present approaches or that can be formalized as I've done here with narrative film. Their arguments at present are more like a theory in search of a practice.

The narrative film still beguiles us as the dramatic narrative has since the times of Sophocles, Aeschylus and Euripides and from even earlier shadow memories of figures gathered attentively around cave firesides. We like a story, even as we like to see ourselves in our myths. And aren't the mass media our great contemporary mythmakers?

I've given many examples both to illustrate my points and to provide a sense of the range of possibilities available to you from which you may draw your own conclusions. I encourage you to look for your own examples. See what has been done in order to realize the options that you can use in your own writing.

Many of the examples are from films that are readily available through rental distributors or that are frequently shown on television. The television series referred to are generally viewable as syndicated reruns or as current series. Some of the film examples are available as published screenplays.

Rather than continually repeat the phrase "film and television program," I've decided to use "film" as a simpler shorthand term when both media are meant. Similarly, what is said of "screenplay" can generally be read as also applying to "teleplay."

A difficult decision was to use the ecumenical pronouns "he, him, his" in a unisex fashion to refer to both/either male and female. I do so with apologies and the regret that there is no convenient neutral alternative.

—WCM
March, 1980

1

Creator and Craftsman

> Before I met Don Juan I would spend years sharpening my pencils, and then getting a headache every time I sat down to write. Don Juan taught me that's stupid. If you want to do something, do it impeccably, and that's all that matters.[1]*
>
> —Carlos Castaneda

WRITING IS a very demanding profession. Sitting at the typewriter for hours on end requires a self-imposed discipline that doesn't come easily. In spite of those extraordinary individuals we read of now and again who turn out a pulp novel every two weeks, most writers find the process of writing very difficult. Coming up with ideas is hard enough, but then working them out on paper with just you and the typewriter can seem to rival the labors of Hercules. But when it works, when a scene takes off and crystalizes just so, or a character does some extraordinary and beautiful thing, at that moment there's a deep satisfaction not unlike giving birth. In this act of creation the writer is the creator, so it's appropriate to begin by looking at what we know about the process of creation and how we might use it to develop our own experience of creativity.

Creativity has been a ripe area for study over the past few decades. A raft of books and articles have been published about it and a number of workshops and college courses have appeared to help develop creativity—I've taught some myself. But it's difficult to deal with something as personal and unconscious as creativity. Often a student is presented a number of exercises, such as those suggested later, to stimulate the imagination. They probably do some good,

*Footnotes are listed as references at the end of each chapter.

especially if they show us that we can be freely imaginative and more trusting in the products of our imagination. Education has a nasty way of undercutting our faith in our own inner wisdom, and courses like this help right the balance. Still, as we approach a study of creativity, let's realize how hazy our understanding of it is. The exercises suggested won't work for everyone. They won't work at all unless you really get into them in a positive way. They are like catalysts, which you can use to teach yourself what is involved in freeing your own creative energies. The studies of creativity can give us some guideposts for that discovery.

The Creative Process

It is convenient to look at the creative process as broken down into a number of stages, which seem to occur as step one, step two, and so on, but the steps really intermingle in some complex ways so that we may have a number of stages operating at the same time while we are working out a script idea. The stages are preparation, unconscious incubation, the moment of inspiration, getting it down on paper, and critical revision. Let's see how these work in practice by imagining a writer going through the process.

Our imaginary screenwriter has had sufficient *preparation* before he begins. He's educated enough to know his way around words. At least he is able to spell them decently and to place them into sentences in a reasonable and interesting fashion. He's also knowledgeable about the medium and its techniques. He's developed the ability to think in terms of visual images, since images, not words, are the basic units of screenwriting. He's learned the script vocabulary to translate these images to the page (CU, MS, LS and so on). He's rather sensitive to himself and the inner journey he's made to become the person he now is. He's similarly perceptive of others and of their uniquenesses. He's tuned to the world around him—to its social problems, inequities, joys and follies. He's done concrete research about the world. He's studied locations, people and institutions. He's developed an ear for dialogue and the unique ways that people communicate, both verbally and non-verbally. All of these have been the long-term preparation to make him a creative screenwriter.

However, the preparation stage has a more specific application to the film he's now writing. It refers to that time he's spent involving himself in the first thoughts about the script and the initial ideas and vague hunches he's entertained and the notes he's taken when something strikes him as a possible idea to be developed later. He's done a lot of thinking about what he wants to write, about the characters he'd like in the story and about how he sees them. His pockets contain little memos he's scribbled about a character or a line of development. Other notes are scattered around the house. Some of these will be elaborated or modified and take form in the finished script. Others will be dismissed with barely a glance. At times he's expanded his notes into pages of longhand sketches of scenes or character descriptions or plot outlines. If he's doing an adaptation, it means he's carefully read the original work and taken notes on it. If he's writing for a television series, then he's studied the series well so that he knows its style, characters and story parameters. If he's working with a producer or story editor, he's hashed over their expectations in some initial story conferences. In sum, he's done his preparatory work and has some idea of what he wants to do. If we keep in mind that the stages of the creative process are not so neatly divided and much of what we're about to describe has already been going on, then we can say our writer is ready for stage two.

If we didn't understand what was happening, we'd be very puzzled by the *incubation* stage. Our writer seems to be doing nothing! Well, not really nothing. He putters around the house doing things with his hands in an absent sort of way, perhaps even humming a little to himself. He doesn't talk very much, or read or watch television. He keeps pretty much to himself. He takes long walks, especially at night when no one's around. And he doesn't write. This can be very irritating to those around him who wonder why he isn't working (our puritan work ethic is deeply engrained). It isn't always as peaceful as this for him either. He often has periods of tension and frustration as he tries to force the writing but nothing comes. If he doesn't understand the importance of an incubation period, it can be a difficult time for him indeed. Even if he realizes how important it is to let ideas simmer in his unconscious, he's nagged with a bit of doubt, since there's a thin line between productive gestation and wasteful procrastination. Part of what it means to be a professional writer is being able to incorporate the incubation process into your working regimen in a productive way.

The incubation stage is most intriguing, since it's so mysterious and elusive. It's the period during which the unconscious organizes into meaningful form those ideas we've been developing in our conscious thinking. There's a great deal of evidence that this is what happens even though we don't know exactly how it happens. We're not even quite sure what the "unconscious" is. However, this shouldn't bother us if we use it to refer to an activity, that, like dreams, goes on in our brain outside of our regular consciousness. The connection of conscious thought to sleep and dreaming gives partial evidence of the work of the unconscious. It's quite common to struggle with a problem—anything from math homework to a plot development that isn't working out—and then go to sleep on it only to wake the next morning with the answer. "You've" worked out the answer while you were sleeping, but the "you" is the unconscious you. We don't know how it happens, but it happens. When we turn off our conscious thinking, our unconscious is able to take over and do some rather remarkable things. It's the source of tremendous creative energy.

This process doesn't just go on while we sleep. It frequently happens just as we fall asleep and enter that twilight state between sleep and waking, which is called the hypnagogic—characterized by theta brain waves, imagistic thinking and mystery. This is a prime period for getting ideas. Every writer should keep a pen and paper beside his bed to jot down any inspirational ideas that come just as he's falling asleep, or he may lose them. The temptation is to say to yourself that you'll remember them in the morning and go on to sleep. Don't. It doesn't seem to work that way. If you don't write it down, the chances are it won't be available in the morning.

This doesn't mean that incubation is only associated with sleeping. Any time you put your conscious mind to the side, you facilitate the working of the unconscious. It's as though the unconscious can't be active if the conscious is filled with busy things—watching television, reading, talking or doing any sort of consciously involved thinking. After looking into the activities of creative people, Dorothea Brande[2] concluded that creativity is most encouraged by doing things that are rhythmic, monotonous and silent. These would have the effect of tuning down the conscious so that the unconscious can proceed with its mysterious yet essential work.

How long does the process go on? How long must an idea simmer in the unconscious before it emerges ready to be written? Of course the answer is as long as the unconscious needs to do its work, but that's not very helpful if you're staring at a deadline. One of Wagner's operas took years to incubate, but then he wasn't fighting a production schedule. The big ideas for our story and characters or for the development of a major scene may need to gestate for days or weeks. When we're writing and things seem to reach an impasse, it may be time to knock off for a while, perhaps to take a walk while things sort themselves out. This is a good way to treat the so-called "writer's block." Get away from it for a bit—maybe even for a couple of days—to give the unconscious a chance to work through the block. (In a sense, the incubation process goes on continually during the process of writing itself as a sort of dialogue between our conscious and unconscious, as ideas flow back and forth, forming and re-forming with only minutes or even seconds of incubation.)

We can make the incubation process work more effectively for us by understanding its importance in our creative thinking and by setting up conditions under which it best operates. We might take walks or find those wordless, monotonous and silent activities that invite the creative state. It all sounds pretty mystifying, but it really isn't. Once experienced, you'll have a rather good idea of what it feels like. Unconscious activity is an integral part of the creative process; we all go through it even though we aren't always aware of it. For the professional writer, it's part of his working routine. Now let's follow him into the next stage.

Our writer has been dreamingly musing about his story idea in a relaxed way while his unconscious goes about its work. Then suddenly the whole thing comes together and pops into his head in a flash of illumination. It's the moment of *inspiration*. Eureka, he has found it! The muse has arrived. The work of the unconscious leaps into the conscious with a burst of insight. Sometimes it is just as dramatic as this. At other times there is just the low-key feeling that it's now time to begin setting things down on paper. Either way, the connection has been made.

Now our writer enters the stage where he *gets it down on paper*. He sits at the typewriter and works. Some prefer to write these early drafts in longhand and type later. A few of the more affluent dictate into a tape recorder and have a secretary transcribe it. The important thing is to get it down. The moment of inspiration is something like opening the floodgates of the unconscious—everything comes pouring out in a rush. The writer needs to let all of this flow freely and spontaneously. It's going to be a mixture of words, images and ideas—some good, some not so good. But this is not the time to start severely judging the output, or it can choke off the creative flow. This doesn't mean writing a stream-of-consciousness garble. You'll write sensibly, but you'll set your major critical sense off to the side for a while so that it won't inhibit the current from the unconscious. At this stage, let the emphasis be on keeping the flow going and getting it all down. It might be an entire story outline, or some crucial character scenes or the final act of a teleplay. Or it might be only a few key lines of dialogue or a decisive story point that had been hanging up the story. Our imaginary writer had a good time of it. He sketched out a fifteen-page outline.

The last stage in the creative process is that of *critical revision*. This is when what's been written is critically evaluated, revised and reworked. The unconscious mind has been likened to a creative child—marvelously imaginative, but also capricious and very much in need of the discipline of rational judgment. "Scripts aren't written, they're rewritten" is an old Hollywood maxim. We'll leave our imaginary writer now as he sits pen in hand assessing the effectiveness of what he's written. He marks out, scribbles margin notes on things to be changed, becomes involved in the whole process again as he thinks of an alternative for something that doesn't work and prepares to be back at the typewriter soon, pounding out the revision.

Every writer will use the creative process in his own individual way. There are still a few things to be said about it to make it more accessible, such as what does it feel like to be in a creative mood? Again, granting that there will be a wide range of differences between individuals, we can make some generalizations. There's a paradox about it. It involves both tension and relaxation at the same time. There's a feeling of heightened awareness. Distractions are shut out. There's an intensity in your concentration. Often the tension is seen in nervous mannerisms—jiggling the knees or tapping a pencil or endlessly sipping a beverage while at the typewriter. If out for a walk, the energy naturally goes into the rhythm of the movement, which should be easy and unhurried, more a stroll than a stride. But along with the tension goes a relaxation—sometimes physical but more often and most especially mental. The mind is held in *relaxed awareness* so that ideas can flow in and through it. When the creative flow is at its best, there's a certain effortlessness and spontaneity about it. It just seems to come naturally. A feeling of confidence accompanies it, for you know you're working effectively. In all, it's a great feeling.

In the early stages of writing a script, it's important to get as many ideas going about the story as possible. If you're too quick to judge an idea and reject it, you can miss something. The early notions we get about a script are often samples from the unconscious—incomplete bits that represent a certain stage of our unconscious thinking. If they're rejected, it can cut off the process. Keep them around, and they may surface again and again in modified form until something useful comes out. If something you jot down as a note doesn't appear valuable at the time, it may later tie in with something else in an unexpected way. These first ideas you get about a script don't necessarily come whole cloth; rather, they are bits and pieces which you don't want to lose until you're certain they aren't needed. This is why it's so important to avoid being critical in the early stages of work. Be open to anything. Be almost childlike in your innocence of acceptance. There's a reason why an idea comes to you. Keep it around long enough to find out what that reason is. Explore it long enough to see where it takes you. Then if you have to leave it, let it go. Sometimes the initial impulse for a script—a scene or a story point—becomes superfluous as the script develops in a different direction. It's hard to give up that initial idea even though it no longer fits. But if later critical evaluation convinces you that it no longer belongs, eliminate it.

Saying that it's important to be open to your ideas is like saying that you must have a certain amount of faith in yourself. It's the conviction that you can write something decent if you are willing to work at it. The key is that you're willing to work at it until you've mastered the necessary skills. You should recognize that this will take time and effort. You must accept the fact that there's a lot to learn about screenwriting. In spite of the number of poorly written television programs that we can view on any given night, it isn't as easy as it looks. A friend was recently made story editor of a television adventure series. Commenting on the poor quality of scripts he's reviewed, he said that any of my students could do better. Well, they tried. We had a special course to write something for that series. And, although this was not one of the more quality series on television, the students found how very difficult it was to come up with even one workable script idea. If as a beginning writer you realize that you have much to learn, you'll be less likely to set yourself up for a letdown by thinking that if your first scripts aren't masterpieces they must be useless flops.

Getting ideas is a problem only if you aren't getting any, and then it can be a vexing problem indeed. If you're a professional writer and stuck for ideas, you can tag it a writer's block and try to wait it out until the juices flow again. If you're a student in a writing class, you've got a different kind of deadline problem with your course grade in the balance. How do you come up with an idea? Sometimes it seems the well is very, very dry.

But look. How many years have you been around as a thinking and feeling human being? How many emotions have you experienced? How many joys?

fears? romances, real or fantasied? How many peak experiences have you enjoyed or depth experiences endured? Somewhere in all of that isn't there something that would suggest a story idea? We're all on this spaceship earth together and what we've felt in our deepest recesses are similar for all of us. Yet we've each felt with our own unique and individual perceptions. There's something in your perception which you can share to illuminate mine. What moves you? What are you concerned about? Is there a story around that? What of the people you've known? Couldn't they serve as the basis for a character or two? Imagine someone you find intriguing in a certain situation. How would that person act if . . . ? And you supply the "if."

See if what you know about the creative process and some of the additional suggestions you'll read in this chapter can't help if you're really stuck for an idea.

Whatever ideas you finally evolve, let them be an honest expression of yourself rather than an imitation of the once-removed reality of television or film. This is hard to do, since we've all been so steeped in television that its myths have invariably colored our view of the world, especially during those susceptible years of our childhood. It's easy to get trapped into drawing characters and situations from media stereotypes rather than from our own imagination and experience. And for a beginning writer, it's very important that he discover what he has to say. That's why in my beginning classes I avoid having students write for existing television series and their set characters. It's too stifling.

If you're really serious about being a screenwriter, then you're going to have to invest your time and energy into becoming one. It will be something that takes a good part of your life. The discipline of writing—of actually sitting down at the typewriter and working—is the other side of the coin to the incubating evening walks. It's the grain of truth in the old saw about creativity being 10 percent inspiration and 90 percent perspiration. Such a consistent commitment to actually doing it doesn't come easily. There are all sorts of fears involved with putting the words and images on paper. What if they're no good? What are other people going to think? There's a lot of you going into that writing, and it can make you feel exposed and vulnerable. Besides that, writing something as long as a film script, and rewriting it again and again, is hard work. But if you find that you have difficulty in getting started, you can take some comfort in realizing that you are not alone. It's a common feeling for writers. They get very adept at thinking up all sorts of excuses to avoid the typewriter. There's always something around the house that needs fixing, or the car needs some attention or there's that friend you haven't seen in so long . . . and isn't there a good film on television tonight? Any of those ought to be good for a postponement of a few hours, and with any luck you can stretch it out for another day. If nothing else, there's always the typewriter that needs cleaning. But who are we kidding? It may take a certain amount of ritual puttering to get in the right frame of mind to begin writing, but beyond this it becomes the nagging procrastination that so many writers know about. Deadlines are a godsend for many of us; they force us to turn out the work. The bottom line is that if you're going to be a professional writer, you have to discipline yourself to a regular habit of writing.

To get this habit going, it's good practice to sit at the typewriter at definite, scheduled periods for four or five days a week. If in the beginning you have to just sit there staring at an empty piece of paper, then do that. But try to get something down. Read over the last page or two to see if that doesn't stimulate things. Some writers begin work by rereading everything they wrote the previous day. You might try retyping the last page or paragraph from the previous writing session. This may smooth up some of its rough spots as well as spur you to keep going. Whatever works best, do it. Because when it's time to do the writing, it just has to be done. And nothing takes the place of conscientiously developed, disciplined working habits.

If the thought of a full-length script is staggering, it might help to start by setting a series of small goals for each day's work. This might be a scene or two, or so many pages. The amount of work writers actually turn out each day varies considerably. Hour television programs have been written over a weekend—a very busy weekend. But this is rare. Six to a dozen pages a day is a decent bit of work. In the beginning, it might be considerably more than this as you're getting down the idea flow. But when polishing a final version, six to twelve is a respectable output.

The best time to work will vary from writer to writer, although early morning or late evening have been traditionally preferred. The best environment in which to work is the one that presents the fewest distractions. Someone once suggested that a writer should work by a large window that opens on a brick wall.

When you're enjoying that marvelous excitement that comes as the story is developing well, there's a temptation to share your ideas with friends. It's a natural impulse, but one best resisted. It's too easy to talk away a script idea instead of writing it. And you never seem to get the exact response that you want from others. Soon your motivation drains away, and you're not working so well. It's really best not to talk too much about the script while working on it. Let wellwishers wait until it's finished before they see it.

You can learn much of the technique of screenwriting by watching films and television in ways suggested by the examples in this book, that is, as a writer. Take a step back from your usual involvement in the film and see it as it was originally conceived and developed by the writer. Learn to identify the different storylines in the narrative and to trace their development from scene to scene. Take the film apart and restructure it as it was originally written. You'll pick up those moments of characterization when we're brought closer to the reality of a character. And you'll notice the way the writer builds effective suspense, prepares us for later developments and smoothly works in exposition so that we aren't too aware of it. Of course you'll also see a great deal of poor writing, but that's part of the fun. Comic devices are a delight to identify. You let out a laugh at something—now think back and analyze what it was that made you laugh, what made it funny? Begin to listen to dialogue, not as words spoken by seemingly real characters, but as dialogue conceived by a writer. You might even imagine this dialogue as it appeared written down the center of a page in the screenplay. Most of the time we willingly suspend disbelief and immerse ourselves in the fantasy world of the film. This is how we've come to enjoy our media. But when you look at it as a writer, you demythologize the experience by not only viewing it as a staged production but by going a step earlier to see it as a designed, imagined and written conception.

Developing Creativity

Our discussion of creativity would be more useful if it were possible to somehow make the process more accessible to us. If we could only systematize it in some way, then we could work with it. There have been a number of such attempts. In theater, Stanislavski developed a training method for the actor. His exercises were designed to release the unconscious creative power of the actor.[3] But there's a nagging doubt when we start to do similar things for the writer. The creativity of writing may be too elusive to permit us to capture it with a set of imagination exercises. On the other hand, we may be in the position of nineteenth-century pre-Stanislavski actors, who had no concept of the possibility of such a systematic approach to their poetic calling. The model of actor training—with its theater games and sensitivity encounters—is a venturesome one for writers. Still, we may yet move toward a more consistent approach to utilizing our unconscious creative forces. The exercises suggested here are some steps in that direction; they are drawn from theater, from creativity workshops and from a slim volume, long out of print, by Dorothea Brande,[2] whose innovative imagination has my appreciation.

Undertake any exercise with the expectation that it will work for you if you give it a wholehearted try. Explore it fully, and then let it lead you into other imaginative places. These things work best if you can follow the direction of your own inner leanings. If you try but can't really get into a particular exercise, accept that it isn't something that you can work with right now and go on to something else.

Morning Inspiration

The unconscious is apt to be accessible in those preconscious moments between sleep and waking. There isn't much we can do with this at night except try to scribble down a few ideas before we drift off to sleep. But maybe we can catch that morning period when we're not quite asleep and not quite awake. So allow some extra time in the morning—a half hour up to an hour. Immediately upon awakening—without talking with anyone or doing anything that is not an absolute necessity—go to pen or typewriter and begin to write. Write whatever comes into your head as automatically and uncritically as possible. Let whatever wants to come out flow down on paper. It may be any sort of morning reverie, snatches of a dream or anything whatever that may be there. Write rapidly and without judgment. Only you will read this, so there's no need to worry about what another might think of it. Now, this is important—don't reread any of what you have written. Not a page nor a paragraph. For then you will be tempted to start evaluating it. Just let it flow out. Try to write a reasonable amount. A paragraph is too little; a few pages would be useful. When you've finished for the morning, set it aside somewhere safe and out of the way, still without reading it. Do this each morning for a week or two, trying each day to increase both the time spent writing and the output. It would be helpful to double the number of pages within a week so that there's a substantial amount of material available for later analysis. Continue putting aside each day's writing without reading it. If the process is working, those pages will contain material strongly formed by the unconscious. After a week or two of this, you can analyze what's there. But before giving some guidelines for the analysis, there's a second exercise that you might want to try at the same time. You could then analyze both together.

Writing to Schedule

This is a possible exercise to use any time you have something to write; it will help you develop the consistent writing habit of a professional writer. However, we'll treat it as though you have no particular project in mind but wish only to use it to discover ideas and style.

Begin sometime in the morning—such as when you're relaxing over breakfast—and review the coming events of your day. Then pick a time during the day when you will commit yourself to write. (This can be a different time each day.) A half-hour would be sufficient time; fifteen minutes should be an absolute minimum. Once you have set the specific time, consider it a debt of honor to stick to. If you've made your commitment for 5:00 to 5:30, when 5:00 comes, seat yourself at the typewriter. If this sounds inflexible, it's meant to be. You must be a tyrant in rigidly allowing yourself no exceptions, even if it means excusing yourself from friends or other pleasures. Discipline is the purpose of the exercise, to discipline the creative unconscious, which is full of marvelous ideas and excitement but rebellious against rules and control. It's necessary to take this free spirit in hand and put him to work for us. This may not come easily. Brande goes so far as to say that if you fail repeatedly at this exercise, you should give up writing, because your resistance is greater than your desire to write. But, if you keep at it, you will soon find that you are beginning to write with fluency and control.

If you are using this process to discover more about your writing, then write freely rather than on a particular project. Don't give too much thought to what comes out (but don't expect the very personal outpouring of the morning writing). This might be a good time to explore story ideas or character sketches. If you have difficulty coming up with ideas, write about that. This work can also be placed aside, unread.

A good way to do this writing is in the third-person present-tense form of a screenplay, describing only what can be seen or heard on the screen. It would still be in a narrative mode, but it would be the narrative of that which could be seen or heard by an audience.

After a few weeks of writing on schedule (as well as in the morning), it's now time to bring out all those unread papers to see what can be learned from them.

There will be a certain exhilaration in holding those pages in your hand and wondering what they contain. There may also be some trepidation about their unknown quantities. This is a time to pull the ego back from the evaluation in order to better discover what's there. Set aside ambitions, fears and preconceptions and instead adopt a detached attitude toward the material, as though you were examining the work of a stranger and wished to discover the tastes and talents of this unknown writer.

Make the first reading a quick one to gain an overall impression. Then go back and do a more detailed reading. Avoid the tendency to be overly critical; look for positive things on which to build future writing rather than for negative things. There are all sorts of things to be learned from these exercises. Look for subjects and themes that could be developed into more complete stories, especially noting those that suggest, by repeated recurrence, that they have special meaning for you. Are there any striking images or metaphors that could be expanded further? What can you discern about the style? Any patterns or rhythms here? Anything striking about the tone—comic, lyrical, ironic, fantastic, desperate, ponderous, cynical? Are there any people in the writing who could be the bases for screen characters? Let's take that last question a step further and ask if there are any insights into character—including your own—that could form the dominant image or spine of a fictional character? These are only the most general suggestions for your analysis. What you should do is examine the pages to discover what they reveal about what you write and how you write it. Then you can take the clues and use them as you develop ideas into stories and screenplays.

Your analysis should emphasize the positive, but not only the positive. It can also indicate things in the writing that you can correct. Some frequent problems are writing that is too melodramatic and sensational—a legacy from the worst of television and film—or writing that is too superficial in its appeal to immature taste. Morning writing is often personal, symbolic and abstract, but if this dominates the scheduled writing as well, it could indicate the need to develop more of a sense of narrative as communication with an audience.

Some day's writing will be prolific and satisfying, while at other times, the well will seem dry. This might also be something to learn. What contributed to an effective writing period? Or a poor one? Was there anything in the course of either the day or the evening before, or the things you did at either time that might account for the difference? Are there any clues to the sorts of things that seem to turn you on and get your creative muse going, or things that turn the muse off?

A Creativity Microcosm

With what we know of the creative process, it would seem natural to try to concentrate on the process to speed it up. How much we can push something which ordinarily we should just let happen is uncertain. Like many of these suggestions, it works marvelously at times and not so well at others. It's certainly worth a try, especially when facing the problem of developing a simple idea into a useful film story.

Start with a basic idea which really hasn't been elaborated. Immerse yourself in the idea for a day or two. Begin to flesh it out by thinking of possible directions for the action and the characters without being too concrete with the development. Alternate between focusing conscious thought on it and musing about it in a sort of reverie state. Dream about it if you can. Then set a definite time and place two or three days in the future when you will sit down and write the idea into a full narrative story. Give charge to your unconscious to develop this story over the next few days. Then dismiss the idea from your conscious mind. Should you find yourself starting to think about it, put it out of your mind, for this is a time of concentrated incubation. The unconscious is aware of the deadline you've set; let it do its work toward that time.

When that day and time arrive, sit down and write. Work as rapidly as possible, letting it come easily and quickly with as little conscious attention as possible. Avoid reading what you're putting down. Keep at the work until you have achieved a complete narrative story outline—beginning, middle, end. You may be pleasantly surprised at the result.

Another Creativity Microcosm

Here is another way to try to accelerate the incubation period and develop a story or scene. It requires an uninterrupted period of three or four hours which you will spend working out an idea. An evening is a good time if there is nothing pressing happening later. Begin alone and away from distractions. Get into a relaxed, pleasant, indulgent mood. Maintaining this mood, review your story idea to yourself. Visualize any scenes you've imagined; visit with your characters and observe what happens with them. Do all this in a light, easy way, allowing things to come to you rather than struggling for them.

Then take the rough idea out for a walk. Begin the walk telling your unconscious to work out the story. Stroll at an easy, loafing pace while maintaining a mood of reverie or daydreaming. Avoid distractions. You are engrossed in your story but on the unconscious level. Don't be concerned about what you will be writing; let it work itself out. Walk until you are mildly tired, pacing yourself so that you've reviewed the story in a very leisurely way. Return neither too soon, nor too late when you've exhausted the idea to the extent that you're impatient about it.

When you've returned from the walk, relax. Take a warm bath if you desire. Continue in your light trance, your reverie state, avoiding distractions. Think of the story only in a desultory way, without consciously focusing on it. Relax in a dimly lit room, quieting both your mind and body. Be not quite fully awake, yet not drifting into sleep. Remain like this. Then after awhile—twenty minutes perhaps, or an hour, maybe even longer—you will feel a surge of energy impelling you to write. Don't force it; rather, permit it to come of itself. When it does come, go to the typewriter and write. The unconscious work has been coaxed and focused. Get down on paper what it's done.

Inviting Imagination

Stories spring from a fertile imagination. So do characters and images and sounds and ideas. There are things we can do to spur our imagination. Perhaps a better way to think of the task is as a series of new doors that we can open, allowing our imagination to move into areas it doesn't usually visit. We can begin by considering ways of opening the doors of our perception. Most of our perception is by habit. We observe a friend just enough to recognize him and to see that nothing as unusual as a black eye or new hair style graces (or disgraces) the familiar visage. So it is with most of our perceptions. We recognize just enough of our world to get by and little else. This isn't enough for a writer; we need to learn to see anew. There are many ways to describe this change. It means to dishabituate perception. We should see as if for the first time with the long-forgotten innocence of eye. It means noticing things that haven't been noticed before or that have for some time become the unnoticed or to become as a stranger in your own streets, to make the familiar unfamiliar so that it can be perceived anew. What can be done with the eye can also be done with the ear and the voice and sound. When is the last time you really listened to the sound of a friend's voice? It can also be done with smells and with touch, with temperature, and with the inner sounds of our own bodies.

There are all sorts of things to do with this process once you get it started. Imagine perceiving the most everyday events as though through the eyes of one of your characters. Or you might try it through the eyes of a person of the opposite sex, or of a repressed minority, or of a drunk on a binge, or of someone who is angry, of another who is frightened, or of the eyes of one planning a crime or . . . whatever you can come up with.

Have you ever tried turning yourself into an object of your own attention? Imagine observing yourself as from a camera located, say, a little above you and off to the side. How do you look doing even simple actions such as typing, entering a room, making a purchase, walking the streets, relaxing with friends? What do you look like right now? If you knew nothing of yourself, what would you learn about yourself if you were observing as that camera above you? How do you stand? Sit? Walk? Smile? Imagine yourself in a social situation. How do you relate to the people around you? How do you feel about them?

Body language is an entire dimension through which we reveal ourself. Kinesics and gestures are especially important in the way they define your characters. You can learn much by observing how people, including yourself, express or conceal themselves without words and how non-verbal behaviors elicit responses from you and others.

Did you ever try speculating about the lives of the strangers you observe every day while shopping, eating, traveling or working? What are they like? Where are they going? What for? What are they feeling? What secrets are they harboring? What adventures are they having? What would they be like as characters in a script?

Choose an episode from your day and see yourself approaching it, involved with the action and coming away from it. How might it have looked to a stranger?

Without using gestures, tell yourself, step by step, how you do some simple act such as combing your hair or brushing your teeth.

When performing such a simple act, do it as if you had to remember it in order to describe it afterward. Repeat it again, only this time in slow motion. Then repeat it at double normal speed. Perform it as different characters would. You might try it as a person in an imagined situation: about to accept an honor, going for a job interview, prior to a critical final exam or an important championship tennis match, before a big date, after having suffered a loss or on the verge of committing murder. How would this simple act feel in different settings: a grand hotel, a camping trip, on a sailboat, under combat conditions—or wherever else your active fantasy can take you.

There are many imagination exercises like these. Actors use them in their training all the time. Have fun with them. They encourage you to walk in the twilight land of fantasy. It's not a bad place for a writer to spend some time.

Creativity in the Classroom: A Note to Writing Teachers

Ideally a writing course should stimulate student creativity; however, it doesn't necessarily happen that way. Writing courses are often built around the practice of reading aloud and criticizing student work. They quickly become experiences in criticism. This can be destructive to students trying to develop confidence as writers. I question whether students benefit that much from open class criticism. There are some advantages to sharing initial ideas so that the class sees how to form basic story lines. Selected examples can be instructive to illustrate some particular point. As a general practice, however, I prefer to confer privately with students about their writing. Where large classes make individual conferences a difficulty, audio cassettes can be used to give personal and extensive comments.

Another effective procedure—especially during the early story development stages—is to break a class into groups of four or five and have them discuss their story ideas among themselves. Students find this useful and less threatening than formal exposure before the entire class.

A writing course should emphasize writing. Nothing can substitute for weekly writing and subsequent feedback about that writing.

REFERENCES

1. Carlos Castaneda (I have been unable to locate the source of this quotation in his work).
2. Dorothea Brande, *Becoming a Writer* (New York: Harcourt, Brace and Co., 1934).
3. ". . . the fundamental objective of our psycho-technique is to put us in a creative state in which our subconscious will function normally." Constantin Stanislavski, *An Actor Prepares* (New York: Theatre Arts Books, 1936), p. 266. And he states this again: "Through conscious technique to the subconscious creation of artistic truth." *Building a Character* (New York: Theatre Arts Books, 1949), p. 266.

Also:

Arieti, Silvano. *Creativity: The Magic Synthesis*. New York: Basic Books, 1976.

Gallwey, W. Timothy. *The Inner Game of Tennis*. New York: Random House, 1974.

Ghiselin, Brewster, ed. *The Creative Process*. New York: Mentor, 1955.

Huang, Al Chung-liang. *Embrace Tiger, Return to Mountain—The Essence of T'ai Chi*. Moab, Utah: Real People Press, 1973.

May, Rollo. *The Courage to Create*. New York: W. W. Norton & Co., 1975.

Privette, Gayle. "Factors for Peak Performance." *Psychology Today 11* (February 1978): 110.

2

Narrative Structure

> Let's begin with the story. Human beings are storytelling animals. We domesticate our world by narrative, by myths. . . . We are hungry for a story that will dramatize some meaning we can hold to. The need for a myth that begins "Once upon a time," and ends with "The hero finally triumphed after many trials and returned home," still sleeps in our substance.[1]
>
> —Sam Keen

THE ENJOYMENT OF a story is a pleasure deeply embedded in our cultural traditions. Today, film and television have become our preeminent narrative storytelling media. Whether for escape, amusement or aesthetic pleasure, they command our attention. We'll begin the study of story structure with a look at some fundamental ways that this structure works to maintain our interest in the film, for narrative structure not only patterns the film story but also structures our experience of that story.

One part of a story's attractiveness comes from our tendency to perceive patterns and wholes. We appreciate the sense of closure and completeness that rounds out a story. It gives us a unified experience.

Another part of our response is our ability to empathize with or project ourselves into the dramatic situations of the story and to identify with the story's characters and their aspirations and struggles. We participate in the film through the characters and through the tense situations in which they are placed. To see empathy in action, watch young children at a horror movie. (There is evidence that empathy may be an inborn capacity; altruism has been found in infants of quite young age.)[2]

There's an empathic aspect to our kinesthetic response to rhythm as we project our rhythms and movements into those on the screen. It's the idea of our rising with the pole vaulter as he makes his jump or leaning in the direction of the running back as we urge him toward the goal line. Or in the obvious way that the audience swayed to the rhythm of the reaper's scythe in an Eisenstein film. Rhythm and motion in film affects us physiologically and emotionally. There may well be an empathic response also in connection with the narrative rhythm of a story which builds to an exciting climax.

There's a certain cause-effect logic to a story's structure. One event leads to another, which in turn leads to the next. The problem presented at the beginning of a story goes through increasing development, until it is finally resolved at the end. This story design leaves its traces on us, creating a series of expectations about what will happen next. We find pleasure in the process of anticipating a certain development and then enjoying watching it happen. (Like the child in a theater who nudges his companion and asserts, "See, I told you it would happen.") This is the *suspense principle,* and it is basic to dramatic structure. Any aesthetic experience contains some expectation and the fulfillment of that expectation. It's the idea behind surprise parties, hide and seek, planning a vacation or the unfolding of a new love affair. We enjoy tracing a pattern.

However, the expectation inherent in dramatic structure is not the same as the curiosity in a cheap whodunit as we focus on the conclusion when the culprit is unmasked. Once we know the butler did it, there is little interest in going through it again. Dramatic suspense is different in that we enjoy tracing the process. The interest is not just on the outcome but on the development as well. This explains why we enjoy repeated experiences with *Hamlet,* Beethoven and our favorite films, even though we know how each comes out in the end.

Dramatic suspense is one of a writer's most powerful techniques. Creating anticipations in the audience means creating concerns about what will happen next, about whether (and how) the hero will triumph, about whether everything will come out successfully in spite of the enormous odds stacked against him. Through his structuring of the story, the writer creates such anticipations in the audience. The audience in turn cooperates by willingly suspending disbelief and accepting the fictional illusion of the narrative. We know that our favorite television series hero will not be eliminated during an episode, but we accept the pretense that it could happen in order to enjoy the suspense of the story. We know that Charles de Gaulle of France was not assassinated, but this doesn't lessen our enjoyment of the last minute capture of a potential assassin in *The Day of the Jackal.* As long as the film is credible within its own fictive world (its diegesis), we accept the illusion.

So emotionally powerful is the anticipation of an event that studies have shown, for example, that stress measured hours prior to a dental appointment is as high for some people as the stress when they are actually in the chair. Psychological testing with films containing stress scenes showed that the emotional response to anticipation of a stressful event was higher than the emotional response to a surprise occurrence of the event.[3]

But if interest is stimulated by anticipation it can also wane if the events in a story are too predictable. To maintain our interest, we also need a certain amount of the unexpected—the *surprise principle*.

A film must keep the audience in constant expectation that something is going to happen, and then when it does happen, it should be different, but not too different, from what we had expected. Too much expectation and we become bored. Too much of the novel and we become frustrated trying to fit it in. When both interact effectively, we have an involving story. The balance between the two is like a joke punch line which, though it fits the context of the joke, does it in such an unexpected way that it provokes a laugh. As someone announces "The garbageman is here," Groucho Marx responds "Tell him we don't want any."

Traditional Dramatic Structure

Since the dramas of the ancient Greeks, the rising dramatic curve has been part of our tradition. It sketches out a simple dramatic story with a conflict near the beginning which undergoes increasingly intense and suspenseful development before reaching the climactic conclusion, when the conflict is resolved and the story is over. (There may also be a "letting down" time at the end—called a denouement—when loose ends are tied up and things are capped.)

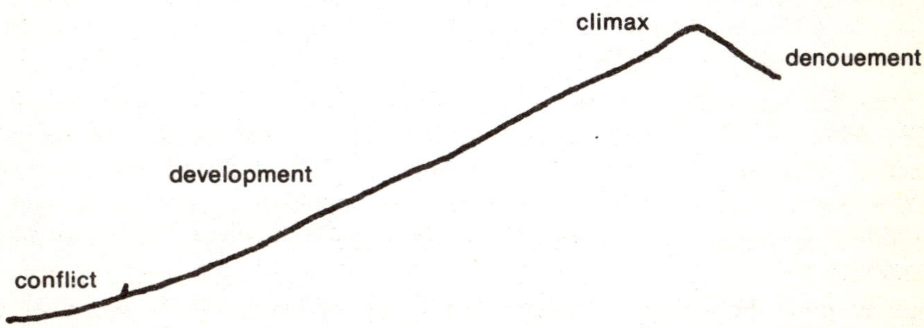

Actually, it would be more accurate to sketch the curve with a series of sawtooth points to reflect that the development moves through a rhythmic series of high and low moments ("beats"). The suspense—and surprises—build through a set of crises alternating with quieter moments, during which we catch our breath and assimilate what we've seen before being thrust into a new development.

In a simple detective story, the conflict is between the detective and the criminal. We wonder if the hero can achieve his objective to bring the culprit to justice. As the story develops, complications place obstacles in his way so that we doubt if he can succeed, even as we expect that he will do so. The complications become more intense. A crooked lawyer helps the criminal beat an arrest charge. Witnesses are intimidated. Evidence disappears. Public pressure mounts on the police to get results. The criminal has a powerful political ally. Another major crime is committed. Finally, the detective must meet a personal threat from the criminal. At the climax, the two confront each other, and the detective triumphs. He has achieved his objective and resolved the conflict. The story is over.

From Deep Structure to Screenplay

If a free-lance television writer wants to write for a new series, he first makes a verbal presentation of some story ideas for the program to the producer or story editor. If one of his ideas is promising, he is given an assignment for the *story*—a narrative outline of some ten to twelve pages. In preparation for this, he'll probably develop a shorter outline of a few pages in which he sketches out the story in terms of its highlights or "beats." If the story is acceptable, he will undoubtedly be given an assignment to do the script (although in theory he could be paid for the story and another writer could do the script). The professional writer starts with the idea and expands it until it is a completed screenplay. There are economic and traditional reasons for this, but also creative ones, for a screenplay grows organically from the seed kernel of the idea into the final script. This is how most writers work, and it is the best way for a promising screenwriter to learn his craft.

Here is the process. It begins with a *basic story idea,* which contains the complete story in capsulated form. This is a concise statement expressing whose story it is and the conflict-development-resolution storyline that patterns the narrative. For the next stage, the basic story is expanded into a *narrative synopsis outline,* which fills in more details and clearly shows the plot developments of the story. (This may range from six or so pages for a half-hour television program up to thirty pages for a feature film.) Then comes a *scene outline* or *scene breakdown*—a scene-by-scene narrative outline of the film, which allows the writer to organize the flow and rhythm of his scenes. Finally there is a *first draft* screenplay, followed by subsequent drafts, culminating in the *final draft* script. (Written in motion picture script format, a screenplay times out at about a minute a page, so a half-hour teleplay is just over 30 pages, an hour teleplay from 60 to 70 pages, an hour-and-a-half teleplay from 90 to 110 pages, and a feature film script anywhere from 130 pages up.)

Wolf Rilla makes an analogy comparing the successive stages a writer goes through in creating a script with those steps taken by an architect. The early narrative outlines give an overview of the story much as an architect's original drawings indicate how the completed building will look on its site. A scene breakdown is comparable to the ground plan and elevations—more detailed but not yet complete. The detailed script is then analogous to the completed blueprints.[4]

In the early stages, the writing should be a narrative story in the third person present tense, using the direct, lean and economic style of screenwriting and avoiding literary stylization or embellishments. Dialogue is avoided in the early narrative stages (except for an occasional phrase or two to spice the reading). The story should read as if it were happening in the present, as it will be seen and heard on the screen.

This organic approach helps the writer better conceptualize his story at each stage of its development. It also gives the practical benefit of permitting the writer to work out script problems in the preliminary narrative versions before going on to a more involved stage. It's always easier to rework a page or two of narrative than to rewrite an entire script.

A theoretical justification for this organic approach is found in the concept of *deep structure*. Underlying any narrative is a deep structure, which forms the spine of the work. Beneath the artistry of the completed film is a deep-structure story outline that gives it unity, coherence and meaning. A writer begins with this deep structure—the basic story of the film. He then transforms it through each successive stage until it becomes the final screenplay. The starting place is a statement of the deep-structure story.

Beginning writers sometimes balk at the idea of a basic story foundation for their screenplay. It sounds so prosaic and dull, not at all like the exciting screenplay they hope to write. What they don't realize is that at this stage it often doesn't sound very exciting. Yet it's as important as the framework that undergirds a building. The beauty of a love sonnet has at its base the simple "I love you" deep-structure message, which is then transformed through images, metaphors and other poetic devices into the lyrical sonnet.

Beginning, Middle, End

If we try to take a dramatic story down to its most essential deep-story structure, we discover the traditional beginning-middle-end pattern. In the time-ordered medium of film, the organization of the film structures not just the work itself but also our experience of it. Functionally, the beginning-middle-end structure corresponds to the requirements of a dramatic story to engage our interest, to hold this interest over the length of the story and to leave us with a feeling of completeness when it is over. In terms of the story, the beginning initiates the problem, the middle develops it through various complications and the end resolves it.

The *beginning* wins our attention, involving us in the nascent story and building tensions and anticipations about the way the story will develop. We meet the principal characters and begin our involvement with them. Through exposition we obtain the necessary background to understand the story. We are introduced to the world of the film—its diegesis—and to its style, tone and atmosphere. We also meet the major conflict or problem that begins the story and will concern us throughout the film.

The *middle* maintains and deepens our interest, intensifying our expectations through a series of story complications, crises, conflicts, subplots and similar difficulties, which make us doubt an easy resolution of the problem.

The *end* is the resolution of the story and its problems and conflicts. It includes the climax of the story and sometimes a denouement, which ties up loose ends and brings us down from our tense involvement. The end resolves our tensions and concludes our aesthetic experience of the film.

Conflict

Conflict has been mentioned a number of times because it is so basic to dramatic narrative. The concept typically refers to an opposition between two forces, the outcome of which is in some doubt. This uncertainty helps keep us involved with the story. It holds our attention and makes us want to know how the conflict will be resolved. Because it is so important to a film story, conflict deserves a closer look before we continue with the idea of the basic story.

There are two senses in which conflict figures into a film story. The most general sense is that of the web of oppositions, which can be found within the film story. Often these are typed as one person versus another person (as sheriff vs. desperado), opposition between one person and a group (the black detective vs. the small southern town bigots), a person opposing some natural force (climbing a difficult mountain, catching a killer shark) or a person in conflict with himself and his values (Hamlet faced with his indecision, Guido in *8½* trying to find artistic purpose). Some conflicts are unique to the story, while others present cultural and social conflicts that may only be explored, since they are too complex for ready solution (such as bigotry, social inequality or injustice).

Here are some of the conflicts in John Ford's *Fort Apache*. The first mentioned are endemic to the story and are resolved within it (although they may reflect continual social problems). The later conflicts are cultural themes that are explored in the film.

The new colonel's rigid, by-the-book approach vs. the more relaxed and realistic fort atmosphere.

The new colonel's destructive authority (since he is ignorant of how to deal with Indians) vs. the comparative powerlessness of those who know what should be done.

The colonel vs. the captain (who understands Indians and how to deal with them).

The colonel vs. the young lieutenant (who has romantic feelings toward his daughter).

The lieutenant's love and desire vs. his shyness and uncertainty in wooing the colonel's daughter.

The lieutenant's inexperience vs. his father's honored example (his father, once an officer, now a sergeant, was decorated for bravery).

The continual chaffing against army restrictions by the sergeants who love drinking and roughhousing.

The evil Indian agent vs. both the Indians and the cavalry.

The cavalry vs. the Indians.

Indian culture vs. White oppression.

The coming civilization vs. the vanishing frontier wildness.

The proper, restrictive Eastern influence vs. the more relaxed atmosphere in the West.

As another example, Sam Rohdie in analyzing *Mr. Deeds Goes to Town* finds a number of thematic oppositions, stemming from Deeds as a naive, honest, rural populist clashing with the hypocrisy of the city (a common American cultural theme). He includes in his list:

country vs. town
deeds vs. words
honesty vs. hypocrisy
naiveté vs. sophistication
human relations vs. cash relations
band vs. opera
popular art vs. art
crowd-community vs. individual
privacy vs. publicity
clean-shaven vs. moustache
nature vs. culture
fun vs. wit
modesty vs. excess
real vs. superficial
private vs. social
"real" sentiment vs. "fake" sentiment
mad (sane) vs. sane (mad) [5]

Whether as themes or as plot elements, such conflicts add interesting dimensions to the story as we watch the different forces interact.

But of more immediate interest to us now is the second sense of conflict—that which initiates a storyline.

At the beginning of any storyline there is a situation that needs some sort of resolution. Usually something happens—an event such as a crime being committed, boy meeting girl with resulting entanglements—and this works itself out in the storyline. This can be seen as a *conflict* to be resolved, but it also can be viewed in other ways:

A *lack* to be corrected,
A *problem* to be solved,
An *obstacle* to be overcome,

A *threat* to be handled,
A *decision* or *choice* to be made,
A *pressure* to be relieved,
A *tension* to be eased,
A *challenge* to be met,
An *imbalance* to be balanced,
Conflicting values to be reconciled,
A *clash, disharmony* or *discord* to be resolved.

In *Fort Apache,* the colonel with his by-the-book approach clashes with the more sensible officers in a conflict that is finally resolved when his stupidity leads to a battle in which he is killed. But if the story is about a detective trying to solve a crime, a doctor fighting a spreading epidemic or a discouraged character needing something to renew him, it might be better to consider it a *problem* to be solved. Climbing a mountain may be a challenge. A woman choosing between a husband and a lover, or a prominent politician deciding whether or not to declare his homosexuality are choice or decision stories. Any one of these choices may be a more effective way to think of the initial conflict rather than in terms of an opposing conflict.

Another useful way to think of a storyline conflict is as an *objective* or goal to achieve. Following the suggestion of the director and acting teacher Constantin Stanislavski, such an objective is best expressed as an active verb form: "to———." To catch the criminal, to win the lady, to solve the mystery, to beat the system, to choose between alternatives. This has the advantage of being dynamic rather than static. While the conflict in *Jaws* is man vs. shark, it takes on a dynamic, animated quality if defined as "to seek and destroy the shark."

Often the story objective—Stanislavski would have said its superobjective—and the central character's objective are the same, as when the detective seeks to catch the criminal. But this is not always so. The central character doesn't have to know the actual conflict of the story, although he is affected by it. Imagine a film story in which the character has the objective to win a tennis tournament while the story objective is for the character to learn to overcome his destructive competitive compulsion and become a more complete person. The character won't know this at first, although the audience probably will.

If the idea of conflict is seen in this broader context, it suggests more complex story possibilities than the more rigid X vs. Y. Now we are ready to begin approaching the basic story. Here are some interesting starting places.

Starting Places

There are two common starting places for a story. Neither present a complete basic story but either can be developed into one.

A *premise* is an interesting and challenging idea for a story which begins

"What if . . ." and then follows with the description of an exciting situation. What if Archie Bunker unknowingly gives mouth-to-mouth resuscitation to a transvestite? What if an ocean liner flips upside down in the water after being hit by a large wave (*The Poseidon Adventure*)? What if a resigned secret service agent finds himself imprisoned in a strange village and must try to escape (*The Prisoner,* a TV series)? What if all the birds unite to attack the human race (*The Birds*)?

A premise usually defines a striking predicament and thereby implies a conflict and shows its obvious audience appeal. It is not a complete story, and it carries the danger of trading on gimmickry. Effective stories come from the actions of characters rather than from a gimmick. But an exciting premise is a good starting place.

A *situation* is another good start for a story, even though it is incomplete since it doesn't include important developments or the resolution of the story. A situation describes the predicament of the central character much as a program description in *TV Guide*—"Archie Bunker has difficulty getting his grandson baptized over Mike and Gloria's objections." It's incomplete because it doesn't describe the story's development and resolution (*TV Guide* wouldn't want to give everything away, now, would they?). It's a good enough place to begin, but it needs to be expressed as a complete story. Too many beginning writers try to work from a situation and then complain "I can't come up with an ending." This difficulty is avoided by sketching out the basic story first.

The Basic Story

The basic story is a deceptively simple concept—so deceptive that it's easy not to realize that you don't understand it. Yet it is one of the most important concepts for a screenwriter. The basic story is a deep-structure statement of the story; it is the writer's concretion of the deep structure. In capsule form, it shapes the spine that unifies and integrates the story. As it is gradually expanded, it guides the writer in keeping a balance between various story developments. It's as valuable in a loosely structured story as in a tight one, since a loose story needs a strong, organizing spine. (Even as abstract a film as *Last Year at Marienbad* is basically a variation on the classic love triangle of two men and a woman.)

The basic story is a present tense, capsulized-statement outline of the film story which summarizes the beginning-middle-end or conflict-development-resolution structure. It expresses the essentials of the story. And it does so in a way that indicates the development of the story through later narrative and script versions.

The classic "boy meets girl, boy loses girl, boy gets girl" expresses a kind of story idea, but it's a bit too general. Suppose we make it into a basic story statement as follows:

> Approaching middle age, a lonely, homely man meets a nice but not especially attractive woman and they get involved. But he loses her when his own ego and the jibes of friends pull them apart. However, he comes to realize how much she means to him and at the end goes back to her.

This basic story statement contains a beginning, a middle and an end. It presents the conflict and the character's motivation (he is lonely). The development shows any major plot twists—his ego and his friends' taunts separate them. At the end he turns to her again. These are the essentials of the story (and may well describe the story of *Marty*).

This looks simple enough, but it is really quite difficult for a beginning writer to develop the sense of thinking of stories as complete entities and expressing this in a basic story. It is important to keep the basic story short and concise—written in a page or less. This is a challenge. It is easier to write two or three pages about a story than to construct a single paragraph which presents the story. Yet this economy is important, since too much detail at this early stage can get in the way of the story as a whole. It's as though the writer first needs to see the entire forest before he starts moving toward the individual trees. If the story can't be sketched out completely in a paragraph or so, then it may not be a story. It's as though you had an appointment with a producer who is giving you thirty seconds in which to tell the story. You must do it coherently and succinctly in that time. If it can't be done, then you might not have a story.

The basic story is an outline for the screenplay.

It presents the following information:

1. The locale and time period of the story.
2. Whose story it is—the central character plus other major characters.
3. The conflict that initiates the story.
4. A *brief* description of the dominant developments of the plot.
5. The climax and resolution.

This can be done in two paragraphs. The first gives us the locale and time period of the story—contemporary New York City, a California beach town in the 1950s, London in the mid-seventeenth century. It can happen in a baroque chateau or in the Seventh Avenue garment district.

The character description is also brief, and includes age and other relevant demographic information. For example, a character may be fifty years old, overweight and a blue-collar WASP bigot. The description should include some rationale for why the character is involved with the conflict and why it is important to him. What motivates the character? What is his intention that involves him in the conflict. There is no problem with the motivation of a detective going after a criminal, it's his job. We can also understand why Archie Bunker wants to get his grandson baptized. But we need to know of Sol's concentration camp experience in order to understand his actions in *The Pawnbroker*. In some film stories, the motivation is so much a part of the total character that it would be difficult to point to a single intention; in fact, we might not want to make the motivation so obvious (as with Thomas in *Blow-Up* which will be shown in Chapter Four).

Here is such a paragraph for a screenplay of *The Four Feathers* from a novel by A. E. Mason (1903), which has been made into at least three different film and television versions.

> England in the 1880s is fighting a war in Egypt and the Sudan. Harry Faversham, twenty-seven, comes from a family with a proud military heritage. His father, as his other ancestors, is a career military officer. His friends are fellow officers. Even his fiancée is the daughter of a military man. However, Harry would rather settle down to a life of quiet marital bliss than rush off to fight with his regiment in the Sudan.

This sets the scene for us, introduces Harry, whose story it is, and gives us an understanding of the pressure on him to distinguish himself in the military. Now we are ready for the second paragraph, which sketches out the story proper: Beginning-middle-end, conflict-development-resolution.

> When Harry rejects his marching orders, he is ostracized by his father and other family friends. But the strongest insult is the four white feathers of cowardice which he is given by his three friends and his financée. To overcome this shame, Harry steals away alone and incognito to Egypt. Disguised as a mute native, he leads one of his friends, who is blinded by the sun, across the desert to safety. Then he breaks into a prison to rescue his other two friends. By these heroic actions, he has regained his honor and the four feathers are taken back. He is reunited with his fiancée and enjoys the respect and admiration of all.

Once having sketched out this basic story outline, the writer knows that he has a complete story. He will then expand it to a longer narrative outline by filling in more details of the story's development.*

Here is the basic story of Archie Bunker's wanting to get his grandson baptized. It clearly defines the development of the action.

> Archie would like to get his baby grandson baptized, but the parents, Mike and Gloria, object because they are not religious. Archie tries to get Edith to support him, but she feels that the parents should decide. Archie tries to sneak off to have it done but is abashed when he goes to an Oriental minister (Archie wonders if he is a Christian). The minister sides with its being a parents' decision. But in the end Archie achieves a personal victory when he baptizes the child himself in an empty church.

This sketches out the essentials of the story. Since *All in the Family* is a television series, we already know the characters and setting. The conflict is clear:

* At the most elementary deep-structure level, one might say that the story of *The Four Feathers* is about how a man who is branded a coward by his friends overcomes this dishonor by becoming a hero—by saving his friends' lives—and thereby making them take back their accusation. Expressed in such compressed form, this shows how basic stories can be generalized to fit different situations. This idea could fit stories about different wars, different historical periods, even apply to something as diverse as the story of some young men taking a white-water camping trip.

Archie has the objective to get his grandson baptized. There may be a number of other things going on in the program—Archie might be having trouble at work, he and Mike might argue some point of politics, Mike and Gloria might be quarreling, Edith may have done something crazy that day.

But all these are secondary to the dominant storyline—can Archie get his grandson baptized? The story goes through four *beats** or developments, each of which can be considered complications to the story or obstacles to Archie's achieving his objective. These are: (1) Mike and Gloria's refusal, (2) Edith's support of them, (3) the Oriental minister perceived as possibly non-Christian and (4) his siding with the parents. The story climaxes and is resolved when Archie does his own baptizing and thereby achieves his objective. The story is over.

Let's take another look at the beginning-middle-end, conflict-development-resolution structure of a basic story.

Near the beginning of the script is the *conflict,* which begins the essential story. It might be a crime committed, a catastrophe to be overcome, perhaps just an interesting character with intriguing contradictory characteristics. (Recall that while we follow tradition in calling this a "conflict," it might appear in different guises as an objective, a choice, a lack, a problem or the like.) This conflict is the start of the story. And it is *this* conflict that is developed to a climax and resolution.

It is important to accurately define the conflict (or problem, objective), since it determines the storyline. This is more difficult than it might seem because often the real conflict that impels the story is a personal and internal one for the main character and defies a quick description. A complex character may overcome many problems, but which is the central problem of the story? One way to discover this is to look at the climax and ask what is being climaxed and resolved and then trace this back to the original conflict. Imagine a story in which at the climax a character wins a championship tennis match. Ostensibly it would appear that the conflict is to win the match. But the actual story may be more subtle. The primary conflict may be the character's internal need to overcome a psychological block against winning. Precisely defining the exact conflict of the story is not simple. It often means looking beneath the surface to discover the actual story you are telling. A clear understanding of the conflict is important to knowing your story.

The *development* is the middle section of the story in which the conflict goes through increasing complications. The basic story gives the *beats* or story highlights of this development. These are the crises, confrontations, threats, twists and hurdles that carry the conflict along its uncertain road to resolution.

*"Beat" is used in the sense of a major story development. A story develops by a series of beats. This usage is different from that found in the theater, where a beat is comparable to a motivational unit and is a basic script unit used for rehearsing. "Beat" has still another usage within a script—that of signifying a short pause. When used as "(Beat)" within a dialogue speech, it means to pause for a moment—or a beat.

In trying to solve a crime, a detective may be thwarted by a lack of clues; a major breakthrough turns out to be a dead end; a suspect turns out to be the wrong person; junior officers act rashly and precipitate a community confrontation; a new crime increases the pressure . . . and so the story progresses.

The development also involves increasing tensions. Recall the rising intensity of the dramatic curve. The developments become more intense as the story nears its climax. (Otherwise our interest might slacken.)

The development may unfold as a series of different objectives or different problems to solve. For example, a detective has to pacify angry community reaction before he can get on to the business of solving the crime. Or he may have to complete a complex chemical analysis of a clue before continuing. The resolution of one problem may lead us directly into the next: the search for a missing witness ends up in finding her corpse—and there's a new crime to solve. These objectives and problems which form the development of the story carry us along in suspense as we anticipate the handling of each new crisis, and we are pleasurably surprised by the unexpected twists and turns this takes.

The *resolution* is the end of the story. Most stories are resolved at the *climax*—that final, dominant crisis toward which the story has been building. With the climax, we are no longer in doubt about the resolution of the conflict, and our suspense about the story is over. It is the marshal shooting the gunfighters in *High Noon* and then rejecting the town which refused to help him. It's Michael becoming the new godfather (*The Godfather*) or Bobby chucking it all and running away to Alaska, his search still unrealized (*Five Easy Pieces*).

Many films end with the high point of the climax, but other films have a short *denouement* to tie up loose ends and bring us down from our involvement. In television programs, the denouement may be a short tag after the final commercial break. The old *Perry Mason* television series did this. A typical episode would climax dramatically in the courtroom when Perry would point out the real murderer among the courtroom spectators. Then, after the commercial, came the denouement tag. Usually it found Perry talking with his client, secretary and private investigator friend. Perry would accept his client's grateful thanks and in a word or two explain what put him on to the real criminal. Things would then conclude on the light note of who would pay for lunch that afternoon.

Denouements may or may not be used in a story; however, if one is used, it should be kept short, since the story has already ended and you are just wrapping up the traces.

Structure is not the only element in a film story that gets us involved, but it is one of the most authoritative. Some otherwise fine films would have been even better if they had a stronger story. I felt this about Antonioni's *Red Desert*—a classic in its use of color, but regrettably weak on story and dramatic interest, I also noticed this when viewing Woody Allen's *Love and Death*. At one point in the film, my involvement lagged. It happened when the girl asks Allen's character to marry her (for other than romantic reasons). Up to this point I was involved with the character's objective to win the girl. Then suddenly he got her, and though the film was far from finished, the story lagged. So often when a film seems to drag at a certain point, it's because it has moved away from its central story. Working from a basic story helps keep a writer's focus on his story's structure.

Some films concentrate on involving us with an interesting character rather than presenting an immediate external conflict. This is a rather good indication that there is a personal conflict underlying the film. We feel this in *Blow-Up,* when we are immediately intrigued by the contradictions and attractions of Thomas; it isn't until part-way into the film that there is the clash with the woman in the park and the discovery that he has photographed a murder. There is no question that Thomas learns something by the film's end, something more important than knowledge of the crime, which remains unsolved. Can we spell out exactly what has happened with Thomas? I'm not sure. Like most good character stories, it's somewhat ambiguous. Whether the ending is a final affirmation or a final surrender depends on your perspective. Either way, Thomas has lived his story.

Examples: All the President's Men, The African Queen

Simple basic story outlines reflecting deep structure can be seen in these two film stories, which are strongly dependent on plot. In *All the President's Men,* the conflict is in how the two reporters uncover the details surrounding the Watergate break-in and expose the venality of the Nixon White House. They are opposed by the government officials involved. We know how the story ends but are still involved in *how* it happens. The reporters' objective is *to uncover* the Watergate story. To achieve this, as the story develops, they have to overcome one obstacle after another. Here is a basic story statement for the film story:

> Bernstein and Woodward are two young reporters on *The Washington Post* at the time of the Watergate break-in. They set out to uncover the real story behind the Watergate break-in and the government officials that this might implicate. At first their editor doubts that they should be on the story because of their inexperience. Then they are frustrated because their mysterious source ("deep throat") knows more than he is saying. They get discouraged when the *New York Times* beats them to part of the story. They are almost removed from the story because they can't get enough material. Possible sources are scared and won't talk—a possible break when one woman agrees to talk fizzles because she is the wrong woman. Bernstein goes to Florida to get some information but can't get it until he uses subterfuge. They can't get enough leads, and things look discouraging. A crisis occurs when they falsely accuse Haldeman and it backfires—it appears they are being set up to be discredited. Finally, they have reason to believe their lives are in danger. But then they succeed in getting the story, and it goes to press.

Early in *The African Queen,* the two characters determine to try to go down the uncharted river and sink the German gunboat, *The Luisa.* As the story develops, they encounter one obstacle after another that threatens to destroy them and thwart their mission. As often happens in film stories, the crises they encounter increase in intensity as we near the climax. At one point near the end, they resign themselves to death. Then later it looks as though their deaths are a sure thing. A number of surprise twists hold our interest. For example, they are just a few yards from the lake but can't see it through the tall swamp grass. Just when it appears they have failed, *The Queen*'s hull, with homemade torpedoes sticking out, refloats to the surface and the German gunboat rams it. Here is the basic story:

> This is wilderness Africa at the time of the First World War. Rosie is a rather spinsterish sister of an English missionary, probably in her forties. Charlie is about the same age, a drunken riverboat bum, who makes his living carrying supplies on his derelict boat *The African Queen*.
>
> When the Germans destroy their village and cause the death of her brother, Rosie persuades Charlie that they must travel down the river and sink *The Luisa*—the gunboat which assures German control of this part of Africa. Only reluctantly does Charlie agree, since the river is hostile and may be unnavigable, and *The Luisa* is heavily armed. But with true British pluck, they start off. They encounter rapids, waterfalls, gunfire from a German fort on the river, a broken propellor, a mosquito swarm, leeches and the disappearance of river channels. They are ready to give up to death, certain that they are hopelessly lost, when rising water from an overnight storm in the mountains floats their boat the few yards onto the lake, which they couldn't see through the swamp vegetation. They make homemade torpedoes, but just as they start after *The Luisa,* they sink in a small storm and are captured. They are about to be hanged as spies when *The Luisa* steams into the raised, upturned hull of *The Queen,* hits the torpedoes and blows up. Charlie and Rosie swim toward the British shore of the lake, having succeeded in their objective.

A basic story is a means of organizing the film's story into its primary components so that as the story is expanded in later stages, each story element is correctly emphasized and the story moves along at a suitable pace. The two examples are of plotty films which clearly show how an objective develops through a series of obstacles and crises until it is ultimately resolved. (*The African Queen* also shows some of the surprise plot twists near the end which are so typical of many stories.) In both examples, the *action*—what happens—corresponds to the story's development. But this isn't always the case. One mistake of beginning writers is to confuse the action—what happens—with the structure of that action. Whether developing your own idea or analyzing a film or television program, it's important to get down to the organizing structure of the story rather than simply telling "what happens." The action includes the embellishments, transitions and other events that comprise the final film story, while the basic story structure lies underneath like the skeleton supporting the body. The skeleton doesn't contain a body's beauty or uniqueness, but where would we be without it?

Whose Story Is It?

In Truffaut's *Day for Night,* each of the three central characters—actors in the film-within-a-film—are interviewed about this film. What is it about? Alexandre, the father, replies, "Well, it's the story of a man in his early fifties who has a son . . . ." Alphonse, the son, says, "Well, it's the story of a young man who marries an English girl . . . ." And Julie, the English girl, gives her version as: "*Meet Pamela* is the story of a young Englishwoman who falls in love with . . . ."[6] Each sees this film as his own story. While this says something about actors' egos, it also describes what is frequently a writer's dilemma: whose story is it? That is, who is the central character, the character who experiences the conflict, development and resolution of the story?

Usually it is the dominant character and the one with whom we can strongly identify and empathize. He is typically the first major character we meet and the last we see at the film's end. Through his experiences in the story, he will undergo change and growth. While it is often a single individual, this needn't be so. The story may belong to a couple (as in *The African Queen*) or to a group.

In some cases, it is necessary to tell the story of a dominant character through another character. This is often true when the dominant character is unsympathetic and we resist identifying with him. Thus, while one character dominates the film, it is, from a structural standpoint, another character's story. *I Am a Camera* and its musical version, *Cabaret,* are structurally the story of a young man, although the dominant character is the exciting woman he meets. The same thing happens in *Auntie Mame,* where Mame dominates by her extravagant personality; structurally it is the nephew's story.

While the figure of Jesus dominates the television film *The Day Christ Died,* structurally it is organized as Pilate's story, a dramatizing technique not found in the original book. Pilate is the first main character we meet. His conflict is to find a way to conveniently avoid crucifying the revolutionary Barabbas. Because Caesar wants to crackdown on revolutionaries, and Barabbas moreover had killed a Roman soldier, Pilate had condemned him to death. To free him would offend Caesar. But if he crucifies Barabbas, the angry mob will riot. His solution is to ask the mob to choose between Barabbas and another prisoner to receive the Passover pardon. It will have to be a prisoner who committed an equally important crime and whom the Jews hate. Jesus then serves this purpose. Typical of the structure, Pilate appears in the film's last scene, his objective now accomplished.

A similar problem occurs with a television series that has a continuing series star but also has special guest stars in particular episodes. The answer to whose story it is depends then on how the story is handled.

A Frame Story

One contribution of story structure to a film is that it tells the audience what to expect in the story's development. We have some sense of where the story is going from our understanding of the conflict. We then enjoy the dramatic suspense of anticipating the story's development. So important is this function that some films adopt an unusual structure to achieve it: the frame story. Frame stories use a brief, informing framework, then tell the bulk of the story in flashback. They usually have characters who serve as presenters in narrating the story. The short, present-time events set the story and let us know where it's heading; the story then develops in flashback. *Citizen Kane* uses the present to establish the reporter's search to learn about Kane and the meaning of Rosebud, and then tells of Kane's life in large flashbacks. In *Dr. Zhivago,* the meeting of General Zhivago and the young girl who may be the daughter of Dr. Zhivago and Lara occurs in the present. It tells us that we shall learn of the love affair between Lara and Zhivago; then we go into the flashback to watch this develop. *Lawrence of Arabia* opens with Lawrence being killed in a motorcycle crash. We then get different impressions of him from newsmen interviewing people who knew him. Then we go into the flashback and follow his adventures. *Serpico* opens with his being rushed to a hospital with a gunshot wound. A fellow policeman asks another: "Think a cop did it?" The other replies, "I know six cops I think who'd like to." Then we enter the flashback, beginning with his becoming a policeman and following the story's development to the place where we can answer the question which hooked us on the story—did some fellow officers contribute to his being shot and why?

Presenting a narrative in extended flashback is one solution to handling a sprawling story, such as one tracing a young man's growth and adventures. The frame supplies the direction for the story. It gives us the objective or conflict which will hold our interest and keep us in suspense through the development of the flashback story.

Before going into the complexity of story structure, be certain that you have an understanding of simple basic story. Try to formulate basic stories for your own ideas. See if you can identify the dominant storyline in various television programs or films. The concept is a deceptively simple one; it always gives trouble to beginning writing students (and to some advanced ones as well). Yet the idea is so important that it's worth spending a good deal of time making sure that you understand it. It will be time well spent.

Complex Structure

Film structures are more complex than a simple basic storyline. We will now examine that complexity.

As we've seen, a storyline is a narrative pattern having a beginning-middle-end (or conflict-development-resolution) structure. The storyline defines the main story of the film. It begins near the beginning of the film and resolves itself at the film's climax at the end. But there are usually other storylines as well. Some storylines parallel the basic story. Others develop as subplots. Often we will find that storylines develop from conflicts of the major characters in a film. In order to more clearly define these various storylines, we should see that they are of three different kinds: external or task storylines, interpersonal storylines and internal or personal storylines.

External storylines are about a task to be done. The objective is to sink *The Luisa,* to catch the criminal, to save the dying patient or to successfully complete the secret mission. External storylines are common to melodrama and plotty films.

Interpersonal or "people" storylines are about relationships between characters. We are social beings involved with each other. A story often involves relationships that characters have with each other: to win a lover, to make a friend or to gain another's respect. In a film such as *Paper Moon,* the story is primarily interpersonal—the developing relationship between an itinerant con man and a nine-year-old orphan girl.

Internal storylines concern some internal change in values, morals, attitudes or beliefs. A character may need to learn something about himself, make a choice or decision, achieve personal insight or affect some sort of personal growth and change. This might mean overcoming false pride, developing confidence or resolving a conflict between personal desire and a sense of duty.

These different sorts of storylines interact within the film story. A character may accomplish some external task and at the same time go through some internal changes. Or, while completing the external objective, a character may get involved with other characters and win a lover or straighten out a relationship with a doubting colleague.

Storylines interweave in different ways. The primary, basic storyline dominates the narrative of the film. Another storyline may develop along with the primary line. The lines may climax and become resolved together—as when both an external objective is achieved and the woman is won at the film's end, or when an internal change and external task are accomplished together. *Subplots* are independent storylines that are nested within the story. They often involve minor characters, such as the romance between two young lovers (in *Fort Apache,* it is the young lieutenant and the colonel's daughter).

Not every sequence that has a beginning-middle-end is a separate storyline. Many scenes use this conflict-development-resolution pattern as part of the development of the main storyline. In *The African Queen,* there's a sequence in which Charlie and Rosie have to sail past the German fort guarding the river. A shot ruptures the steam line and they risk going dead in the water. Charlie is almost shot by the German commander but is saved at the last minute when sunlight reflects in the telescopic sight of the rifle and *The Queen* rounds the bend to safety. This sequence has dramatic build, but it is part of the development of the primary storyline and not an independent storyline.

Each major character in a film may have his own problem to be resolved, so there may be a separate storyline built around each such character. Ingmar Bergman's *Through a Glass Darkly* is the story of Karen and her breakdown and search for God. Other storylines are formed around the other major characters. The father is having an identity crisis; he can't interact with his children nor handle his feelings about Karen's madness. The son, Karen's brother, is having difficulty defining his sexuality and relating to his father. This same multiple-storyline pattern appears in *Cries and Whispers*. The dominant storyline—basic story—centers around Agnes as she searches for affirmation in life in the face of her coming death. Karin and Maria share an interpersonal storyline as they try to achieve a belated reconciliation, but their moment of contact is too fragile and they fail and separate. Each character has her own storyline. Karin has an unhappy marriage, which leads her to turn off sexually and mutilate herself as a significant gesture of this. Maria's selfish love for the doctor leads to her husband's attempted suicide; the doctor wisely rejects her later approach. Anna, the housekeeper, achieves in fantasy her need to care for the dying Agnes as she once cared for her own now-dead child.

Now let's go back to our basic story for *The African Queen*. We sketched out the story but omitted another storyline. We can include it now as a separate paragraph in our story outline. Paralleling the external storyline of *The African Queen* is a strong interpersonal romance line:

> Rosie and Charlie develop a romance. At first they are uncomfortable together. He considers her too prim; she finds him too uncouth. But they are united in their mutual goal. As they overcome some of the river's hazards, their enthusiasm with success leads first to a hesitant kiss and then to a romance. They kid and joke and enjoy being together. They share a tender moment as they go to sleep in their swamp-mired boat, expecting death. They quarrel before going after *The Luisa;* Charlie wants Rosie to stay safely behind and she insists on coming along. The climax to their romance occurs when they are captured and about to be hanged for spies—Charlie persuades the captain to marry them first. He does, announcing, "I pronounce you man and wife, proceed with the execution." Then, after *The Luisa* is blown up, they swim together toward the British shore and a future life as man and wife.

Different storylines add variety to a story. They also give the writer a chance to vary the rhythm (and suspense) in the story as, for example, when cutting away from the central storyline in order to have a scene or two which develops a secondary storyline. A complex story can be graphed in order to see which storylines are being developed at what point in the film. The following is a graphic representation of a story in which the main storyline is accomplishing a mission, while secondary storylines are built around the central character's need to develop confidence (internal), a romance (interpersonal), and another

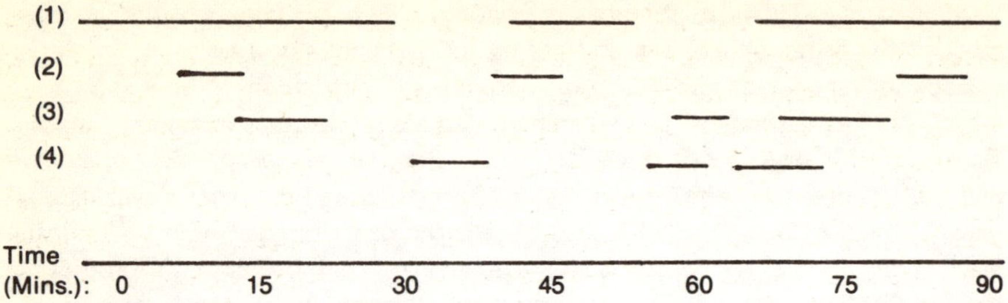

(1) Main storyline—to accomplish the mission
(2) Internal storyline—to develop confidence
(3) Interpersonal romance storyline
(4) Subplot involving another character

character's need to become less selfishly egotistic as developed in a subplot. The graph represents the film developing over time from beginning to end. The lines show the amount of screen time that is given to each storyline. Since the main storyline (1) is the dominant story of the film, it is given more time than the other storylines. Other lines are seen developing along with the main storyline. This is typical, since they often have some bearing on the main storyline. The subplot (4) is independent of the main story. It develops over three scenes. Two of these scenes deal only with the subplot and not with the main story. The third scene overlaps the main story somewhat. It shows that the subplot's resolution has some connection with the main story. The internal storyline (2) develops along with the main story. The romance storyline (3) is interrelated with the main story except for one scene about two-thirds of the way through the film.

Analysis of films and television programs will reveal how different storylines interweave to produce the complex structure of the film. We'll now consider some examples of complex structure to reinforce the concept.

The most prominent storyline in Hitchcock's *The Birds* is for the principal characters to discover, then escape from the threat from the attacking birds. This external storyline builds through the following stages:

> Wildly fluttering birds appear indistinctly behind the titles, prefiguring what is to come. The characters notice that birds are flocking together in an unusual way. Then a seagull attacks Melanie. Farm chickens aren't eating. A seagull crashes into Annie's door. Seagulls attack children at a birthday party. Sparrows invade the house through the chimney. A neighbor is found killed by birds. School children and townspeople are attacked by birds. Annie is killed by the birds. The birds attack the house, and Melanie is almost killed in a personal confrontation with the birds. Finally, the characters drive through the birds and escape (although the ultimate fate of the world is left up in the air).

A second strong storyline in this film is the interpersonal love story between Mitch and Melanie. However, there's a surprise in this, since from a structural point of view the romance line may be the basic storyline. It develops long before we are aware of the threat from the birds. The romance line functions as the peg on which to hang the more striking external line. After all, the romance line is the one we first meet when Mitch and Melanie interact in the pet shop at the beginning of the film. We wonder how these two will come together.

Let's consider this storyline in terms of the obstacles or hurdles to the romance. First there is their own natural reluctance, especially from Melanie, who is always talking about returning to San Francisco. There is an implied threat from Annie—an old love of Mitch's. While not a strong threat, she might be at least perceived as a potential threat, for we find her a sympathetic character and wouldn't like to see her rejected without some compensation. There is opposition from Mitch's mother, who doesn't want anyone taking away her son. The final hurdle to the romance is the threat from the birds.

Let's see how these obstacles are overcome in the story so that the romance can flourish. Melanie's attempt to return to San Francisco is thwarted by the threat from the birds. This threat also brings her and Mitch closer together in mutual support. The mother's opposition fades when Melanie gives her support and strength during the bird attacks (and significantly, at the end, as they drive off, the mother cradles Melanie's head and smiles at her, showing acceptance). Annie is eliminated as an obstacle by her being killed by the birds. As they drive away at the film's end, there is the promise that the romance will continue.

The Godfather is a story that develops over a number of years. Whose story is it? The older Don Corleone dies during the film and Michael dominates the narrative, but in a real sense, it is the family's story. The central storyline is the survival and prosperity of the Corleone family in the face of threatened destruction from the other crime families. As the story develops, the family's survival depends on overcoming a series of complications: the shooting of Don Corleone and then of Sonny, doubts about Michael's being able to take control of the family, internal betrayal, crooked cops and external opposition from the other families. At the end, the family kills off its enemies and survives.

Another storyline closely related to the primary line is the internal change in Michael's values from being a relative outsider opposed to the activity of the family to being the vicious new head of the family. Michael's change is motivated by a series of events. His father is shot and nearly killed then almost assassinated at the hospital because of the complicity of crooked police. The police captain hits Michael, breaking his jaw. Michael is the only person who can avenge his father's shooting, which he does by killing two men. Hiding in Sicily, Michael's new wife is killed by an explosion meant for him. His brother is set up by the brother-in-law and killed. A Las Vegas casino owner roughs up Michael's other brother and refuses to sell out to the family. Finally, a traitorous friend sets Michael up to be killed. These events all contribute to Michael's change of values.

Three subplots appear in the film's structure. One is the romance of Michael and Kay. In the beginning, they are a loving couple. They have difficulty when the family problems hit but finally marry and have children. The romance concludes on an ironic note at the film's end when a perplexed Kay observes what Michael has become.

A second subplot shows Michael falling in love with and marrying a Sicilian girl while he is hiding out overseas. This subplot occupies a small portion of the middle of the film. It concludes when the girl is killed in an explosion meant for Michael.

The third subplot centers around a popular singer, godson to the Don, who asks the family head to help him land an important lead in a film. This is done when the studio head is given an "offer he can't refuse," and it is punctuated by the movie mogul finding the head of his prize race horse in his bed. The singer gets the film role. This subplot is unrelated to the central narrative storyline other than that it shows the ruthlessness of the family.

An interpersonal storyline defines the story in *Paper Moon,* as we watch to see if the itinerant con man and the nine-year-old orphan girl, who is his match at cons, will stay together in a father-daughter type of relationship. After being thrown together in the beginning, some of the beats in the story are: she saves him from possible exposure by a peace officer (increasing his respect for her); a woman almost romances his interest away, until the girl exposes her as a slut; he outwrestles a tough opponent and wins additional respect from her. The final and most difficult complication occurs when he drops her off at her aunt's house and it looks as though they will be separated for good. But they both realize how much they care for each other and get together at the end. (A parallel external concern is whether they can survive and avoid being caught pulling their scams.)

An interplay of character relationships helps define the new western film which appeared after the Second World War. *Shane* is an example of such a film, combining traditional western themes with strong interpersonal involvement. The basic storyline is one common to westerns: will Shane be able to help the homesteaders in their struggle with the villainous cattleman? Paralleling this—and it could be argued that this is the primary storyline—is the personal storyline of Shane wanting to give up the unsatisfying life of a wandering gunfighter and settle down. The antagonism of these two lines adds to the tension of the film.

The central storyline develops through a series of complications: challenges by the villains, fist fights, a hired gunslinger, a homesteader's murder and Shane's forced fight with his friend. Finally, Shane straps on his gun. Although wounded, he kills the villains. He rides off at the end having saved the homesteaders, but failing in his attempt to hang up his guns and escape his destiny as a gunfighter.

There is a strong interpersonal fabric to the film. The homesteader husband wants to build a town. He is opposed to violence but is finally forced to it. His son—the boy—finds a hero in Shane. The boy becomes the focus of conflict between the two contrasting ways of life represented by his father and Shane. The wife also reflects this conflict. She is true to her husband, but there is the suggestion that she is strongly attracted to Shane. However, this interpersonal romance remains on the platonic level.

Shane and the husband become friends. Shane works for the man and gains his admiration. They fight the villains together. But near the end, this interpersonal storyline takes a surprise twist—so typical of storyline development—when they fight each other over the right to confront the villains.

Shane and the boy share a special relationship, but it too takes a surprise twist. The boy sees Shane knock out the father with a blow from his gun during their big fight. This, of course, violates the unwritten code of the fair fist fight. Speaking from his anger, the boy says he hates Shane. Then he runs after Shane to apologize and witnesses the final shootout and Shane's departure.

As a final example of complex narrative structure, we'll do a detailed analysis of a half-hour *Mary Tyler Moore* television program.[7] This shows how, even with a half-hour program, there can be an involved complex structure.

For those unfamiliar with the series, here is a review of the characters. Mary Richards, the leading character, is a young woman working as producer in a television newsroom in Minneapolis. Lou Grant is her hard-boiled, sentimental boss. Murray is a newswriter colleague. Ted Baxter is the clownish news announcer. Georgette is Ted's flighty girlfriend (they were married in a later episode). Sue Ann is the bitchy hostess of a cooking program.

The following is a sketch of the action of the show—of what happens in the program.

> Ted Baxter comically sneaks into Lou's office, late for a staff meeting. The others are waiting for him. Lou announces that he has decided to hire a woman co-anchor newsperson to work with Ted. She will provide a woman's point-of-view editorial segment. Lou is setting up auditions for the job. He says that he wants a woman very much like Mary—attractive like Mary, about Mary's age, bright and well-dressed like Mary. But when Murray asks Why not Mary? Lou firmly says that she would be wrong for it. After the meeting, Ted lingers and offers to change his image—even grow a moustache—if Lou would not hire a newswoman but give Ted the additional money instead.
>
> Mary's apartment. Georgette enters and tells Mary how Ted is pushing her to try out for the job, since Ted wants them to have the additional money. But Georgette doesn't want to audition. She urges Mary to try it, saying that Mary would be perfect for it. But Mary is reluctant, and only says that she might consider it.
>
> At the office the next day, Murray urges Mary to audition, But she is still unsure. Ted is peeved that Mary didn't support Georgette for the job.
>
> Lou and Mary talk in his office. He explains that he doesn't want Mary auditioning because he wouldn't want to disappoint her if she didn't get the job, for Mary has succeeded at just about everything she has tried. She hasn't had such a disappointment. Mary objects that once she ran for a high school office and was disappointed. Did she lose? No, but she didn't win by as much as she had expected. Lou finally agrees that Mary can audition.

After Mary leaves Lou's office, Ted enters. He has overheard Lou saying that Mary can audition. Ted accuses Mary of intrigue in order to get more money, of being a schemer and conniver. Then Ted concludes to a flabbergasted Lou: "She's my kind of woman!"

COMMERCIAL BREAK

In her apartment, Mary is practicing saying "Thank you, Ted" as she might if she were closing the news show. Sue Ann, hostess of the Happy Homemaker program, comes in and tells Mary that she is going to try out for the job. Sue Ann is sick of eleven years of smiling in the role of the kitchen-trapped Happy Homemaker. Mary tells Sue Ann that she, Mary, is also auditioning. Sue Ann's phony smile appears as she accuses Mary of conflict of interest, of using undue influence and of being a two-bit, double-crossing fink. Mary protests that she wants to be fair, but Sue Ann leaves with the exit line: "Mary, dear, in the language of the kitchen, that's a crock!"

In the newsroom, the audition is under way. One candidate finishes her editorial using large words which are completely incomprehensible to a bewildered Ted. Then Sue Ann auditions. She tries to do a story describing destructive mud slides in Alaska but keeps breaking into the artificial smile and kitchen chatter of the Happy Homemaker, mixing up information about the mud slides with material from old Happy Homemaker shows.

Mary arrives to audition just as Enid, an attractive Black woman, finishes her reading. During a five-minute break, a well-meaning Ted gives Mary some advice on speaking to the camera. He urges her to personalize the camera, to caress it with her eyes, make love to it with her eyes, letting her eyes say to the camera, "Be my love." Ted claims that this is his secret. But when Mary tries it, she looks absurd, causing Lou to comment about her weird eye business, "Mary, whatever you got in your eye—you wanna get it out?"

Later in Lou's office, Murray and Lou are talking. We learn that Mary didn't get the job; Enid did. Enid bursts in to give an embarrassed Lou a hug of appreciation and joy.

Murray and Enid leave. Mary enters, and is now alone in the office with Lou. Lou can't bring himself to tell Mary that she didn't get the job. Instead, he dissembles by saying it hasn't been decided yet and offers to let her make the final decision. He shows Mary the videotaped segment made by Enid. It's well done. Enid says that there is no such thing as a woman's point of view but that she can speak honestly for herself. Lou is confident that Mary will recognize Enid's obvious talent and declare the woman the winner. But Mary doesn't do so. Rather, she says that she honestly feels that she is the best one for the job. She likes Enid's tape but sees the statement as a one-time thing. For the day-to-day presentation of the news, Mary feels she is the best one.

Just then Enid bursts in, interrupting, and thanks Lou once again for the job. Then she leaves as quickly as she came in. Mary learns of Lou's deception. Lou confesses to Mary that he lied to spare her feelings. Mary is genuinely hurt by this and close to tears. She asks Lou how she did. Lou says she finished fourth.

Mary: Fourth!?
Lou: I didn't want to hurt you.
Mary: Fourth!?!
Lou: Sixth!

COMMERCIAL BREAK

In the tag, Mary is alone in the office getting ready to go home. Enid enters and says she's sorry that Mary didn't get the job, then adds: "Hey, you wanna go have a drink?" Mary responds: "Sure, I'd love to." And they start to go out together with the strong implication that a new friendship is developing. Ted enters to supply the final comic touch when Enid asks if he remembers her and he replies, "Sure, you're the black one."

Before reading further, why not take the time to sketch out your own story analysis of the program. Define the basic storyline and any other storylines. Place yourself in the position of the writer and determine the deep structure which underlies the action of the program as described above.

Here's the situation of the program as described in *TV Guide:* "When Lou announces that he wants to hire a woman reporter to share on-camera duties with Ted, Mary musters up her courage and decides to audition for the job." This gives the viewer an idea about the show, but it isn't a complete basic story.

Here is the basic storyline:

> Mary accepts the challenge to audition for a job sharing on-camera duties with Ted, even though it means risking failure—something new for Mary. She has to overcome: Lou's doubts, her own initial reluctance, Ted's conniving, competition from Sue Ann and competition from Enid. She thinks she has the job, only to learn that she didn't do well and lost out to Enid. But in the end it looks as though Mary gains a friend in her new co-worker.

Two storylines develop around Mary: (1) the external storyline—will Mary get the job? and (2) the internal storyline—how will Mary cope with the personal disappointment if she fails? Both are prominent storylines, but which is the most dominant? At first glance, it would seem that the external line of winning the job is primary, but a closer look suggests that the internal line is structurally dominant.

Here is the evidence favoring the internal line about Mary's disappointment as being the basic storyline. Early in the program we learn of Lou's concern should Mary fail and be disappointed. We are clearly told that she has succeeded at virtually everything she has attempted; this seems to be setting us up for concern over her response should she fail. We also learn about Mary's failure before she does. This is a suspense device designed to make us wonder how Mary will respond once she finds out. The climax then occurs when she learns that she didn't get the job. Although we've been concerned about Mary's reaction, our concern is moderated by the scene's ending with a joke ("Fourth?! . . . Sixth!"). Then the tag further resolves things by showing that Mary gains a new friend.

Why is it so important to correctly identify the primary storyline? Because this is the main story the writer is telling. In this example, it is the story of Mary facing a failure experience. It is *not* fundamentally a story about Mary's almost getting a new job. The distinction is critical, for it determines the focus of the entire narrative. While both storylines obviously interrelate, the central focus is on Mary's internal response and not just on whether or not she succeeds in getting the job. If there is any doubt, look at the climax and work back to see what it resolves. The important question can't be whether or not Mary got the job, since we learn quite early that she didn't. Instead, the emphasis is on her personal reaction. She is upset. How does she deal with the disappointment? The joke is a subtle answer to this. And the tag reinforces that things will be fine. In this story, the internal and external storylines develop together. Mary's auditioning for the job is a necessary prerequisite to her being turned down for it. While the basic story is Mary's internal problem, the action of the story is largely the external line. Here are the complications in the development of the story:

1. Lou's doubts and opposition are an early stumbling block. He doesn't want Mary, just someone like Mary. She finally overcomes his opposition and gets permission to audition, but his doubts remain.
2. Mary's own reluctance is another initial hurdle to surmount. Urged on by Murray and Georgette, she finally decides to try.
3. Ted's conniving isn't really a serious obstacle, since we can't take him seriously, but he does try to keep her from getting the job in the beginning. Later he tries to be genuinely helpful and ceases to be an obstacle.
4. Sue Ann is also too ridiculous to present a serious hurdle, but she stings Mary by her accusation of unfair competition. Sue Ann ceases to be an obstacle when we see her do so badly in the audition.
5. The final complication—which Mary doesn't overcome, unlike most happy-ending stories—is Enid's effective competition. The story reaches a strong crisis point when Mary is asked to decide between herself and Enid. Mary's choice of herself is the unexpected twist which then precipitates the final climax between Lou and Mary.

Some secondary storylines enrich the story's pattern. Lou has the problem of dealing with Mary's failure and disappointment. He shies away from this. The subterfuge he tries backfires. Just as we identify with Mary and her problems, so we identify with Lou and share his concern. Both Ted and Sue Ann also have problems. Ted doesn't want to share his news anchor role; Sue Ann wants to break free of her Happy Homemaker role. These might be considered minor storylines, but we don't take the characters too seriously. These are best considered as complications to the main storylines.

There are some other things to consider about this narrative. There is a surprise twist when Mary is asked to pick the winner and picks herself over Enid in spite of the excellence of Enid's presentation. Some such surprise near the end of a narrative is a frequent device. We can also note how the various problems and developments of the story hold our interest. We wonder why Lou doesn't want Mary to audition. Then, when she does, will she win the job?

How will Lou tell her if she doesn't? How will she take it if she fails? Will she decide to audition? How will Sue Ann handle the audition? Will Mary pick Enid over herself? And so on. Such suspense questions hold our attention to the story.

Finally, here is a graphic representation of the structure of the program.

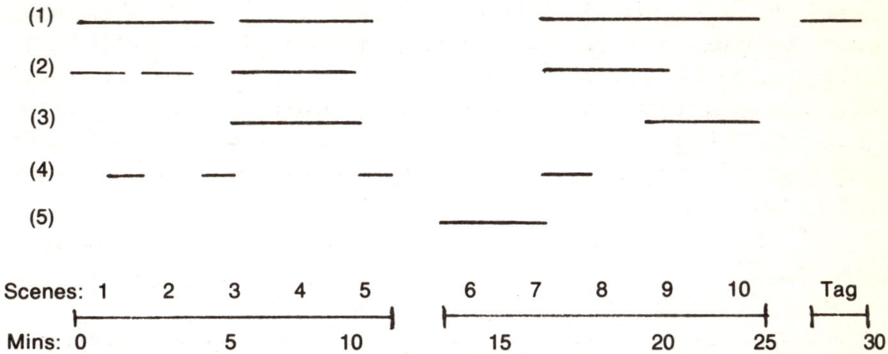

(1) Mary's personal storyline—risking and handling disappointment
(2) Mary's external storyline—will she get the job?
(3) Lou's personal storyline—dealing with Mary's disappointment
(4) Ted's storyline—eliminate competition
(5) Sue Ann's storyline—get the job

This shows how Mary's personal (1) and external (2) storylines develop simultaneously until nearly the end of the program. Lou's personal storyline (3) overlaps Mary's. So does Ted's storyline (4), except for part of scenes 3 and 5. Sue Ann's storyline (5) is developed in only two scenes, 6 and 7. Mary's storyline may also overlay scene 6, although it is not shown that way in the graph. The primary storyline is so much present in a story that except for some obviously independent subplots with other characters it is difficult to say when it doesn't occur.

Narrative Structure: A Review

A film story* is not simply a series of happenings. It has an underlying deep structure which both forms the material and informs the experience of the viewer through such techniques as suspense and surprise. Traditional dramatic narrative structure follows a beginning-middle-end pattern as expressed through conflict-development-resolution. In order to maintain this structure with unity

*A distinction is often made between story and plot. The story is the structure underlying the action, while the plot is the way that the story works itself out through actions and events. The same "story" might be plotted any number of different ways. This is a meaningful distinction in some contexts, but less important here.

and a proper balance of the elements in the pattern, a screenwriter works from a basic story. This basic story is an economical statement which establishes whose story it is as well as the conflict-development-resolution storyline that underlies the narrative. While one storyline usually dominates the narrative, other storylines enrich the complex pattern of the story. Such lines may be external, interpersonal or internal. There may be a separate storyline about each major character in the film. When the narrative structure is completed, the writer has outlined the screenplay and knows how the story develops.

Then what? Once the outline is set, the next step is to expand the initial paragraphs into a narrative story that fills in more details and clearly shows the beats—the plot developments—of the story. If the narrative story works, it is expanded into a scene breakdown—a scene by scene outline of the screenplay—and then finally into a script. And so it grows. At each step it is checked by the writer, and perhaps by the producer or story editor, to be certain that there are no problems. If something isn't quite working well at any level, it should be reworked until effective. This organic approach permits reworking the story at each level—because it is easier to see story problems this way, and a rewrite is easier to do in earlier stages than when dealing with a full script.

Do all writers work this way? Not necessarily. Many do because they find it the most effective way to develop a film or television story. Others do so because of the exigencies of the business. They need to get approval of preliminary outlines before going on to the next level. Some professional writers may not appear to follow the approach since they have so learned a sense of structure that it is second nature to them. They can tackle a story from almost any point and still insure that it is adequately structured. They have an understanding of structure, which is so important to a screenwriter—or to a producer, director, story editor or other creative filmmaker. But it is especially important to the beginning screenwriter to follow this approach. Perhaps no other skill that a screenwriter needs is as important as an intuitive sense of story structure. The beginning writer should work with the concepts presented in this chapter until they are clearly understood. (My experience in the classroom suggests that this is rarely as easy as the student thinks it will be. An understanding of basic story structure is one of the most difficult skills for a student to learn.)

One way to help with this is to analyze films and television programs, working from the surface structure down to the basic story deep structure. Try to reconstruct the basic story as did the writer of the film. Sometimes it helps to go to the climax and work backwards—what is it that is resolved? Be careful of the tendency to take the external storyline as the primary one that structures the narrative. It may be, but it might also be subordinate to an internal or interpersonal storyline. Once you have mastered the concept of narrative structure, you have taken a large step toward becoming a screenwriter.

Don't be discouraged in your analyses if you discover some badly structured stories. There are nearly as many of these as there are films or television programs with weak characters, bad dialogue and pretentious themes. If you happen to hit a bad one, try again with another. (And see how much you can learn from identifying the structural weakness in a film or program.)

Now we want to consider some techniques in developing a story structure.

REFERENCES

1. Sam Keen, "Don Juan's Power Trip," *Psychology Today* 11 (December 1977): 42.
2. Maya Pines, "Good Samaritans at Age Two?" *Psychology Today* 13 (June 1979): 66–77.
3. Cf. Markellos S. Nomikos *et al,* "Surprise Versus Suspense in the Production of Stress Reaction," *Journal of Personality and Social Psychology* 8 (1968): 204–8.
4. Wolf Rilla, *The Writer and the Screen* (New York: W.H. Allen, 1973).
5. Sam Rohdie, "Totems and Movies," in *Movies and Methods,* ed. Bill Nichols (Berkeley: University of California Press, 1976), pp. 469–81.
6. Francois Truffaut, *Day for Night,* tr. Sam Flores (New York: Grove Press, 1975).
7. This program was aired on June 21, 1975, and has subsequently been shown in syndicated reruns.

Also:

Swain, Dwight. *Film Scripwriting*. New York: Hastings House, 1976.

Vale, Eugene. *The Technique of Screenplay Writing*. New York: Grosset and Dunlap, 1944; revised and reprinted, 1972.

3

Selected Narrative Techniques

> The rule of the "story" is so powerful that the image, which is said to be the major constituent of film, vanishes behind the plot it has woven . . . so that the cinema is only in theory the art of images.[1]
>
> —Christian Metz

THIS CHAPTER WILL begin by discussing two narrative techniques, exposition and preparation. Then it will consider some things that a writer will decide about when writing his story: point of view, point of attack, pace, tone, subject matter, the title and television format. Finally, we discuss some other things that affect the film: openings, contrasts, story patterns, genre and filmic tradition, film technique, realism, the audience and the tension release laugh.

Exposition

A film will rarely show us every detail that is important to the story. Film stories usually start "in the middle of things" (in medias res) so the story events are underway before the start of the film. We need to learn about these past events in order for the story to make sense to us. In other cases, something will happen offscreen that we need to find out about. Exposition is the technique of giving us this information. It helps us understand and appreciate the story. *From Here to Eternity* is a complex story with a number of different storylines. In order for events to make sense, we have to learn about things that took place prior to the film's beginning. We need to know that Pruit was replaced as bugler of his previous army company because the position was given to a friend of the commanding officer. Pruit is a boxer who won't fight anymore because he once blinded a man in the ring. His new captain is obsessed with having a successful boxing team; they just missed winning a championship the previous year. The captain's wife lost their baby through her husband's drunken, cheating inconsideration. And so on. Obviously we won't understand the conflicts and the character's reactions unless we know these things. This prior material is called the *backstory*.

We also have to learn about offscreen action in this film. A prime example occurs when Maggio enters the stockade where Fatso, the stockade sergeant, is waiting to get him. We expect the worst, but we don't see the actual beating. Rather, we learn of it later when a soldier newly released from the stockade describes it to Pruit. Giving us this information is the technique of exposition.

Handling exposition effectively is often a thorny problem for the writer. How do you say these things without it seeming awkward and obvious, without breaking the continuity of the narrative or without hurting the credibility of the film or the interest of the audience? (These problems are worse if the audience is being given information which the characters already know. Why rehash it again if they already know it?) The challenge for the writer is to tell us what we need to know without having it sound unrealistic, obvious and spoon-fed.

Let's begin by looking at some *poor* ways to meet this challenge. These are examples of exposition that don't work. They seem too awkward, obvious and dull.

The classic illustration of blatant exposition is that of the "well-made play" of the late nineteenth century. Such a play might open with a maid and a butler setting the table for a formal family dinner in an English mansion. As they lay out the silverware, they gossip together—and thereby inform us about everything we need to know about the characters and action to this point—the backstory. "Isn't it exciting about Master Harry returning after ten years lost in India?" "Yes, but what will this mean for his half brother, Lord Paddington, who inherited all when the old lord, Harry's father, died?" "And what about Lady Marion? She was Harry's fiancée, but thinking him lost is now betrothed to Sir Percival!" "Yes, and. . . ." And so it goes, piling exposition atop exposition until the table is set, and they have said it all. Then they leave and the family enters; and we watch the characters we have just learned about. Such exposition is laughable today, or is it? Do we detect the writer giving us exposition when in a monologue phone conversation the heroine lays out her problems to a girl friend while seemingly asking her help?

Since exposition means giving us information, it is often done in dialogue. And since we need to know the backstory in order to understand what's going on, we often get it in a big dose near the beginning of the film. The combination can be deadly.

Paddy Chayefsky's original screenplay for *The Hospital* won critical acclaim, but still has a strong dose of talky exposition near the beginning when the main character unloads his problems on a friend. We learn that he and his wife have broken up, that he's kicked out his "Maoist" son, that his daughter is a hippie who's had two abortions and that he's thought of suicide a number of times.

A more difficult talky scene appears at the beginning of the undistinguished film *Nine Hours to Rama*. A young terrorist suspect is being mildly interrogated by the chief of police in a town in India. We are given a short history lesson about India and Mahatma Ghandi and the turmoil now afflicting the country. We learn of an assassination plot against Ghandi. The policeman, once a terrorist sort of radical himself, lectures the boy about the plot. And on and on in a very talky scene.

One of the worst offenders in presenting unmitigated exposition was a television movie: *Mr. and Ms. and the Magic Show Mystery*. It opens on an attractive couple getting ready to go out. She is sewing a skirt; he's getting dressed. We learn that they are married and that he has not worn ties nor she a skirt for some time now. She graduated from a prestigious woman's college. He is now a beach-bum lawyer. She is from Shaker Heights (an expensive Cleveland suburb) and has money. His father is a police lieutenant. The woman who invited them to a magic show that evening is a former date of his and a skilled magician. And . . . so it continues with all sorts of bits of information. The action during all of this has been nothing but their dressing. We have had our noses rubbed in this glaring exposition.

Well then, how can we effectively present exposition? While dialogue is the most common way to give exposition, it can be done by other means, such as a flashback (if appropriate), a narrator, or even, succinctly, by a title such as "Berlin, 1946." Most of the time, however, it will be in dialogue, and the writer will try to present it as naturally and unobtrusively as possible.

One way to do this is to place it within an emotional situation in which we become so involved that we are unaware of being fed exposition. It's the idea behind exposition given while a couple are arguing—"Your mother is . . . !" "But if you hadn't . . . !"—and we're caught up in the emotion of the relationship while at the same time we're being given needed exposition. Something like this is cleverly done in *The Goodbye Girl* when we and the woman learn that the man trying to take over her apartment is an actor. (The man she had been living with subleased it to him without telling her.) They are arguing. Then he says a dialogue line about going to see a lawyer friend. She blurts out: "Oh, God, another actor!" For she recognized the line from the play *A Streetcar Named Desire* and realizes that he is an actor. From this discovery, they go on to talk about each other, about theater and the like. How much better to have the information come out this way instead of the trite "What do you do?" or "Here's what I do . . ." If something has to be explained in dialogue, it's nice to have something else—such as character interaction—going at the same time to involve us.

While exposition often comes near the beginning in order to give us the backstory, it's better not to give this all in one obvious dose. It is more effective if it is revealed gradually over the length of the story.

It also helps if exposition can be presented in a way that seems natural. One such way is when a character needs to know something. Perhaps he has even been trying to discover it. Then, when the character finds out, so do we. In *Chinatown* we learn that a young girl is both the sister and daughter of the female lead character as a result of the latter's incest with her father. This is given to us in a powerful, emotional moment as the male lead character discovers the information from the woman while slapping her again and again as she keeps repeating: "my sister . . . my daughter . . . my sister . . . my daughter . . ."

Pick the right moment to reveal some exposition. Often this is the most dramatic time for us to learn it. It's after he falls in love that we might most dramatically learn that a man is impotent. In *Butch Cassidy and the Sundance Kid,* we learn that the Kid can't swim just before the two must leap off a cliff into a river in order to escape pursuers. And it's when Butch is facing a gunfight showdown that we learn he hasn't killed a man before.

Exposition is awkward when it's just ladled out to us in a way that makes us realize we're being given exposition. But it isn't offensive if we're being told something we want to know at that point. The mental hospital ward in *One Flew Over the Cuckoo's Nest* is an unappealing place, but McMurphy is overjoyed to be there. We want to know why. So when we are told, it doesn't seem like blatant exposition, since it's satisfying our need to know. In the *Mary Tyler Moore* episode analyzed earlier, we hear Lou saying: "A woman . . . like Mary . . . like Mary . . . but Mary wouldn't be right for it." Why wouldn't she be right, we wonder. Later it's explained.

One type of film is structured around the idea of a horrible past event affecting the present. We want to know what the past event was and usually learn it only later in the film. Often such a film features a stranger who rides into a town to revenge something the town has done previously. In *High Plains Drifter,* the central character returns to revenge a vicious whipping that took place in the town years before. *Bad Day at Black Rock* presents a town that is hostile to a curious stranger; only later in the film do we—and the central character—discover that the town had burned out a Japanese family during the Second World War.

In *The Midnight Man,* the central character is a college security guard who was formerly a metropolitan homicide detective but is now on parole from prison. We learn near the beginning of the film about his former job and his parole. But it isn't until nearly halfway through the story that we discover that his crime was shooting a man who was in bed with his wife. By the time this is revealed, we've been wanting to know it for some while.

Here are some effective examples of exposition. *Husbands* opens on a series of still photographs behind the titles that show four friends clowning around together while posing for candid shots. Thus we already know the relationship of the men when the story begins at the funeral of one of them. *Citizen Kane* uses an eight-and-a-half minute newsreel in the beginning to give us information about Charles Foster Kane. We see his palatial home, Xanadu, his funeral, shots of his early life, different opinions about the man ("Communist," "Fascist"), his marriage, love affair, his political life and the like. The reporter's search for information serves as motivation to have others talk about Kane.

Patton also uses a newsreel as a device to give us information about Patton's background and to cover events that had happened offscreen. We also learn about Patton from the captain in the German High Command headquarters, whose job is to psych out this enemy general and report his findings to the command. He tells us that Patton is a sixteenth-century man, a romantic, who would conquer Sicily first. (The film events confirm this even though the German generals don't believe him.) This is a clever way to give exposition without seeming to break the story development or the suspense involved.

Annie Hall begins with Woody Allen as the character Alvy talking directly to the camera and the audience about his life and about the film. *Hour of the Wolf* begins with a written prologue, and with the wife of the deceased painter being interviewed by an offscreen interviewer and telling us what we need to know to set up the story and our involvement with it.

Television series have some special exposition problems. It may be necessary to fill in the background of the series on each episode for any new viewers. This is done in the opening and often integrated with titles, as when *The Fugitive* tells us why he is fleeing and *The Six Million Dollar Man* recaps his construction. Situation comedies can do this with theme songs, which explain the background of the series—*Gilligan's Island, The Beverly Hillbillies, Green Acres, Rhoda, The Jeffersons, All in the Family*.

Star Trek uses the captain's log with Captain Kirk's voice-over commentary as though he were dictating to the ship's tape-recorded log. *Mission Impossible* uses taped messages that self-destruct after we learn about the mission on which the team is being sent. *Charlie's Angels* uses a phone call from Charlie to the girls explaining their assignment.

Giving information or revealing the backstory or an offscreen happening needn't be obvious if the exposition is handled skillfully.

Preparation

In *Deliverance*, the Jon Voight character has an arrow aimed at the mountain man who has been shooting at them. Suddenly he begins to shake with buck fever, a nervous response some people get when about to kill something. This gives us a tense moment, but is it a legitimate bit to suddenly get buck fever at a life or death moment like this?

In *Duel*, the main character is escaping from a demonic tractor-trailer truck which is bent on his destruction. He finally reaches an upgrade where he thinks he can outrace the slower truck, only to have his car overheat and slow to fifteen miles an hour. Meanwhile, the truck gains on him. Suspenseful, yes; but isn't there something fraudulently coincidental about his losing radiator water at this tense moment? Can't we complain that the film gratuitously brings this incident in from left field just to increase suspense?

If that were all there was to it, we could. But in each of these films the events were acceptable because we had been prepared for them beforehand. In *Deliverance,* another character explains buck fever earlier in the film, and we see Voight come across a deer in the woods, draw a bead on it and then start shaking. The nervousness causes his shot to go awry, and the deer escapes. We fully accept his later action as probable because of this earlier experience. Early in *Duel,* the central character stops at a gas station and is told that he needs a radiator hose, but he ignores the advice, thinking it just a sales pitch. At a second station later on, he asks the attendant to check the hose, but she doesn't have time to do so. It is no surprise then that the hose ruptures and he loses water, power and speed. We had been prepared for it.

Preparation sets things by raising events from the merely possible to the probable—or perhaps even to the inevitable. The technique prepares us for certain actions or events, or for the use of a special object or person. When these actions happen later, they don't seem coincidental and convenient. Even the most casual plant can unconsciously prepare us for the ready acceptance of a later development. Not to prepare us risks breaking our involvement as we wonder "Where did that come from?"

We speak of preparation in two senses. *Foreshadowing* is a way of setting up actions, events and story twists. There are many ways to foreshadow. The mood and atmosphere of the setting can foreshadow what might occur there. A look from a character may presage a future killing, or a romance. A howling wind can set up mystery. A *plant* is an object, a person or information which is established early so that it can be used effectively later. Paraphrasing Chekhov, if you want to use a gun in Act III, show it in Act I. Preparation will become clearer as we consider a number of examples.

At the end of *Slaughterhouse Five,* Billy Pilgrim is comfortably settled on the planet Tralfamadore with the starlet Montana Wildhack. He chose her from among all women, but it's not been an arbitrary choice. We've been prepared for it. We first see Montana's picture as the centerfold pinup in a girlie magazine that Billy takes away from his son. Later, Billy and his family are at a drive-in movie where Billy watches Montana perform on the screen while his family bickers among themselves. It's no surprise then that he chooses her.

In *The Birds,* the first attack by sparrows through the chimney leaves the house in a shambles. In the aftermath of the scene, we are casually (but carefully) shown the mother picking up pieces of broken crockery while the conversation continues. The mother later visits a neighbor. Getting no reply to her knock, she enters the house. There are pieces of broken crockery in the room. It's a fine suspense device since we know what this means. It foreshadows her discovery of the neighbor horribly killed by the birds.

In the violent conclusion of *Straw Dogs,* the protagonist kills an assailant by catching his neck in a large and gruesome springhold bear trap. It's a shocking instrument to use. It was planted early in the film when we see him buying it "to hang over the mantlepiece" and being warned that it's dangerous.

At the end of *One Flew Over the Cuckoo's Nest,* the Chief picks up a large marble sink, throws it through the window, and escapes from the mental hospital. This is a symbolic fulfillment of an early foreshadowing when McMurphy bets others he can do it, tries, but can't.

In *Young Mr. Lincoln,* attorney Lincoln uses an almanac to prove the innocence of his client (there was no moon that night, so the witness was lying when he said he saw the client commit the crime). The almanac is first seen as a writing support when the mother asks Lincoln to write to her imprisoned sons. On the first day of the trial, the book is on Lincoln's table near his hat. Then, in a quiet night scene, Lincoln is shown fingering it with apparent casualness. He finally produces it from his hat at the end of the second day of trial and makes his point.

While we don't learn the meaning of "Rosebud" until the end of *Citizen Kane,* we've been prepared for the revelation both by the "snow scene" paperweight Kane is holding when he dies and by scenes showing young Kane playing with the sled in the snow.

In *A Touch of Class,* the protagonist mentions that he sometimes gets back spasms. This prepares us for a later moment when he is trying to make love and his back goes out before he can get very far (just one of a number of obstacles which keep him from culminating his affair).

The President's Analyst is a comedy about the President's psychotherapist, who flees his job because of the pressure it puts him under. But because he possesses confidential knowledge about the President, he is pursued by various enemy agents as well as by the FBR and CEA. A surprise twist occurs near the end when we discover that the most serious threat is from TPC—The Phone Company! This comes as a comic surprise, but we really have been prepared for it. Phones are prominently featured in the film. Once when the analyst calls his girl friend, we observe that she tapes his call, then later plays the tape back over the phone to whomever. Hiding out at a citizen's house, he makes a desperate phone call for help—and we see it's being taped by the young boy of the family. Later, when being shot at by enemy agents, one of his assailants gets stuck in a phone booth and can't open its door. These are subtle incidents that set up the unusual plot twist.

A skillful screenwriter can use the principle of preparation in some interesting ways. The future development of *Blow-Up* is prefigured early in the film when a painter friend discusses one of his paintings with Thomas. "They don't mean anything when I do them—just a mess. Afterwards, I find something to hang onto—like that—like—like—that leg. And then it sorts itself out. It adds up. It's like finding a clue in a detective story." This symbolically foreshadows what Thomas will do with the photographic blow-ups. It's underscored later when Thomas shows the painter's wife the grainy, extremely enlarged photograph of the murder and she responds: "It looks like one of Bill's paintings."

Preparation, then, is the technique of planting or foreshadowing so that later developments seem probable rather than coincidental and solely for the convenience of the author. The plant may seem very casual when it appears, but it will unconsciously prepare the audience for a later happening. Surprises can be exciting but not if they break the fabric of probability of the film. A development frequently takes an unusual twist different from what we expected, but not so different as to seem implausible. By preparing us, things do fit.

You can familiarize yourself with methods of preparation by discovering them in films and television programs.

As he writes the script, the writer will have to make decisions about point of view, point of attack, pace, tone, subject matter, the title of the film and the demands of the television format if writing for that medium.

Point of View

Generally, point of view is the perspective from which the writer tells the story. This gets quite complex in a film where it involves narrator, narrative, character presence and the use of the camera. Here are four traditional point-of-view approaches found in literature.

1. *The First Person*—in which the author appears as a character telling the story using the "I" form of address.
2. *Omniscient*—where the analytical author knows all about the characters and events and may go into the thoughts of various characters or comment on the story itself.
3. *Scenic* or *Objective*—in which the author seems not to be there. He is objective and exterior to the story as would be an observer or a recording camera.
4. *Central Intelligence*—where the author tells the story through one of the characters depicted in the third person "he" or "she." We are limited to the point of view of that character and what he/she perceives of the action or feels about it. This approach shares much with the other three. The author can give background and description as in the omniscient. Like the scenic, the author doesn't seem to be there. Like the first person, we're limited to the feelings and perceptions of a single character, although he is depicted in third and not first person.

Film uses uniquely cinematic variations of literary points of view. There are a number of different senses in which we speak of filmic point of view. There's a general sense of point of view as it fits the story, sort of corresponding to the literary points of view. This refers to the perspective from which the story is told, the "narrator" in the story. Because the camera records the surface of what it is filming, some points of view are more suitable to film than others. The first person is difficult to do in film. A voice-over narration can have a character using the "I" form, but the images of the camera quickly pull us back from the purely subjective.

The omniscient point of view appears variously in film. The film's "author" may appear to know all about the characters and events. He may even go into the thoughts of various characters, although it is unusual to do this with too many characters. It is rare for the filmmaker to comment directly about the film although sometimes a voice-over narrator can express commentary about the main character, as in *Tom Jones*.

The scenic or objective point of view is commonly used in films and on television. The "narrator" of such films is the recording camera—the unseen, outside observer of the action. We get this feeling in a film such as John Ford's *Fort Apache*. Now the camera is on one character, now with another. No single perspective dominates the film.

The central intelligence point of view is also commonly used in film. The narrative story is presented through the perspective of a particular character. We see those things that are important to the character and observe his reactions to the various events. We may be restricted to knowing only what the character knows and seeing only what he sees; or we may be restricted to what happens in his presence, his immediate surroundings. This happens whenever a film revolves around a particular character. This point of view dominates when the character appears in virtually every scene, as does Benjamin in *The Graduate,* Thomas in *Blow-Up,* Bobby in *Five Easy Pieces* and Guido in *8½*.

Multiple points of view are commonly used in film. Points of view can shift as the action shifts focus from one character to another. *The China Syndrome* begins as the reporter's point of view (it is her story). At one point, we shift to the point of view of the nuclear power plant's chief engineer. The film alternates between these two points of view—now with the reporter, now with the engineer. A number of scenes feature both characters together. Only once or twice does the film deviate from these characters. A television dramatization of the killing of Israeli Olympic athletes (*21 Hours at Munich*) was told through the points of view of a security supervisor, a reporter and one of the terrorists. The two television programs dramatizing the Israeli raid on Entebbe to free captive airline hostages developed through a number of points of view, including Israeli politicians and generals, a leader of the raid and the hostages.

Rashomon is an interesting experiment in differing points of view. It tells the story of a rape and homicide (or possibly suicide) in retrospect as perceived differently by four persons. Three are the participants: a notorious bandit, who may have committed the crimes; the dead Samurai warrior (as told through a priestess medium); and the latter's raped wife. The fourth is a woodcutter who alleges to have accidentally witnessed the event, although his version is also questionable. Although none disputes the facts of the event—the violation of the woman and the death of her warrior husband—each has a different version of how it happened. These are shown in flashbacks as each gives testimony before an (unseen) police magistrate. The episode is told and shown four times, from each person's point of view. However, the camera is not used subjectively in any case.

Whenever he is presenting a presumably historical event as history—an airline crash, a nuclear power plant incident or a crime—the writer has to choose the perspective(s) from which to tell the story. If the event were a famous crime, it could be told from the point of view of the detective, a reporter, the criminal, the victim, a lawyer, an involved observer, a detached observer or from no particular perspective at all. A television special presented the Watergate affair from the perspective of John Dean, since it was based on his book about the incident. The same story could have been told from any number of other points of view.

There is a sense in which point of view refers to the camera placement within a scene. As viewers we may be located within the scene, as an observer who is very close to the action or a part of it; or we may be set outside the scene, looking on from a distance.

There's another sense in which a point of view is created by the degree to which the camera is subjective or objective. A subjective camera assumes the perspective of a character when, as in a point-of-view shot, we see what the character is looking at. The camera subjectively becomes the eyes of the character. These shots appear frequently in a film, but rarely will a subjective point of view dominate an entire film. *Lady in the Lake* tried this as an experiment. The camera is the character's eyes for the entire film. We see only what the character sees. The camera is kissed, punched and responded to as the character would be. The only time we see what the character looks like is when he looks into a mirror. This approach wasn't really successful; the gimmickry called too much attention to itself. A similar approach was used in the beginning of *Dark Passage,* as we see the world largely through the eyes of an escaped convict. We never see his face, except for a newspaper picture, until just after he has undergone plastic surgery, and then we view only a bandaged face. At this point the largely subjective camera approach is abandoned. (When he removes the bandages, we see his "new" face, that of Humphrey Bogart.) The television series *M*A*S*H* successfully used a subjective-camera point of view in one of its episodes. The entire program was filmed through the eyes of a wounded soldier who is patched up by the MASH doctors.

There is a subtle sense of point-of-view change when the camera moves closer to or further away from a purely subjective position. From one standpoint, a subjective camera is an either-or matter—either the camera acts as the character's eyes or it does not. But subjectivity is also a matter of degree. An over-shoulder shot is close to a subjective one (although it introduces the added complication of our seeing the character whose viewpoint we share). The camera can give us a shot close to a subjective one or increasingly away. Imagine two characters facing each other having a conversation. We can be purely subjective if we see one character as if through the eyes of the other character. Or the camera can shift around through an arc until it presents the most objective point of view—a two-shot perpendicular to the plane of the two characters. However, camera point of view gets even more complex. For, while the camera can act as, or close to, the eyes of a character, if the shot is of another character, this character's presence dominates the screen. It is an involved topic. Camera placement is often determined by the director, but there is no reason why a writer shouldn't specify the degree of subjective-objective camera if he feels this is crucial to the meaning of a scene.

Point of Attack

If the story is considered in its broadest sense to include all action leading up to the central events, if it includes the complete backstory, then there are many choices possible as to when to "attack" or begin the actual film story. A film that begins with the central character as a child and follows him/her through adulthood is one that attacks the broader story early. *Little Big Man* is such a story. However, a film, like a short story, usually attacks the story in the middle of things (in media res), that is, it starts at some point after things have already happened. The backstory has already happened when the film begins. *Dr. Strangelove* begins with the bombers already at their fail-safe point. Karen has already had her earlier breakdown when we meet her in *Through a Glass Darkly*. Guido already has his problem of not being able to complete his film in *8½*. Exposition then fills the audience in on the backstory.

The point to attack a story depends on the writer's conception of the story. It also depends on the demands of the basic story. If the storyline seems too rambling to sustain continual, taut suspense, it may be necessary to attack the story further along. If the conflict is one that holds our interest over a vaster narrative, then the story can be attacked earlier. A disconnected narrative might best be told by a later point of attack, using exposition to concisely provide needed backstory information. If the amount of exposition seems too overwhelming for the story, the writer might choose an earlier attack on the story. Generally, the writer will consider different points of attack and choose the one which seems most appropriate to him and then adapt the necessary story mechanics to realize his choice.

Pace

Pace refers to the speed and tempo of the film. A fast pace conveys vigor, excitement, confusion and drive. A slower pace is associated with thoughtfulness, languor, oppressiveness, tenderness and the like.

There are two aspects to the impression of pace in a film—speed and forward movement. We'll first consider pace in the sense of speed of activity or movement.

Rhythm, tempo and pacing refer to movement in the film and our perception of it. Rhythm is the pulse we feel as we view the film. Tempo is the rate of this rhythm—how fast or slow it moves. Pacing refers to the various changes in the tempo and rhythm. However, in practice, any distinction in these terms is largely academic. What is important is to realize that how a scene is constructed contributes to the pace of the film. Pace comes from the lengths of scenes and of speeches within the scene (as well as the speed of delivery of the lines). It comes from the action on the screen, from camera movement or from changes brought about through editing, lighting, sound and music. (The rhythm of *American Graffiti* is set largely by the rock music from Wolfman Jack's radio show.) Fast pacing comes from short scenes with fast-paced action. Slow rhythms develop from longer scenes with slower movement and less activity. Slower scenes are useful in building a mood, in giving us a chance to get to know characters or in providing a break from faster sequences. Fast and slow rhythms intermix in a film for desired effect; most films increase in tempo as the action builds toward the climax.

Another aspect of pace is the idea of *forward movement*—the subjective impression the audience has that the film is moving along at a progressive pace. Forward movement develops in the mind of the audience and is a function of our immersion in the narrative. If we are involved with the action, with dramatic suspense in the development of the story, we will have the impression that the film moves quickly. If we lose interest, the film seems to drag. This effect is clearly seen in a comparison of two television programs—an *All in the Family* episode and a situation comedy made in an advanced production class at a university. The *All in the Family* program had a slow tempo with many pauses and sustained reaction shots. The student production had some very brisk moments and snappy, escalating dialogue. Yet in spite of the fact that it physically seemed to move much faster, the subjective *impression* from this sit com was that it dragged. The audience was not involved in either the characters or the dramatic suspense of the story. In contrast, the *All in the Family* episode seemed to move much faster, even though it had a slower physical tempo. If the audience is continually involved, moving from one crisis to another in their concern for the story's development, the film will seem to move quickly for them. If they are not involved in the story, the film will seem slow. The writer achieves a strong sense of forward movement by using the suspense principle to construct a taut story that involves the audience in a developing conflict. If the conflict escalates with dramatic build, the audience will feel that the story is moving.

Pace will be discussed further when we consider the arrangement and structure of sequences and scenes.

Tone

Tone—mood and atmosphere—is the emotional climate of the film as can be described by such adjectives as: lively, sparkling, tame, vapid, insipid, violent, erotic, racy, florid, ponderous, warm, obscure, taut, crude, lyrical, delicate, heavy, somber, sordid, mysterious, forceful, bright, dignified and so on.

Many things contribute to the overall tone of the film—subject matter, settings, themes and the way that the characters feel about themselves and the other characters in the film. Perhaps as much as anything, the tone is set by the screenwriter's attitude toward the film, its characters and subject.

We can always expect a rather heavy experience with an Ingmar Bergman film. Fellini seems to have an easy-going, pleasurable relationship with his characters. Perhaps Fellini's influence helped Lina Wertmuller develop her striking contrasts of light and heavy moments in *Seven Beauties*. The horror and degradation of the concentration camp contrasts with humorous moments in the film. The central character kills a man and tries to cover the crime by chopping up the body and sneaking it away in suitcases. But the barbarity is mitigated because it is handled comically. We laugh at his reactions, for he can hardly bring himself to do the grisly deed. Then he fumbles with the suitcases. A dog follows him sniffing at what he's carrying. And so on in an effective interplay of the comic and the gruesome.

Kurosawa made his *Dodes'ka-den* about miserable persons scratching out a meager existence while living in shacks and junked car bodies. Yet he takes an easy, sympathetic attitude toward them, not a strongly polemic one. We sense that he likes these characters, and thus so do we. This is most pleasurably revealed in his treatment of the retarded youth who imagines himself a streetcar operator, as he moves around the junk area paths sounding like a trolley with his "Dodes'ka-den, dodes'ka-den." Kurosawa shows his sympathy for the boy in the way the sound track carries the actual sounds of a streetcar in sync with the boy's movements.

A screenwriter needs to decide rather early whether the tone of the film will be serious or humorous, heavy or light—or some variation or mixture of these. The subject matter largely determines this but not completely. There's a great deal of impact in the contrast of serious and comic in the same film. There is also a tradition in film and television of the non-heroic hero—the character who doesn't take himself too seriously in what are typically serious situations. There's much that is humorous about characters such as Jim Rockford, Columbo, McCloud, McMillan and the Mavericks. In one episode of *The Rockford Files,* Jim Rockford is pursued by a killer. Instead of being handled in a ponderous, deadly way, however, there's a feeling of humor, wit and tongue-in-cheek unselfconsciousness. The killer is paunchy and balding. He and Rockford complain and bicker to each other. He openly lets Rockford know his intentions, yet they both treat the threatening killing in a matter-of-fact, non-serious way. Other films have presented characters as likable and amusing who might just as well have been portrayed as stronger "heavies," for example, *Butch Cassidy and the Sundance Kid* and *Bonnie and Clyde*.

A satiric tone has a questionable reputation in Hollywood since it has often failed at the box office. However, this attitude is somewhat undeserved as demonstrated by the success of *If . . . , Dr. Strangelove, The Graduate* and *Carnal Knowledge*.

Irony is a commonly used device in film as well as in literature. It appears in the poetic justice of *Straw Dogs,* when the mathematician turns and devastatingly avenges himself on the men who pushed him around. Irony can make a comment at the end of a film to give impact to its meaning. In *All about Eve,* the young Phoebe is about to repeat Eve's destructive success scenario with Eve as the victim. Near the end of *The Godfather,* Michael is in church affirming the morality of his religion while his henchmen are murdering his enemies. At the end of *The China Syndrome,* the reporter has just made her live telecast about the catastrophe at the nuclear power plant, which resulted in the death of the conscientious engineer and near-devastating accident. The shot is of two television monitors in the station's control room. On one monitor is the continuing shot of the reporter at the power plant after she has given her story. She is no longer on the air. Instead, the air monitor shows what is presently being telecast: an ironic commercial for microwave ovens.

Comic irony frequently happens when we know something that the character doesn't and enjoy the joke being on him. It's the idea of hearing a character boast about how faithful his wife is to him, while we know that her lover is under the bed (which is just about what happens to poor, cuckolded Inspector Clouseau in *The Pink Panther*).

The screenwriter chooses the appropriate tone for his story. Part of it is how he feels about his characters and the subject matter and how he presents his characters' feelings about each other. Part of the choice of tone is deciding how much humor would benefit the story.

Subject Matter

Because a film has to attract an audience, a writer can't ignore the fact that some subjects have more intrinsic popular appeal than others. *Jaws,* with the threat of shark attacks, captured the popular imagination. *Star Wars, Star Trek* and *Close Encounters of the Third Kind* sparked widespread interest in futuristic science fiction. A film on an interesting subject will spawn imitators and soon a genre is born. It wasn't long ago that we were besieged with disaster films (*Earthquake, The Towering Inferno, The Poseidon Adventure*) and occult films (*Rosemary's Baby, The Exorcist, The Omen*). Television tastes run in similar fads. At one time or another the tube was rife with westerns, medical shows and lawyer shows. Now, it's situation comedies and jiggling pretty girl adventure shows like *Charlie's Angels*.

Just because the screenwriter recognizes that certain subject matter is intrinsically more appealing to the general audience doesn't mean that he has to follow every fad that comes along or that he should deliberately seek out exploitive and titillating material. Hopefully he has more integrity than that. It does mean that he has to ask—rather cold-bloodedly at times—if his idea for a film or television program will interest an audience.

One type of subject that seems to have consistent appeal is the "inside look," where the writer takes us into the inside of some operation or adventure and shows us how it happens. How would someone go about robbing the crown jewels or staging a successful raid to rescue terrorist hostages? *2001* shows us what it may be like to travel in space in some future time. *Dr. Strangelove* and *Fail-safe* illustrate how the Strategic Air Command conducts a bombing mission. One of the appeals of early episodes of the *Hawaii Five-O* television series was the way they took us into the inner workings of a police department; we get similar insights, at times, from *Police Story* and *Adam 12*. *Quincy* shows us what a medical examiner from the coroner's office does in his work. Doctor programs undoubtedly appeal to our interest in disease and its treatment or give us an idea of what it means to be a surgeon in a large hospital. Lawyer programs made many people more aware of courtroom procedure, even if in an overdramatized way.

Part of the appeal of historical films is what they tell us about the period that they represent. There's a certain interest in different life styles and in strange and exotic locations.

A film needn't have an exciting subject to attract an audience if it has other things going for it. But it doesn't hurt to have some intrinsic subject matter appeal.

The Title

It seems almost trivial to mention, but the title of a film or television series is a selling point. A vivid, promising title can arouse interest and help attract an audience. (For a film it is also helpful if the title can conveniently fit on a theater marquee.) Consider the intrinsic interest in such titles as: *Blow-Up*, *Casablanca*, *The China Syndrome*, *Dirty Harry*, *Easy Rider*, *The Exorcist*, *The Godfather*, *Hour of the Wolf*, *Jaws*, *The Love Boat*, *M*, *Midnight Cowboy*, *The Paper Chase*, *Soap*, *Star Wars*, *The Sting*, *2001* and *Z*.

Television Format

American television has some special format considerations based around the series itself, the presence of commercials and the notion that it is important to hook the viewer quickly to keep him from switching channels to a competitive program.

The half-hour and hour weekly series are the staple of television. A series offers the advantages of being on at a regular and expected time each week—at least in theory (network program directors have taken to shifting series around in search of ever-larger audiences). A series also offers faithful viewers the opportunity to get to know a "family" of characters and to watch these characters develop and grow with the passage of time.

A short, crisp, punchy teaser—often developing behind the opening titles—is frequently used to catch the attention and interest of the viewer.

On commercial television, the writer must deal with the presence of commercials and the corresponding need to write in "acts" around these. Most programs try to build to a high point prior to a commercial—a "strong curtain." Often there is a strong "curtain line" or joke—if the program is a comedy—just before the commercial break. It is important to try to carry the viewer's interest over the commercial break so that he doesn't switch to another channel to see what is being offered there. A strong story development just before the commercial break entices viewers to continue watching the program.

Act III of an hour program, which starts just after the half-hour commercial break, often begins with some subtle rehash of what has happened thus far in order to bring up to date any viewers who have switched over from another channel. If done, this should be short and should seem natural. For example, Jim Rockford driving in a car with a friend reviews some of the perplexing aspects of the case so far. This doesn't review everything, but it at least gives a new viewer some idea of what the basic storyline problem is. Like any exposition, this should seem unobtrusive and natural.

There are a number of other things that affect a film and its writing. These are: openings, contrasts, story patterns, genre and filmic tradition, film technique, realism, the audience and the tension-release laugh.

Openings

The opening is especially important because it is the audience's first introduction to the film. It should win their attention and interest. It sets the mood of the film. Some films use a shock opening to immediately involve us. *Halloween* begins with a long, sustained moving camera shot taken from the point of view of one whom we soon discover is the killer. The camera peeks in a window, sees a necking teenage couple going to an upstairs bedroom, moves around to the back door and enters the house. We see a hand picking up a knife. The camera continues up the staircase and finds the girl undressed and alone. We watch her through the eyeholes of a Halloween mask as she is slashed to death. Then the camera turns around, goes down the staircase and onto the front lawn. Then we cut and see that the killer is the victim's brother, an eight-year-old boy!

Other stories need time to develop, time to involve us with the characters and their relationships and conflicts, time to let us develop empathy and character identification.

The tone or mood of a film is set by the opening. The titles help to do this: *The Pink Panther* titles set the comic mood before the story begins. Music helps set the mood, as in *2001* and *Star Wars;* so, too, does sound, as with the haunting animal-like sounds and pounding rhythms of Sergio Leone westerns.

The television teaser is often used to hook the audience to the program. It may present the problem or conflict. We see a crime committed and wonder how the criminal will be caught, or we see a powerful threat which the series' characters will have to meet. Not all television programs have teasers, but those that do can use them to hook the audience or otherwise preview the coming program.

There's an instructive anecdote that illustrates how important an opening can be in cuing the audience as to how to respond to the film. When the theater musical *A Funny Thing Happened on the Way to the Forum* first opened, it didn't get the laughs it should have gotten. The creative talents of the show got together to diagnose what was wrong and came up with this: The show began with a love song; could this be cuing the audience to expect a light romance rather than a comedy? So they wrote a new song—"Comedy Tonight"—which informed the audience that there would be tragedy tomorrow, but comedy tonight. It worked. It cued the audience to expect a comedy and be prepared to laugh, and the show got even more laughs than had been expected.

Here is a review of some effective film openings. They set the tone for the rest of the film. *Jaws* opens tensely, as a woman swimmer is slowly discovered, then attacked by a shark. *8½* opens surrealistically, with Guido first trapped inside his car in a traffic jam, then floating high in the air like a balloon. A helicopter carrying a suspended statue of Christ flies high above Rome in *La Dolce Vita*. Smokestacks belching smoke and pollution establish a theme in *Red Desert*. *Seven Beauties* opens with orange-tinted newsreel footage of the war, jazz music and a rhythmic commentary punctuated periodically by "Oh Yeah." *Hiroshima, Mon Amour* presents a couple making love in what seems to be radioactive dust and intoning a strange litany: "You saw nothing in Hiroshima. Nothing." "I saw everything, everything." *Last Year at Marienbad* opens with the camera moving over the ornate baroque ceilings and walls of the chateau, while a man's voice recites a poetic commentary of remembrance. The opening of *El Topo* is as surreal and symbolic as the rest of the film. It features a man dressed in black riding a horse with his seven-year-old son seated behind him, the boy naked except for a hat and moccasins. They stop and the boy buries his first toy and his mother's picture in a strange and personal rite. Then, after titles, they ride into a town to view the bloody aftermath of a massacre. The old television series *Ben Casey* began with the camera in the point of view of a patient being rushed into an emergency operating room. We see the faces of doctors anxiously looking down on him. *Cria* opens on a child hearing her father making love to a best friend's wife. The father has a heart attack and dies during the lovemaking. *Pretty Baby* begins with a close-up of a twelve-year-old girl watching what we assume to be a sexual act (because of the offscreen rhythmic cries of a woman who seems to be approaching orgasm). It turns out that the cries are really those of the girl's mother giving birth to a baby brother.

Contrasts

Contrasts of all sorts appear in a film story, for they suggest conflict and tension: good and evil, strong and weak, youth and age, comic and serious. From their study of myths and folk tales, structuralist critics have concluded that there's a sense in which oppositions function as a basic characteristic of narrative. There will undoubtedly be many diverse contrasts and oppositions in a film story. These might be character contrasts, ranging from the stereotyped good guy and bad guy to the rich bitch and communist worker in *Swept Away* or HAL the computer and the live characters in *2001*. Comedy may be in contrast to bloody cruelty, as in *Seven Beauties* or Makavejev's *Sweet Movie*. Or the grotesque can stand against the tender, as in *El Topo*. Contrasts will also appear within a character, thereby giving him a more fully rounded sense of being. We all carry many contrasts and oppositions within us. These are the yin and the yang, which make us excitingly human. We live paradoxes and so might our major characters. Isn't a character more interesting if he is both a rogue and a man of character?

There is a value to oppositions, paradoxes and contradictions when the writer is forming his ideas in the earlier stages of the creative process. Research on creativity suggests that an effective way to get ideas is to conceive of two or more opposites as existing together—Janusian thinking.[2] A writer might be forming a character who is distressed over his wife's infidelity. But suppose that the character brought this about by unconsciously wanting her to be unfaithful to him. The character is caught in a love-hate relationship. His own self-defeating behavior underlies his problems. This could be the beginning of a complex character.

Story Patterns

Some films have a multiple story pattern that features separate stories with different characters all linked together by some unifying feature, such as a common location or event—*Hotel, Airport, Earthquake, The Poseidon Adventure*. There is still usually a primary storyline, which is the first presented and the last resolved. In *Hotel,* this is the question of whether the grand hotel can be retained by the present owners or whether it must be sold. Multiple story films intermix their different storylines—now dealing with one, now shifting to another. The various storylines can be resolved separately or together at the climax.

There are many variations to multiple-story films. Griffith's *Intolerance* has four consecutive stories drawn from different periods of history yet linked by theme and subject. In each hour episode, television's *Love Boat* usually tells three separate stories about people taking the cruise. Television medical programs typically feature the doctor involved with two or more patients as well as some sort of personal problem at home or a business problem with hospital administrators. Fellini's *Amarcord* tells a number of stories linked by the common town location and the daily interaction of the characters involved (as well as by his caring and respect for them). Makavejev's *Sweet Movie* features two separate and virtually unrelated stories that connect only once near the ending, when the character from one story looks in a window and observes the character from the other story. Except for a thematic connection, the two stories in Pasolini's *Pigpen* are completely separate; they even take place in different times and places.

Episodes from the television program *M*A*S*H* frequently present two separate storylines. In one program Corporal Klinger is beset by a Korean woman who mistakenly believes he tried to take advantage of her daughter. This storyline alternates with another in which Hawkeye has difficulty consigning the ill-gotten money of a dead soldier. Both lines are resolved at the end when some of the money is used to move the Koreans to a safer town. The two alternating storylines of another program were a water shortage, with the suspicion that Charles was hoarding water, and the problems of an assertive nurse who acts overly affectionate toward Father Mulcahy.

Genre and Filmic Tradition

Film and television have developed traditions which include the conventions and expectations of different genres—western, detective, gangster, horror, occult, martial art, teenage beach party, musical, nostalgia, sexploitation, spy and international intrigue, science fiction, war, disaster, doomsday thriller, samurai, medical, lawyer, relevant situation comedy and the like. Within each genre, there can be identified various forms which appear as the genre develops (e.g., the early western and the later adult or psychological western), and variations of the form (Truffaut's *Shoot the Piano Player* and Godard's *Breathless* both play with the genre of the gangster film and in so doing actually illuminate aspects of the form, which permit us to understand it better).

Genre films that continue the tradition of the genre present the audience with recognizable and attractive characteristics and internal dynamics. A screenwriter shouldn't feel locked into a genre; to do so might mean repeating clichés. But to write without any awareness of the tradition of different genres would be restricting. Like any artist or craftsman, a screenwriter should know the heritage of his medium.

Film Technique

A screenwriter should know the technique of the medium for which he is writing; he should understand the use of camera and editing to achieve visual continuity and desired effects. A minimum amount of such knowledge is essential, for the writer must indicate shots in the script—even if in a general way. (A listing and definitions of common shot terminology as well as sample script pages are given in the Appendix.) A more complete knowledge will allow the writer greater options in visualizing the effect he wants on the screen. A detailed exegesis of cinematic techniques is beyond the scope of this book; books on film techniques are avilable and the writer is urged to study these as well as to gain his own direct experience in filmmaking. The few examples that we present here will suggest only some of the possibilities available to the screenwriter.

Fast and slow motion offer opportunities for unusual effects, although as with many striking techniques, they can be overused to the point of gimmickry. Fast motion is frequently used for comic effect. In *A Clockwork Orange,* Alex enjoys a high-speed orgy with two girls. This was shot at a racy two frames per second. In *Death of a Bureaucrat,* A secretary is talking at the central character, telling him of the regulations that block his getting his work card. Over a close-up of her lips, both camera and sound speed up as she yaps on.

Slow motion has become a cliché means of expressing innocent love—floating hand in hand through a blossoming meadow—and violence—as the fight scenes in the old television series *Kung Fu*. This doesn't mean that it can't be used effectively. The slow motion deaths of *Bonnie and Clyde* and *The Wild Bunch* are vividly powerful.

An understanding of the effects of lenses is also useful to expand a writer's options in visualizing a scene. Wide-angle lenses can be used for deep-focus long takes. An entire scene might be played on one such shot. This permits the viewer to search out meanings in the composition of the scene. Such shots appear in *Citizen Kane* and *Annie Hall*. The telephoto lens' ability to compress distance produces the seemingly endless attack of the dozens of Wild Bunch outlaws in *My Name is Nobody;* the compressed crowds on New York sidewalks in *Midnight Cowboy;* and the impression that when Benjamin is running toward the church (and camera) in *The Graduate,* his effort isn't getting him anyplace.

With a zoom lens we can move in to see, for example, HAL lip-reading the conversation of the astronauts in *2001,* or move out, as in the opening of *Goodbye Columbus* (which begins on a tight shot of a girl's navel and then zooms out to reveal the setting, the girl and then boy meeting girl).

The freeze frame was used effectively at the end of *Butch Cassidy and the Sundance Kid* as they step out of their cover to face what appears to be the entire Bolivian Army. The fusillade of shots continues over the freeze frame, which slowly goes grainy like an old sepia print and then fades. Still frames are often used to convey a montage of different actions, as in this same film when we see Butch, the Kid and Etta enjoying their visit to New York.

Because film techniques create the image and because the image is the basic unit of the screenwriter, the screenwriter must have a knowledge of cinematic technique.

Realism, Credibility, Coincidence

Realism is the dominant mode of narrative in film and television. Most film stories try to create the impression that the action is natural; we view the film "as if" it were real and see the film diegesis as the representation of a realistic, coherent world. Some modern critics attack this assumption by pointing out that verisimilitude is a cultural and artistic convention and not a natural quality of the film content. Yet, it is difficult to see any ready, pragmatic alternatives. Film is highly suited to rendering objects, persons and their actions; it is about as close to actual experience as any medium. Even surrealism and similar experiments build on a base of realism. It is difficult to imagine a narrative story film designed for popular consumption that isn't in some way grounded in our sense of conventional reality.

This suggests that a basic requirement of a film is that it is credible, that is, that what happens is believable within the established world of the film—its diegesis—no matter how unusual or surreal that filmic reality may be. There must be a necessary internal consistency or we reject what happens as incredible. We are willing to "suspend disbelief" up to a point, but not to the point of incredulity.

Credibility depends to a large extent on the characters' behavior being consistent with who they are, what motivates them and the circumstances and relationships to which they respond. They shouldn't "break character" but rather, given their dispositions, act believably within the context of the story.

If the film purports to be historically accurate, then the screenwriter must do his homework. He must *research*. He should know his material thoroughly—subject, characters, settings and the cultural world of his narrative. If his story takes place in the New York Seventh Avenue garment district, it should capture a feeling of the city and of the peculiar subculture of that milieu. If a character goes to prison, then let it be an accurate depiction of a real prison—not a fantasy based on previous films the writer has seen. If the characters inhabit the jet set, what is this life like? The only way to do this credibly is by thoroughly researching the subject. If the writer desires historical accuracy, he must investigate much as an anthropologist does in order to understand the culture of the story.

However, there's another sense in which the writer is free to create his own diegesis and its inhabitants if historical accuracy is not his aim. The village in the television series *The Prisoner* is its own creation. The real Bonnie and

Clyde didn't resemble their re-creations in the film any more than did Butch Cassidy and the Sundance Kid; James Bond, too, existed only in the writer's fantasies.

The question of credibility refers to more than the cultural context of the film; it also includes the quality of the actions that occur in the film. These should be believable. Even the bizarre happenings found in the works of Fellini, Bergman, Makavejev and Buñuel are consistent with the ethos of their diegesis and so seem credible. What most often doesn't seem credible is the intervention of chance and coincidence into a serious story (comedy is another matter). A man falls from a window—and just happens to land unhurt on a passing truck loaded with hay. A policeman is about to be bested by the villain when in the nick of time, without preparation, his partner arrives to save him.

Such things can be made to work if we are properly prepared for them. And they will be acceptable if we are so engrossed in the tension of the story that we ignore improbabilities. This happens typically with the last-minute rescue at the climax (and has become a clichéd convention in television). For example, at the end of the taut melodrama *The Day of the Jackal,* the police inspector bursts in just in time to best the assassin and save the life of de Gaulle. The entire film has built to this climactic moment and so the coincidence of the split-second timing doesn't bother us. We accept the established dramatic convention of the last-minute rescue.

If we are caught up in the tension of suspense, we overlook coincidences. This has enabled Hitchcock to get away with a number of coincidences in *The 39 Steps*. The Hero's Life is saved because a bullet fired at him just happens to hit a hymn book in the pocket of the borrowed coat he is wearing. Later, he escapes his pursuers by ducking into a Salvation Army band, which just happens to be passing by. Then he enters a hall where he is mistaken for an expected speaker. Another time, he escapes from a car that is forced to stop because a flock of sheep block the road. The crucial test for all these is whether or not they work. Hitchcock brings it off because of our involvement in the tensions of the story, whereas most other writers wouldn't be able to. The general principle still holds—beware of coincidence.

Another type of incredibility is the "idiot plot" in which things develop as a result of a character's doing something completely stupid and idiotic. Think of all those B-movie thrillers in which the heroine ingenue is told to "stay here where it's safe; don't move," so naturally she goes adventuring and is captured by the villain. If she weren't such an idiot, the next plot complication couldn't materialize. In a *Medical Center* television episode, a character is warned that after an operation he shouldn't exert himself in the slightest way or he could have a relapse; he shouldn't lift anything. So he tried to lift a girl who fell downstairs and, as a result, collapses. A *Mary Tyler Moore* episode had Mary covering up for an obviously incompetent secretary. The woman was not only totally incompetent—earlier in the show she couldn't even function adequately as a waitress—but was ungrateful for Mary's help and made no effort to improve. She is finally fired at the end of the program, but Mary's attempts to continually cover for her by doing her work only makes Mary appear rather stupid. *Alien* is a very suspenseful movie. As we watch the small crew of a spaceship fall prey to an alien monster, we almost (but not quite) overlook some of the idiocies that produce the suspense. A crewman goes searching for the ship's cat and so falls prey to the creature. Who in his right mind would wander the dangerous ship alone just for a cat? So, too, at the end, the remaining crewwoman goes back for the cat before escaping and leaves the door to the escape shuttlecraft open, permitting the "thing" to sneak in while she is away.

Consider the Audience

Good screenwriting involves the audience; it gives us something to do. We are experiencing the film as it unfolds before us. If it is effective, we are effectively involved with it. The excitement and emotion of a scene need to be felt by the audience and not just by the characters on the screen. When the characters are feeling and expressing extremes of emotion that we don't share, we become bored and the film is labeled heavy-handed, excessive, maudlin or "melodramatic." Ideally, the audience is moving with the feeling and action on the screen—or is even a bit ahead and anticipating. Consider the case of a character feeling an emotion that is painful to the point of tears. If the character is overreacting and gushing out tears while the audience remains unmoved, we'll find it excessive. The more effective course is for the character to fight to hold back those tears while we're feeling the pain *for* the character, wanting him to let loose the emotion. The essential emotion is that felt by the audience.

Similarly, if building toward a strong character action, it's more effective to hold off the response and let the audience really want it to happen. In *Straw Dogs,* we want the beleaguered mathematician to fight back against the goading he's receiving. When he finally does make his move, a cheer comes from the audience (in the showings I witnessed). We were there before he was.

While working on a script, the writer is in a privileged position, for he knows where the story is going, how the situations relate to each other and what the characters are like. The audience doesn't have this special knowledge. They know only what they see and hear on the screen. If a script begins with a description of "an assassin cleaning his rifle," and the audience is expected to read the action this way, there is no guarantee that they will. For all they know, the character may be a hunter or a gun collector. This is the COIK fallacy—Clear Only If Known. With his special knowledge of future developments in the script, the writer knows how to read the scene. But we as an audience may not.

A student script about a freighter that runs aground on a reef contained a tense scene in which the towline from a tugboat clears the water and is quickly cut by an officer on the ship. This is a realistic action, but it makes sense to us only if we realize that when a towline lifts out of the water, there is danger that it could snap, whip around and possibly decapitate someone on the ship. The writer knew this, but we wouldn't unless he told us. A screenwriter should keep a sort of automatic running check on whether the audience will understand what is happening and if they can read screen action as it is intended to be read.

Try to avoid a frustrating audience cheat, such as setting up something disastrous which is about to happen and then doesn't. For example, a television program might end an act with the discovery of a time bomb about to explode, then break for the commercial. When we come back for the next act, we are told it wasn't a time bomb after all. Ugh!

It is tempting for a writer to use a cliché, because its meaning is easily grasped by the audience. However, that is exactly its weakness. We recognize it because we've seen it so much, and this recognition replaces our involvement. How boring to see another example of the bedroom love scene in which the camera pans away from the couple to the night sky framed in the window, or of the couple who "meet cute" when they bump into each other fighting for a seat on the subway as a prelude to a later involvement, or of the obviously emotional "little match girl" scene with its many variants, such as the lame girl who might walk again if she only believes strongly enough. The writer's constant challenge is to transcend such easy stereotypes.

It is generally better to underplay rather than overplay, to use subtlety rather than overkill. Avoid making it too obvious for the audience. By so doing, you leave room for the audience to participate in the drama and fill in the ambiguities that are essential to aesthetic enjoyment.

A screenwriter should by all means avoid preaching and pontificating. It is tedious to hear characters spout platitudes and sermonettes. The worst offenders are films such as *Billy Jack,* which gives us a continual barrage of moral bromides and trite truisms. Some otherwise enjoyable television situation comedies stumble when they insert obvious "relevant" messages as the moral after the humor. There's nothing wrong with saying something meaningful in a script; the audience doesn't, however, like being hit over the head with a "message" and having their noses rubbed in relevance. The most effective meanings we take away from a film are those expressed intrinsically through the drama, not those laid on top of it like a moral preachment.

The Tension-Release Laugh

Here is one of those bits of advice that might come in handy sometime. Often material in a film is liable to embarrass the audience or make them uncomfortable. This might be overt sexual material or something that would embarrass the character and thus disturb us because of our identification with him. Such material needs judicious treatment and adequate preparation; if not so treated, it could cause problems. In *Short Eyes,* there is a scene in which the child molester tells of his past sexual experiences with children. The scene needed more careful handling; it was unnecessarily discomforting.

Disturbing material can present problems even if done credibly and with adequate preparation. Since such material creates uneasy tensions within the audience, there is the risk that the tensions will be discharged through undesirable laughter. In such an audience, a single nervous laugh could trigger mass laughter as a tension release. The laughter is against the film—not with the film—and disruptively breaks the audience's involvement.

This was observed at two separate screenings of *Fingers* when, at the climax, we witness a bloody killing, which includes shooting out a man's eye. It is a difficult scene to watch. Then there is a cut to the final shot of the film, showing the central character, who did the killing, seated naked and distraught at the window of his apartment. He slowly turns to look directly at the camera. This produced a large tension-release laugh from both audiences. The laugh was disruptive and detracted from any intended impact of this last shot in the film.

There is a way to deal with such possible disruptions. This is to consciously place some slight, appropriate, comic touch in the film just after such an awkward, intense or embarrassing moment in order to let the audience laugh and thus drain away their tension. They then laugh with the film, not against it, and their involvement continues unabated.

Something like this happens in *Swept Away,* when the woman, crying, kneels before the man whose dominance she is finally acknowledging. She caresses and kisses his feet and rubs her face against his leg. Played straight, this might seem uncomfortably embarrassing. But in the film, he has an abashed, bewildered reaction with which we can identify and at which we can at least smile. It takes the sting away from the possibly disturbing material.

There are three examples of this technique in *Looking for Mr. Goodbar*. One occurs after a tense sex scene between Terry and the man she picked up. The scene includes his leaping and slashing around her apartment with a knife, frightening both her and the audience. But then he lays his cheek on her bare buttocks and says, "cheek to cheek," which gets an audience laugh and drains off some of the tension. Later, Terry exults in the joy of sex after another experience. She flings her arms in the air and expresses obvious and uninhibited satisfaction. It concludes a sequence in which we in the audience have built up some embarrassing tensions. But then there is a cut to a close-up of her in the class of deaf students that she teaches; she is blowing on some balloons—"puh, pow, puff" (to illustrate to the children the sounds which go "puh" through blowing out air). This gets an immediate loud and spontaneous laugh from the audience, much of which is discharged tension. A similar thing happens later, after another strong sex scene, when we cut to her expressing her pleasure about sex by singing "Volaré" in a weird and funny way. The audience laughs here, too. In each case, the laugh drains away tension which otherwise might have come out in laughter at the wrong time and thus against the film; instead, it is with the film. None of the actions eliciting laughs are enormously funny in themselves, but they serve the purpose of giving the audience a chance to discharge built-up tensions.

REFERENCES

1. Christian Metz as quoted in Morris Beja, *Film and Literature* (New York: Longman Inc., 1979): 54.
2. Albert Rothenberg, "Creative Contradictions," *Psychology Today* 13 (June 1979): 55–62.

Also:

Newcomb, Horace. *TV: The Most Popular Art.* New York: Doubleday, 1974.

4

Characters

> Every single character, even a bastard like Goldberg in *The Birthday Party,* I care for.[1]
>
> —Harold Pinter

CREATING EFFECTIVE and interesting characters is one of the most important challenges for the screenwriter. We have stressed the importance of structuring the story; this is essential. But creating effective characters is equally important, for the story springs from the action of characters in conflict. If the characters are right, the story will develop naturally from the chemistry of their mix. If they are really effective, they will seem to take over and write their own story.

The audience wants to care about the characters. We become intimately involved with them through the psychological processes of empathy and identification. We like or dislike them, feel with them, worry about them, share their problems and adventures and take sides in their clashes. We see ourselves in their struggles, triumphs and failures.

We remember many characters long after the film is over: Rhett Butler and Scarlett O'Hara, Sam Spade, Chaplin's Little Tramp, James Bond, Captain Bligh, Little Caesar, Charles Foster Kane, Sherlock Holmes and Dr. Watson, Dracula, Archie and Edith Bunker, Mary Richards, Lucy, Hawkeye Pierce and many others.

Effective characters can't be so easily structured to be functional as is a narrative story; they are more intangible than this. Still, there are many things that we can say about them. The following are some of the elements that distinguish effective major characters.

Sense of Person

Effective characters convey a sense that they are real people. They give us the feeling that they have a personal history and a past that has made them who and what they are, instead of having been created just to meet the requirements of a plot. They are three dimensional and fully formed, rather than one-dimensional cardboard figures who function as pawns of the plot. They seem to be involved in the process of living their lives and of working out their destinies, rather than being mere puppets of the writer. We see them as human beings within the world of the film.

To help give his characters this sense of person, a writer will often model them on real people. He will incorporate aspects of someone he knows in the character or perhaps combine qualities of several people into a single character. Neil Simon has said that his brother has been the model for six characters in his plays up to 1977. A writer will avoid modeling characters on other media characters as much as possible, since this tends to make them stereotypes. The writer draws on what he knows of himself and of others to create characters who convey a sense of being real persons.

Credibility

Effective characters are believable. Their behavior is consistent with who they are, what they know and what we know of them. Their actions are consistent within the culture—the diegesis—of the film. Credibility in a story depends largely on the credible actions of the characters in that story.

The characters need to have enough complexity and depth to handle any strong feelings and emotions that are called for by the situations in the film. One characteristic of excessively melodramatic films is that the characters leap from one emotional crisis to another without having shown that they have the capacity to understand the situations or to feel the emotions that are laid on them. When this happens, it blocks our empathy. We recognize the reactions of the character, but we can't share them. We are given a display rather than insight; we are shown rather than invited along. Credibility means that the characters respond with a depth and insight that is appropriate to how we see them, that is, to how the writer has presented them to us.

Behavior

Film characters are characterized behaviorally by their actions, by what and how they do and say things. The screenwriter doesn't have the novelist's luxury of describing a character, so he must present that character in specific, observable, behavioral ways. These will include the character's style of speech, vocabulary, mannerisms, choice of dress and all those other qualities that, when added up, give us a sense of the character.

The screenwriter can give us some description—if it comes from the character himself or from what others say about him. Major characters in *Citizen Kane, Laura* and *The Third Man* are discussed so much before they finally appear, we not only know a great deal about them but are curious to see how they compare to their advance notices.

The way characters behave toward each other tells us a great deal about them. How they react to others and how others react to them can tell us much about what they are like. So can the pattern of his likes and dislikes in a film. We will learn much about a character by noticing who his friends and his enemies are. All these will be primarily expressed in specific, behavioral ways that we can see on the screen.

Ambiguity

There is a certain ambiguity about effective characters. Everything isn't laid out for us like parts of a formula. Just as with real people, there's that sense of an unknown area—of mystery. Everything fits with who the character is, but there's the feeling that something more exists. This touch of ambiguity leaves room for us to project our own feelings and motivations into the character.

In *8½*, we are never clearly told why Guido is having trouble completing his film, yet we share his turmoil. Nor are we ever quite sure why Bobby is running in *Five Easy Pieces,* even as we participate vicariously in his quest. In *The Passenger,* we are given only hints as to why Locke switches identities with the dead Robertson. There is an enticing mystery about the hired assassin in *The Day of the Jackal;* even when the plot is exposed and his backers are removed, he continues with the planned assassination out of some sense of professional challenge, and we never really know why. And at the film's end, no one knows who he was, or even what nationality he was. The complexities of *Lawrence of Arabia,* with his strange drive and sense of destiny, are as much a part of the written character as they were of the man himself.

Justification

"In real drama, all characters must be in the right—that is how God sees them, i.e., how they are."[2] Characters should not be simplistically drawn as "good" or "bad" but as persons who are the result of their past experiences. When we understand someone's past and see what has made him who he is, we see how what he does is psychologically—although not necessarily morally—justified. Some psychological researchers found this to be true about men who were subjects of a long-term study: "Another surprise was that there were no bastards. If you know enough about someone, the views they have that you think of as selfish or politically and morally reprehensible fall into place in terms of their lives. It's very hard to do this work and not sympathize."[3] It is the same with characters. The most effective villains are not just "bad guys" but are complex individuals acting out of the totality of their being. This doesn't mean that the writer will present them sympathetically, but that he will understand the reasons for their actions and will thus be able to justify them.

Motivation

Adequate motivation underlies a character's actions throughout the story. There is a reasonable and meaningful "why" behind a character's objectives and behaviors. His wants and intentions are based on who he is and on the circumstances in the story in which he finds himself. Motivations are dynamic; they underlie and impel the actions of the character. Some motivations are deep-seated, influencing an entire life course. These are the kind that would be uncovered in a thorough psychoanalysis of the character. Other motivations are situational and could change with the varying developments of the story. The pattern of motivations gives consistency and thus justifies the actions of the characters.

When forming a character, a writer will have some idea of the motivational dynamics that drive the character. Much of this will come from the history the writer creates for each character. But much will be a product of the writer's own inner impulses and dynamics and thus "unconscious." From this combination of overt and covert motivation, the writer produces a consistent character.

Usually a writer will deal with motivation by determining that a character's motive to achieve an objective is reasonable and consistent. He will define the character's objective by an active verb form: "To ——— ": to catch the criminal, to win someone's love, to discover meaning in a chaotic situation, to master (or indulge) a passion—these are broad objectives that determine a character's actions over the film. Individual actions will also have their objectives: to escape from prison, to repair a malfunctioning engine, to meet a person of the opposite sex, to convince another of a course of action. As the character moves from objective to objective within the story, the writer insures that the motivation behind each objective that is sought is appropriate to both the character and to the situation.

Sometimes, however, the writer desires an objective or action for the character and is puzzled by the motivation behind it. It seems reasonable, but he's not quite sure why. At this point he can use the technique of asking himself questions about the reasons for his character's behavior. For example, suppose a female character becomes angry at a male character who made a sexual advance. Understandable; but the writer sees the character as extremely angry—

more upset than he would have imagined the character to be. The emotion is over-determined. So he asks himself, why? Well . . . because she doesn't feel the man showed enough respect for her as a person and that is important to her. This seems reasonable enough, but there seems to be something more, so the writer presses further. Why is this respect so important to her? Because she feels she's competing in a man's world and has been the victim of sexual prejudice and hasn't been able to get a job commensurate with her talent and education. Now the character's dynamic is taking shape. The writer might probe even further. Are there any other reasons that motivate this response in her? Well . . . her mother was a talented woman who never fulfilled her potential and . . . on and on. A writer can use this inner dialogue with himself whenever he wants to explore the depth of motivation of a character in order to better understand that character and to insure that the action is consistent for the character. (A writer can duck the question of motivation by justifying an action on the grounds that the character was drunk, stoned or crazy. This is a cheap shot, and in all but a few cases when it is intrinsic to the story, it is unsatisfying to the audience.)

While it is important that the writer have an understanding of a character's motivation, this need not be explicitely spelled out for the audience. The most intriguing characters have very complex and unclear motivations. They have a needed amount of ambiguity. Films such as *Rachel, Rachel* and *Midnight Cowboy* are too obvious, as well as clinically suspect, for they lay out simplistic clinical motivations based on flashbacks to traumatic childhood experiences.

Non-stereotype

It is easy and tempting to create stereotyped characters—oversimplified, unidimensional, excessively drawn and with obvious dominant traits. They are easily recognized copies of other media clichés: the starving artist, effete poet, alcoholic reporter, stuffy professor, bigoted and overweight southern sheriff, solemn and pontificating clergyman or whore with a heart of gold. They are exaggerations, phony composites of clichés. Whatever truths they once possessed have become trite through overexposure and distortion. They are not so much typical and representative as they are exaggerated and fantasied. Remember the guy from Brooklyn in films of some decades ago? Wisecracking, gumchewing, talking of dese and dose and da Dodgers. He wasn't representative of a Brooklynite so much as he was a caricature of the most extreme traits of some guys from Brooklyn. Like all stereotypes, he had the advantage of immediate audience recognition. But it was recognition of a cliché. It is more difficult to create real, non-stereotyped characters, especially with minor characters who are on the screen for such a short time. But when we see such real characters, we recognize the difference instantly. And it's worth it.

There are different sorts of typical characters. The *stock character* is a product of a plot cliché. We see stock characters so often that we soon take them for granted—and another stereotype is born. There are many kinds of stock characters: the old sheriff in the western, who's lost his nerve; the acerbic, cynical girlfriend of the heroine; the sidekick of the western hero, who was there to give us a few laughs; the "other guy" of the social comedies of the thirties and forties, who was nice enough, but not of heroic caliber, so he loses the heroine and settles for the second female lead. These stereotypes are sometimes tempting to fall back on but should be avoided.

We can distinguish the type from the stereotype. The type has certain prominent or exaggerated characteristics, but he is also a real individual and not simply unidimensional. From a distance, Archie Bunker is the quintessential bigot. But he is much more than this. As we get closer, we see other aspects of him—a tender, caring side, for example. He is more an individual than a cliché.

Archetypes are prototypes of an ingrained cultural type. Their uniqueness is so prominent that they come to represent a type for others to imitate. Some archetypes in our culture are Faust, Othello, Shylock, Don Quixote, Mrs. Malaprop, Babbitt, James Bond, Frankenstein, Dracula and, perhaps, Archie Bunker, for types can become archetypes if they become ingrained in our cultural tradition.

Strength and Presence

Major characters have to be strong enough to sustain the story and the conflict. Every drama has a larger-than-life quality even as it seems to naturalistically portray life. Characters must have a strong enough presence to gain our attention, invite our involvement and carry the drama. Even "weak" characters must be a strong portrayal of weakness. Both Hamlet and Guido (in *8½*) are characters who vacillate and have difficulty acting decisively, yet they each convey a strong presence.

Be wary of characters who feel sorry for themselves. Their feeling often preempts our feeling it for them. Truffaut's classic *Jules and Jim* is a fine film; however, Jules comes very close to feeling too sorry for himself. He comes across as too weak a character.

Attractiveness

Characters must be attractive—not in the sense of being glamorous, but in having qualities that attract us to them. They are special. We find them interesting people, grappling with life and its problems in interesting ways. We care for them, perhaps because the writer cared for them as he wrote them. A writer who doesn't care about his characters can't expect the audience to do so. One reason that *The Prisoner* television series is so successful is that not only is the central character an intelligent and powerful personality, but he also contends with strong, interesting and intelligent adversaries.

Unique, Individualized

Effective characters are unique characters with their own individualized characteristics: actions, speech, movement, rhythms, dress, values, dominant traits and style. We think of Chaplin's shuffle and flipping cane; Columbo's wrinkled raincoat; or the unkempt, ill-mannered Ronin Samurai of *Yojimbo* and *Sanjuro*. Rizzo, in *Midnight Cowboy*, has his limp, ragged appearance, New York accent and aggressiveness. Minus, the young adolescent in *Through a Glass Darkly*, has his own rhythm—he runs rather than walks, full of the exuberance of teenage youth. Quincy, from the television series of that name, is a touching person; he literally touches people as he interacts with them. Colonel Nicholson in *The Bridge on the River Kwai* is properly English and stubborn and dedicated to the point of obsession. Annie Hall, from the film of that name, has such a characteristic mode of dress that it has come out in fashion as the Annie Hall look.

Certain dominant character traits are inevitably emphasized over others. It is these that would stand out if we were to give a capsule description of the character. They indicate the uniqueness and individuality of the character. So we could say that Jake (*Chinatown*), McMurphy (*One Flew Over the Cuckoo's Nest*) and Harry (*Dirty Harry*) are direct, challenging and aggressive. James Bond is suave and effective. Hawkeye Pierce (*M*A*S*H*) is witty and ironic. Benjamin (*The Graduate*) is uncertain and insecure (at least in the beginning; he changes over the film) and Archie Bunker is bigoted and blue-collar waspish.

Tags

One way to individualize a character is to tag him with some distinguishing label, mannerism, gesture or other special characteristic of appearance, behavior or speech. These are the sorts of things an impersonator exaggerates when he caricatures the essence of a person. They are things such as limps, accents, obesity or even a bow tie. While a tag helps make a character distinctive, tagging shouldn't be overdone, since it can easily become too gimmicky and turn characters into caricatures and freaks.

Some familiar tags are: Kojak's sucker and his "what can I tell ya?"; Captain Queeg's ball bearings (*The Caine Mutiny*); Ironside's wheelchair; Columbo's raincoat and his last minute "Oh, just one more thing . . ."; Guido's hat (*8½*); Belmondo's gesture of moving his thumb over his lips in imitation of

Bogart (*Breathless*); Harpo Marx's business of "giving his leg"; the Chief Samurai's habit of stroking his shaved head (*Seven Samurai*); Lucy's cry, "Whaa" (*I Love Lucy*); Archie Bunker's "stifle it" and abashed facial reaction; Rocky's halting speech, "ya know—"; Mr. Spock's ears (*Star Trek*); a central character with only one arm (*Bad Day at Black Rock*); Oliver Hardy's tie flutter; W. C. Field's voice pattern and unusual style of expression; Chaplin's Little Tramp walk and cane swing; and the harmonica which becomes the signature of the Bronson character in *Once Upon a Time in the West*.

Establishing Character

Some characters develop slowly; getting to know them is a progressive revelation. The writer must give us time to become involved with them. However, it is usually the case that the writer will characterize his principals quickly, giving us an immediate feeling for and involvement with the characters. When we first meet one of the main characters of the film *M*A*S*H,* he steals a jeep, thereby showing the devil-may-care casual attitude that characterizes him. Early in *Dirty Harry,* when Harry clashes with his police department superiors and bluffs down a bank robber with an empty gun, we see him as an aggressive outsider. In *The Bridge on the River Kwai,* we get an immediate feel for Colonel Nicholson when, by defying the Japanese Colonel Saito, he shows his rigid dedication to doing things "by the book" and demonstrates his willingness to suffer punishment for what he believes is right. Both *Once Upon a Time in the West* and *The Good, the Bad and the Ugly* quickly establish the gunfighting skills of their heroes as they outshoot those set to ambush them.

A writer finds ways to quickly characterize minor characters as well. Since they are so briefly on the screen, it is difficult to let us see them develop. In *Harry and Tonto,* the elderly central character decides to visit a former girl friend who he hasn't seen since their youthful romance. He learns that she is in a nursing home. Neither he, nor we, know what she will be like. But we've come to like Harry so much that we wonder if she will measure up to him. As he approaches the table at which she is seated, we smile approvingly as we hear her say to an attendant—even before we see her face—"When in the hell are you going to get me another book!" (That she later turns out to be addled is unfortunate, but inevitable, for otherwise we might want them to become reinvolved.)

Growth and Change

Characterization is an on-going process. Characters learn and grow from their experiences; they develop as they are shaped by events and interactions with other characters. There's always the implicit possibility of some new development, the feeling that there's more to the character than we've seen so far. And so we get increasingly involved with them as we get to know them over the length of the film.

In *The Godfather,* Michael changes from being antagonistic to the family's criminal activities to becoming the vicious Don directing these activities. In *Deliverance,* Ed (Jon Voight) starts off as an average sort of guy planning to enjoy a pleasant river canoe trip. By the film's end, he's had to take control of a nightmarish situation, kill one man, help bury two others and conduct a cover-up of all that's happened. After his many experiences, the cowboy who hoped to make big money as a male stud in New York City is a much different person at the end of *Midnight Cowboy.* There's a numbing change at the end in the characters of *Who's Afraid of Virginia Woolf* after they have been forced to abandon their sustaining illusions.

At the beginning of *Seven Beauties,* the central character is ready to kill another because the man has made his sister a whore. It is important for him to defend her honor. But at the film's end, he asks a young prostitute to marry him. His experiences in prison, war and a German prison camp have destroyed his romantic ideals of honor.

We can chart a capsulized example of growth and change with the Indian called "Chief," a secondary character in *One Flew Over the Cuckoo's Nest.* When we first meet him he is withdrawn, uninvolved. He doesn't speak or take part in any of the activities in the mental hospital. McMurphy then gets him finally to raise his hands with a basketball in them, although he won't put it in the basket; he is then induced to raise his hand to vote to view the World Series on television. He stands a second time on the basketball court and holds the net closed so that the opposing team can't put the ball through. Then he pulls away a guard who is attacking McMurphy. When McMurphy offers him some gum, we hear him speak his first words: "Thank you," then, "Ahh, Juicy Fruit." Now that he talks, he explains to McMurphy why he can't leave the mental hospital and describes how his father went blind from drinking. Finally, at the end of the film, we see him hug and cry over the vegetable-like, lobotomized McMurphy, while he mercifully smothers the life from the body that was once his friend. Then he rips the heavy sink from the floor—the one McMurphy bet he could lift, but couldn't—throws it through the window and triumphantly makes his escape.

It is a bit more difficult to affect major character changes in the short time length of a television series episode. While there may be growth and change, often a story will simply *reveal* something new about the character—something new to us, and perhaps new to the character as well. So it is that when his daughter is about to get married, Archie Bunker reveals a tender side that he has not often shown. In another episode, Archie gets drunk and reveals a lonely and frightened side of his character.

Television series characters often change over the length of the series. Some of the changes are obvious—having children, seeing some characters leave and new characters take their place. As a series becomes established and more sure of its audience, the characters become less extreme, less stereotyped, and more well-rounded. This happened with such series as *All in the Family, Mary Tyler Moore, Rhoda* and *M*A*S*H*. The relationship between Quincy and his boss, Asten, has mellowed, and Asten is more likely to trust the expertise of his medical examiner. Edith Bunker of *All in the Family* started out as being tired, burdened and really quite stupid. As the series developed, she grew more energetic, more honest and compassionate and developed a stronger willingness to assert herself.

Conflicting Values

Frequently characters will have conflicting personal values or styles. Archie Bunker is a bigot, yet he can be caring and tender. Internal storylines generally spring from such conflicts. Bobby in *Five Easy Pieces* tries to span two worlds—his escape world as an oil drill worker, with a socially and intellectually inferior girl friend and bowling and country-and-western music, and the world of his family, with its classical music and refinement. He doesn't know where he belongs. The father in *Through a Glass Darkly* is torn between his love for his daughter and sympathy for her mental illness, and his almost morbid curiosity in watching the degenerative progression of her disease.

Character Interactions

Most film stories develop out of the interactions of characters. Interesting relationships are important within the film narrative. The writer understands these involvements. He knows how his characters feel about each other. What they want from one another. How relationships form and dissolve, grow and change. What of themselves characters share with others and what they withhold. What others know about them that they don't know themselves. What interpersonal strokes they give, receive or withhold. What interpersonal games they play. (*Who's Afraid of Virginia Woolf* is about interpersonal games.) What conflicts they clash over. So much of the film narrative depends on the web of character involvements.

A certain amount of character *contrast* is valuable both for intrinsic interest and to help the audience distinguish between characters. These may be contrasting values, motives, emotions, temperament, verbal qualities and physical appearances. In *Zorba the Greek,* the educated, cautious, sensible and refined Englishman is in contrast to the impetuous, spontaneous, aggressive, Dyonesian Zorba. *Midnight Cowboy* gives us the naïve cowboy and the seedy, streetwise New Yorker. *Swept Away* contrasts the communist laborer and the rich society bitch. In *The Seventh Seal,* the tall, blond, idealistic knight travels with his shorter, darker, and more cynical squire. A nervous, confused, young Benjamin contrasts with the assured, experienced Mrs. Robinson when they first meet in *The Graduate.* At the beginning of *The African Queen,* the two characters are such obvious contrasts—he a drunken, ne'er-do-well river bum, she a prim, proper, prissy missionary maiden lady. In *The Day of the Jackal,* the assassin is a loner, an outsider, a rather mysterious figure; the police inspector is a bureaucratic official and family man. Yet both are expert, efficient and single-minded. They are worthy antagonists.

Complex, intriguing relationships appear in some films. The three sisters in *Cries and Whispers* come together for a moment of interpersonal touching, only to split apart again. Interesting triangle relationships appear in *Jules and Jim,* with the two friends and the woman they sometimes share; in *Last Year at Marienbad,* between the man, the woman, and the man who might be her husband or might not be; and in *Sunday, Bloody Sunday,* in which the triangle is between a woman and a homosexual man who both share the favors of a young lover.

A number of films and television series feature an easy, joking sort of "buddy" relationship, such as between *Butch Cassidy and the Sundance Kid, Starsky and Hutch,* and in *Adam 12.* Variants of this sort of relationship are seen with *McMillan and Wife,* the Thin Man films, *The Rockford Files* and *Laverne and Shirley.*

The idea of a family relationship is important to many television series—*The Waltons, Little House on the Prairie, The Jeffersons, Happy Days* and *All in the Family.* We can also speak of the television "families" of the *Mary Tyler Moore* show and *Barney Miller.*

Selected Character Examples

The following characters are effective. They seem real. They are specifically characterized, yet ambiguous enough to intrigue. They are believable. They are motivated by who they are and by the circumstances of their stories. They are strong characters who command our interest by their sense of presence. They are exciting and special.

THOMAS. Thomas, the photographer in Antonioni's *Blow-up,* is a young man in his middle twenties. When we first see him as he leaves a hostel for down-and-outers, he looks disheveled and unshaven. Then, when he gets into a Rolls Royce convertible, we are intrigued by the sharp contrast.

In his photography studio he photographs a model in an erotic sequence, accompanied by sensual jazz music. This sequence shows that he is very much in control of the situation, that he is sensual and artistic and moves quickly, effectively and confidently. As he photographs some other models, he is demanding and controlling, and he doesn't hesitate to move off and leave them stranded waiting for him.

After photographing the couple in the park, he dupes the woman about the photographs. He plays with her, putting her on. He is mocking, sardonic and somewhat cruel. He deceives her by giving her a blank role of film.

Thomas is shown to be impulsive. In an antique shop, he immediately buys a propeller he sees. He also shows interpersonal skill in the easy and effective way he converses with the young woman who owns the shop. Nor does he think that the propeller might hurt his Rolls Royce as he is about to load it in. This impulsiveness appears later in the film when he is distracted from hunting for the woman involved in the murder by a rock group and a chase over a broken guitar neck.

There is a symbolic relationship between Thomas and his camera. It gives him a sort of identity. He can seduce with it or use it to control the environment and the responses of others.

Thomas can be described as: controlling, strong, impulsive, creative, commanding, adventurous, spontaneous, attractive, mod, hip, ironic, mocking, autocratic, capricious, stylish, brash, abrupt and mercurial.

ALEX. In the first few scenes of Kubrick's *A Clockwork Orange,* we quickly learn about the main character, Alex. He is first seen in droog costume with eye make-up and false lashes on one eye. He is violent and aggressive. As we watch, he and his droogs beat a tramp, fight Billyboy and his droogs, drive wildly and force others off the road and commit rape. We learn that he likes Beethoven's Ninth Symphony, has a pet snake and weak parents and enjoys sexual and violent fantasies. We are also exposed to his unique dialogue expressions with the private meanings that accompany this jargon.

JAKE. Jake in Polanski's *Chinatown* is an interesting character. While not very likable or sympathetic, he is nonetheless attractive because of his strong individuality. He gains much of our sympathy because he is up against a powerful and vicious conspiracy. We can identify with this. Jake is direct, blunt, insulting, cynical, cocky, antagonistic, sarcastic, amoral, pushy, out for himself, confident, gutsy, but really rather naïve in that he doesn't hesitate to confront the multimillionaire murderer about his crimes. Jake is his own man; he shares little of himself. He will lie and mislead if it gets him what he wants. He likes to lay his cards on the table. He doesn't care about the water-dumping cover-up, but he does dislike the fact that his nose was cut up, so he pushes the investigation. He bursts into offices and pushes past secretaries, showing no regard for social and organizational amenities. He'll claim to be a deputy water commissioner in order to get into a restricted area. He rips a page out of real estate records from the Hall of Records because he wants the information it contains. He seems always ready to fight, and we sense that he can be brutal if he wants to be. He is rather cold and distant after lovemaking and doesn't hesitate to break the woman's taillight so that it is easier for him to follow her car.

He continually asks for trouble and risks injury by throwing insults in situations where caution would be more advisable. He insults police officers. When some toughs corner him, he calls one a midget, and so gets his nose cut with a knife. When he is surrounded by three or four tough guys, he shows no caution and calls one a "dumb okie." He is quick to write off people he doesn't like—he mumbles "weasel" under his breath about the obnoxious clerk in the Hall of Records. Overall, he is a striking and intriguing character.

ARCHIE. Finally, consider Archie Bunker of the *All in the Family* television series. He is bigoted, waspish, angry, sarcastic, mocking, but well-meaning and rather tender at times. In his way, he very much loves his wife Edith and daughter Gloria. He has definite mannerisms (tags) in his reactions, glares, shrugs and tongue raspberry. He has a favorite chair and a favorite expression: "Stifle it." He wears a distinctive hat, a special jacket and a white work shirt. He lives in a blue-collar home. He expects Edith to do many things for him, such as fix his dinner on time and bring him his beer when he's home from work. Edith endures him at times, draws the line at other times, but always loves him. Gloria will argue with him, but she also loves him. Even Mike, the son-in-law with whom he argues so much, has some feelings for him. At times we laugh at Archie, at times we sympathize with him, but we always care about him. We've gotten to know him in many different situations as his daughter marries, his grandson is born, as his daughter and his wife are almost raped. When his saloon business does badly, we've seen him get hooked on alcohol and amphetamines. He has become very real to us.

Secondary Characters

Minor characters should be as interesting as the writer can make them, although not so strong that they overwhelm the major characters. The writer will also identify with them and care for them. Otherwise he runs the risk of their functioning as straight men feeding lines to the central characters. If they appear for only a short time, they need to be characterized quickly with only one or two of their main qualities highlighted. They are inclined to be types, since their purpose in the story is often more important than trying to justify the motives for their actions.

Fellini is especially effective in drawing interesting minor characters. In *8½*, he presents all sorts of strange people: the rich old ladies taking their mineral water treatments; the aged cardinal and his officious attendants; the fat, dancing whore from Guido's childhood; the masochistic, erotic American girl; the befeathered showgirl who was Guido's first love; the vexing intellectual; and many others.

The wife of the painter in *Blow-up* appears in only a few scenes, yet she is an intriguing character. She no longer receives satisfaction from her husband, yet she doesn't think she could leave him; she wants help from Thomas, yet she doesn't. She is remarkably unconcerned about the fact that he has photographed a murder being committed.

Anyone who has seen *Five Easy Pieces* will remember Palm, the girl who hitches a ride while on her way to Alaska. There she hopes it will be clean, for all she sees around her is "crap . . . filth . . . a stink." In *Mickey One*, there is the theatrical agent, who we last see singing in a Salvation Army band, and the artist-guru figure, who has no dialogue yet who figures strongly and symbolically in the adventures of the central character.

Comic Characters

Characters are often exaggerated for comic effect. Their range extends from the farcical characters of the Marx Brothers through the *Saturday Night Live* troupe characters—or those of Jerry Lewis or Woody Allen—to the light sentimental comedy of Neil Simon. Many comic characters are built around a popular comedian, such as Chaplin, W.C. Fields, Laurel and Hardy, Bob Hope, Jerry Lewis, Buster Keaton, Harold Lloyd, Peter Sellers or Robin Williams (Mork). Serious dramas often have comic characters for comic relief, as with Falstaff, the porter in *Macbeth*, or the robots in *Star Wars*. Sergeant Concannon fulfills this role as the hard-drinking, hard-fighting, lovable and well-meaning character in *She Wore a Yellow Ribbon*.

Villains

Even villainous characters can have their charms and attractions. Memories of villains played by Boris Karloff, Peter Lorre and Sidney Greenstreet survive long after we've forgotten the heroes of their films. Eric von Stroheim was billed as "the man you love to hate." Actresses like Bette Davis and Marlene Dietrich created memorable characters as strong women rather than as smiling ingenues (although they were not necessarily villains). So care for your villains. Give them attention just as you give your heroes.

Actors

Casting is an important part of the characterization process. Actors have expressiveness. When John Wayne plays an aging gunfighter, he draws on his persona as well as a rich film tradition of Western roles. Marlon Brando, Humphrey Bogart, Bette Davis and so many others were important in forming their film characters. This is less the immediate concern of the writer, unless he is writing for a particular actor. In that case, he draws on the actor's expressive qualities and film tradition.

Non-Human Characters

Much of what is true of human characters is equally true of their non-human counterparts. Animals are noted for capturing audience affection. This happened with Rin Tin Tin, Lassie and the Disney animals. Robots and computers were memorable in *Star Wars* and *2001*. In the short film *The Red Balloon,* the balloon is treated in such a way that it takes on human characteristics. It is a strongly moving moment when the balloon, hit by a stone thrown by errant boys, loses air and "dies." In *Duel,* a diesel tractor-trailer truck assumes menacing proportions as it stalks and attacks the protagonist.

Names

Carrie, Baby Jane, Dr. Strangelove, Barnaby, Angel, Rocky, Kaz, Mork, Fonzie, Archie, Maude, Hawkeye, B.J., Trapper, and R2-D2 are intriguing names. Character names are of some importance.

Names carry associations; they suggest character types and personalities and they convey cultural connotations. Different connotations are suggested by such names as Bruce, Orville, Scott, Joe, Reba, Rosemary, Harvey, Percival, Rodney, Gertrude and Millie. Mary doesn't sound very villainous. James suggests a butler. Agatha sounds like an aunt as does Em (as with Auntie Em of *The Wizard of Oz*). Priscilla could well be quite prim. Havensacker sounds like a bureaucrat. Walter Mitty would be likely to have a secret life. Tabitha makes a nice, friendly witch.

Very simple names like Bill, Tom, Dick, Sue, Jane, Mary, Smith and Brown are probably best avoided. It is also wise to avoid cultural and ethnic stereotypic names such as Mamie (from Brooklyn), Ivan, Hans, Fritz, Gigi and Jacques. A writer can pick a name because of what it connotes, or he may prefer to go against type connotation. (Humphrey is not exactly a macho virile name, but then there was Humphrey Bogart.)

A telephone book is a fine source for names as are those books about what to name your baby. A writer will try out the names he picks for their sound. Soft vowel sounds as those in Lisa and Laura have a different feel than hard consonant sounds like Dick or Buck.

A number of psychological studies have identified some common connotations of names. These aren't necessarily gospel, but they may be useful. A review of such studies[4] mentioned that active names were Sargent, Baxter, Otto, Shepard and Bruno, while passive names were Aldwin, Winthrop, Alfred, Milton and Wendell. Desirable names were Karen, Lisa, David, Michael, Richard, Gregory, Wendy, Thomas, Craig, Patrick, John, James and Jonathan. Undesirable names were Elmer, Adell, Bertha, Hubert, Bernard, Curtis, Darrell, Donald, Gerald, Horace, Maurice, Jerome, Samuel, Alfreda, Percival, Isadore and Roderick. A British study showed that Johns are trustworthy,

Robins are young, Tonys are sociable, Agneses are old, Anns are nonaggressive, and Agneses and Matildas are unattractive. If nothing else, these studies show that we hold connotations around names—whether justifiably or not.

A writer can also use names in unusual ways, as by having characters referred to by nicknames. Such special uses of names can add meaning to character interactions. A friend of Jim Rockford (*The Rockford Files*) calls him Rockfish. In one episode, at an important moment in the script, he calls him Rockford—to the surprise of Rockford and us. Archie Bunker repeatedly calls his son-in-law Meathead. In *One Flew Over the Cuckoo's Nest,* McMurphy is called Mac by the other characters except for his adversary Nurse Ratched, who calls him Randle (his first name). It underscores their antagonism.

Character Description: A Checklist of Characteristics

The following checklist of characteristics can be useful to a writer in forming his characters. However, a writer should avoid trying to construct characters mechanically by list making. The checklist may be a useful guide at times, but it should only be used to supplement the natural feel the writer has for a character.

Physical/Biological Characteristics

- Age (How do the characters show age? Is it important how they feel about their age, as with an aging woman or a young girl trying to appear older? As in May–December romances?)
- Sex (How do the characters affirm or deny their maleness or femaleness?)
- Height and weight
- Color of hair, eyes, skin
- Physical defects (abnormalities, deformities, diseases, handicaps)
- Physical body: carriage/posture (casual, relaxed, rigid, stiff)
- Physical body: build and body type (athletic or not, ectomorphic, isomorphic, mesomorphic)
- Movement: rhythm and way of walking (cat-like, fast, jerky, slow, smooth)
- Facial expressions (as in the reactions of Archie Bunker or Jack Benny)
- Mannerisms ("business," characteristic gestures, ways of non-verbal expression)
- Voice/Speech: texture and quality (high or low pitch, clipped, guttural, smooth and flowing) What's the most striking thing about the character's voice?
- Verbal expressions (favorite expressions, idioms, use of language, use of slang)
- Heredity (What are the character's inherited physical characteristics?)
- Clothing/Dress (style, uniqueness)
- Appearance (attractive, clean, mod, neat, unkempt, untidy)

Sexuality (How do they express their sexuality? How do they feel about it? How important is it to them? How much is it a motivating force? What sexual hangups have they?)

How does the character physically express tension? Emotion and Feelings (joy, anger, sexuality)?

Psychological Characteristics

IQ/Intelligence (intellectual? common sense?)

Abilities (languages, skills, talents)

Ambivert, introvert, or extrovert?

Disposition/Temperament (easygoing, optimistic, pessimistic, rebellious)

Other qualities (awareness, imagination, judgment, poise, sensitivity, sophistication, taste)

Complexes/Maladjustments (compulsions, hangups, inhibitions, obsessions, phobias, prejudices, superstitions)

Frustrations and major disappointments in the character's life

What nicknames have been given the character? What do they mean?

Feelings (What are the character's most common feelings? What feelings are the character most comfortable with, most uncomfortable with?)

Attitudes toward life (militant, nervous, relaxed, resigned)

What does the character most like about himself/herself? What does he/she least like?

What aspects of his/her personality does the character deny, not accept? (anger, sexuality, tenderness)

How does the character feel about himself/herself? How does he/she feel about the other characters in the film (as in "I'm ok, you're ok")? Is the character a winner or a loser in life?

Hidden aspects of the character's personality (What do these reveal? What parts of himself/herself does the character know but keeps hidden from others? What is unknown to him/her but known to others? For example, a character may seem cool and in control, but actually exists on Valium, or may act as an upright citizen while taking part in secret orgies.)

Interpersonal Characteristics

Family and family background

Friends and lovers (and their involvements)

Co-workers, employers and employees (Who are they? What is the character's relations with them and attitudes toward them?)

Other people the character interacts with

Cultural Characteristics

Birthplace (where grew up, hometown)

National, ethnic and racial background

Education

Occupation (How does the character feel about his/her job? What are his/her satisfactions and dissatisfactions?)

Socio-economic status
Environment (Where does the character live and how does this environment affect him/her? Room, apartment house, neighborhood, town or city, car character owns)
Historical period of the story (if not the present) and its ethos
Interests, pastimes, hobbies (such as fast cars, wines, hunting, tennis, growing orchids)
Special abilities, skills (such as martial arts skills, weapons skills)
Religious beliefs (How important to the character?)
Political attitudes (How important to the character?)
Values (morals, ethics, habitual mode of response to life)
Lifestyle (on the street, jet set, hippie, suburbia)
Dominant traits
Major events in the character's life (psychological, sociological, interpersonal, cultural)
Goals/ambitions (Immediate and long range. "I want to . . . ." Consider those that are expressed in the film and those that are not shown.)
Dominant expression and impact of the character (including a vast number of descriptive adjectives such as: active, aggressive, ambitious, amoral, anxious, arrogant, artificial, authentic, authoritarian, awkward, bitchy, bold, brave, cantankerous, careful, careless, caring, casual, cheerful, clever, competent, competitive, compulsive, confident, conservative, cowardly, cruel, cunning, dirty, dominant, domineering, dull, egotistic, energetic, exhibitionistic, extravagant, fast, finicky, fickle, friendly, fun, generous, gentle, graceful, hostile, humorous, immoral, insolent, kind, lazy, loyal, miserly, modest, moral, naive, narcissistic, nervous, open, optimistic, passive, perfectionist, pessimistic, phony, placid, playful, radical, rigid, rude, ruthless, selfish, sharp, shrewd, slow, snobbish, strong, stupid, subdued, submissive, tedious, treacherous, vain, violent, vulgar, weak, withdrawn, worldly)

Character Biography

To better understand a character, as well as to give the character the sense of a personal history, a writer can write out a biography for the character. This serves as a working sketch for the writer. It can help answer questions about a character's motivations. While generally useful, it runs the risk of being too intellectual an exercise; the lifelike quality of the character could get lost in biographic details or in clinical-type rationales.

There are a number of ways to do a character biography. One approach is to begin with the character's birth (or even earlier, with family background) and sketch out the highlights of the character's life through infancy, childhood, schooling and adolescence up to the time of the story. Attention should be given to personal traits, feelings, romances, hates, loves and experiences with friends, parents and other important persons in the character's life. There should also be consideration of the cultures and subcultures that have influenced the character. A character biography can be written as straight narrative or as a monologue from the character.

A shorter, but still effective, variant on the full biography is to describe the five (or so) most important experiences in the character's life.

Another variation is to do an impressionistic sketch of the character. By stressing how the writer feels about the character, this approach can pinpoint character aspects that the writer will want to develop. Here is such a sketch, written in response to a classroom assignment to describe a person who might be an interesting character for a film.

> She comes in all starry-eyed and laughing. Black hair and blue eyes. The face of a choirboy who can't tell a lie. At twenty-five she looks like a fourteen-year-old paperboy. The little munchkin is as explosive as a keg of dynamite. A strike of the wrong word can set her off. "Expose and intimidate, expose and intimidate, a hand in the dark is a hand in the dark, that's what I've always said." A prophet with her hand in the dark. Lyrical lover, she can only read political poetry to her band of followers. That sense of politics. A balance of power. An insulation of emotions. Under the guise of a Gemini, she swings from artificial assuredness to manufactured doubt. She needs all that she can get. She feels sorry and won't forget. A tumbleweed connection, an incessant child. It takes a child to be a woman. A preacher of the faith, the protector of the female species, an incurable realist. She deals with the spaces without. A true utilitarian. A radical at best. Known for her sudden outbursts of radical therapy. A contradictor. T-shirts and painted jeans. A pulse of one hundred fifty. The pride of being Jewish. A sixties hippie child. She broke her ankle during a riot at Kent State jumping off a car. A Walter Cronkite special. A sexual spokeswoman. Anything for an argument. Anything for a scene. She breaks the ice with self parody. "Make 'em laugh and you know you've got 'em." Consistently nostalgic. Painfully self-conscious. An intellectual Pinky Lee. Life of the party. An outgoing recluse. Separation of words and actions. She cares too much. With thumb in mouth, she theorizes Marx and Lenin, folds her pajamas under her pillow, never travels without her bedroom slippers. She doesn't like to sleep alone. Showers constantly, chews gum for hours, hates smokers and wants to be magic.[5]

Still another approach is to sketch a character lifeline. This is literally drawing a lifeline of high and low points in the character's psychological and social development. The line should be drawn from birth to the present of the story, and then projected further into the future, beyond the story. (J.D. Salinger describes his character Franny as a girl destined to marry a man with a hacking cough—there was *that* in her face, too.[6]) What will the character be doing five years after the end of the story? How will the character die? At what age? What will be said in the eulogy for the character? What will appear on the character's tombstone? While these future projections won't appear directly in the story, they can help the writer achieve a better grasp of the character.

Some additional questions to consider when doing a preliminary sketch of the character are: does the character think there is something wrong with him? If so, what? If magical change were possible, what would the character change in himself? What is the character's biggest problem? What is his favorite fantasy? What does the character most want from life? What does he most like about himself? What does he least like? How would the character briefly describe himself?

How does the character appear to the public? to his co-workers? to his friends? to his lovers? to others with whom he has an intimate relationship?

If someone very close to you asked what the character was like, how would you answer? What does the character spend his time doing? What does he invest his energy doing and talking about? What do others know about the character that he doesn't know? What does he do that he doesn't realize he is doing (for example, criticizing others a great deal)? What does the character know about himself that he hides from others?

If you were to describe the character as a metaphor, what would it be? What are the subtle, physical ways in which the character expresses his personality? What do all the major characters want from each other?

When Characters Create

Because characters are in large part a creation of the formative unconscious, at times a very peculiar but very exciting thing happens—the characters seem to come alive and develop a life of their own. The characters have been so formed in the unconscious that at some point their actions seem self-determined. They seem to take over the writing and move the story in directions the writer may not have consciously determined. If this happens—and it could—then the writer will just listen as the characters write their own actions. The writer becomes almost an observer, recording what the characters do and say. All this may sound strange, but it is an experience of many writers. A writer should be open to the possibility. Here is how some have described the experience.

Ibsen describes something like this as the way he wrote many of his plays. He would have the initial conception and, with this in mind, have made a model of the set for the play with small dolls to represent the characters. Then, he said, he would put the dolls on the set and watch, listen and write down what happened.

Charles Dickins received a great many letters objecting to the death of Little Nell, a character in a serial episode of *The Old Curiosity Shop*. (Dickins' novels were first published as serials in the public press.) His reply was that he couldn't help her death; she was suffering from a fatal disease! The response suggests that it was out of his hands; the character determined her own end.

I had a similar experience when writing a play. I had planned it to have a rather negative ending, but by the time I got there, the character had taken over and made the ending positive. That was the way it had to be with her.

Screenwriters have spoken of this. Edward Anhalt said, "I think what Shaw spoke of actually happens. That is, the characters seem to be speaking themselves, they seem to be real."[7] Buck Henry said, "If you can let the characters take over instead of having to force them around. If you really know who they are. If it's that kind of film and you're improvising freely enough, they can control the situation through you. It's like being a medium."[8]

All this is further evidence of the power of the unconscious in creatively developing a screenplay.

Imagination Exercises

Exciting characters are one of the primary assets of a successful film or television program. Following are some exercises that can be used to stimulate your imagination and help bring your characters to life. They will be helpful for some writers, less valuable for others. Perhaps they will be of use to you.

In your imagination, take your character through a typical day. How does he feel when he gets up? What does he feel when he looks in the mirror? What kind of toothpaste does he use? Does he sing in the shower? What does he eat for breakfast? How does he get to work? Does he like his work? What do his subordinates think of him? His superiors? Who does he interact with during the day? What does he think about most? Worry about? Dream about? What events mark his day—lunch?—appointments?—dinner? What does he do in the evening? When does he go to bed? Trace over such a typical day in your imagination.

Sometime, when you are relaxed, sit quietly in a darkened room and listen to your character. Ask him questions and hear his replies. Ask him to describe himself—what he is like, why he does what he does, how he feels. Most important to this exercise is to develop a sense of listening to the character. Don't force his replies; just let them happen. Get into that creative attitude of relaxed awareness and listen to what your character tells you of himself.

Another way to do this is to imagine a screen on which your character appears. See him concretely. How does he look? What does he have to say?

You might try having a similar dialogue with your character on paper by writing out your questions and his answers (and his questions to you if he asks any).

What most strikes you about your character? Physically? Psychologically?

Imagine your character's dominant characteristics exaggerated, taken to extremes. What is your character like now?

Pick two or three of your character's dominant characteristics, then think of the opposite of these. How does your character express the opposites? (Aren't we all mixtures of opposites?) Let your character's opposite tendencies dialogue together to see how they coexist in the character. Let his strong side talk with his weak self, his loving self talk with his hating self, his tender self dialogue with his macho self. How does each of these opposites relate to the other? How does each try to assert control?

Become the character in your imagination and take a walk as if you were the character. Sit like him, move like him, behave like him. Experience like him. Holding your mind still, breathe like your character. Get into his rhythm. See, hear, feel as he would.

Sometime, when walking outside, imagine that you are following behind your character. Observe him. What does he do?

Imagine watching a movie of your character when he was younger, prior to the film you are writing, and in particular situations. What do you see?

Imagine the character in scenes from the script and in other situations apart from the film.

What do the character's surroundings (room, car, books, furnishings) and his clothes say of him?

Pick a minor scene from your script and become the character in that particular scene. Let a free fantasy flow. See how rich the scene becomes.

In a crisis situation from your story, try to experience how the character feels the crisis in his body. How does he express this non-verbally? How does he hide it?

If your character has an internal conflict or conflicting values, let the two sides of the conflict dialogue with each other.

Put two characters together and have them honestly and authentically dialogue and say things that they can't or won't express within the situation of the film.

Imagine your character metaphorically. If he were a car, what kind of car would he be? Why? Or an animal, a novel, a painting, a flower, a tree, a piece of furniture, an article of clothing, some food, drink, a color, a song, a piece of music, a style of architecture, an odor, a metal, weather, a period of history or a historical personage.

How does your character deal with fundamental feelings such as anger? Tenderness? Fear? Hate? Rage? Intimacy? Affection? Aggression?

Place your character in front of a mirror. Have him examine himself. Have him describe himself. What does he say?

Have your character complete such sentences as the following: "I have to . . ." "I choose to . . ." "I can't (won't, need, want) . . ." "I control people by . . ." "I keep people from getting close by . . ." "I refuse to face . . ." "I would let people know me if . . ." "I am trying to give the impression that . . ."

Time spent on imagination exercises like those above help make your character more real, more alive, more of a complete person. They help you know your character better and encourage your character to develop a life of his own.

REFERENCES

1. Harold Pinter as quoted in Lawrence M. Bensky, "Harold Pinter: An Interview," *Paris Review* 10 (Fall 1966): 12–37.
2. Friedrich Hebbel as quoted in Abraham Kaplan, "The Aesthetics of the Popular Arts," *Journal of Aesthetics and Art Criticism* 24 (Spring 1966): 361.
3. George Valliant as quoted in Howard Muson, "The Lessons of the Grant Study," *Psychology Today* 11 (September 1977): 48.
4. Mary G. Marcus, "The Power of a Name," *Psychology Today* 10 (October 1976): 75–6.
5. Darlene Mitera, "For Danni," 1975 (unpublished).
6. J.D. Salinger, *Franny and Zooey* (New York: Little, Brown and Co., 1955), p. 126.
7. William Froug, *The Screenwriter Looks at the Screenwriter* (New York: Dell Publishing Co., 1972), p. 276.
8. *Op cit.*, pp. 194–5.

5

Structure Variations

> There is a time and place even for popular art. Champagne and Napoleon brandy are admittedly the best of beverages; but on a Sunday afternoon in the ballpark we want a coke, or maybe a glass of beer. "Even if we have all the virtues," Zarathustra reminds us, "there is still one thing needful: to send the virtues themselves to sleep at the right time." If popular art gives us pleasant dreams, we can only be grateful—when we have wakened.[1]
>
> —Abraham Kaplan

WE HAVE SKETCHED OUT the basics of a dramatic narrative film story in terms of structure and characters. We've pointed out how the fundamental principles of structure are grounded in audience responses such as suspense and surprise. Now we'll consider some variations on the basic techniques by looking at two poles of film narrative: the formula approach of popular mass art and the more open, looser forms of new narrative cinema.

The Formula

At its worst, the formula approach attempts to take structural principles with their ability to affect an audience and codify them into a formula. The formula is overly structured. Suspense and surprise are exaggerated. Each plot development is milked for its maximum effect and direct appeal to the audience's emotions. In trying for such obvious impact, the formula approach develops its own weaknesses. By attempting to do it all for the audience, it deprives them of direct experience. Instead, it leaves them with mere recognition of the same old formula with the same stars and plot and character stereotypes. Subtleties are lost, since only the most obvious and dominant elements of the story are of interest to the formula. It tries to overcome the repetition by flogging our waning interest with claims of the constantly new and different (although it usually turns out to be merely the old in new guise—"Your favorite star as you've never seen her before," but we have). The ambiguity which draws a responsive audience into the experience is missing. The result is too often superficial, simplistic, obvious, predigested, banal and ultimately unsatisfying—a fact to which we can all attest after spending another night of just "wasting time watching television."

To its credit, formula fare is often diverting, entertaining and pleasurably enjoyable—like a glass of beer on a warm summer afternoon picnic. It's also something that can be quickly mass produced and so meet the demand for material to fill television screens night after night. Nor should we forget when we are tempted to disparage the hack writers of formula potboilers that these writers are professionals who have achieved a level of mastery of their craft. They have the skill to construct a workable even if undistinguished film narrative. Moreover, formula-type programs may be the most open market for beginning writers. In itself, the formula needn't necessarily force the shoddy results we tend to observe night after night on television.

What follows is a rendition of formula as it applies to hour-length, action-adventure and investigative dramatic television programs.

First the writer should approach the script with the realization that there is an underlying three-act structure (which roughly corresponds to beginning, middle and end). Each act should develop in this way:

Act I sets up the problem (or conflict). Some trouble or some disruptive situation personally involves the central character and activates the story.

Act II attempts to solve the problem. But unexpected developments cause things to deteriorate. The problem exacerbates. The hero is deeper in trouble than before. Often just when things look as though they are solved, there comes the realization that they are really worse than they had been. For example, in a futuristic science fiction adventure story, a space station is threatened with destruction due to the malfunctioning of a crucial electronic component. Throughout Act II the crew's attempts to repair the part or improvise other methods are unsuccessful. Finally, the crew believes that they are out of trouble; a space shuttle is bringing a new replacement part. But Act II then concludes with their optimism shattered as they realize that if the shuttle tries to land on their crippled space station it will throw them out of orbit and thus to certain destruction. An added complication is that their transmitting communication system is also malfunctioning and they can't send a message to the shuttle not to land. (This might also be an interesting crisis for Act III.)

Act III sees their problems become even worse, even though extreme measures are taken to try to solve things. However, finally there comes the thrilling climax and the problem is solved.

In addition to his sense of three-act structure, the writer realizes that in an hour television program (for American TV) there are four acts, each act being separated by a commercial break.* The writer will write an exciting ending for each act. This could be a suspenseful cliff-hanger, a new threat or problem, some new and challenging information or some other surprise. (For example, a person thought dead turns out to be alive.) Tense act endings hold the viewer to the program over each commercial break. The cliff-hanger or tense ending is especially important at the end of act 2 for the half-hour break. In addition to the four-act division, an hour show may include an introductory teaser. This is a short segment which presents the trouble or problem. There could also be a short tag at the end to wind up loose ends.

Each of the four acts contain three or four beats. (Recall that a beat is a plot development that advances the story. Beats are generally crises, such as new information or a new problem.) For example, imagine a program in which the teaser shows a person killed and some papers stolen. Then in act 1, the first beat establishes that the private investigator hero is suspected of knowing something of the crime and the missing securities. The second beat introduces two new characters—villainous types—who show an interest in the hero. Beat three presents an interpersonal involvement between the hero and his lady friend. She's upset with him because he stood her up for a dinner date. Beat 4—the cliff-hanger conclusion of act 1—has the hero abducted by the villains and threatened with death if he doesn't reveal the whereabouts of the securities (which he doesn't know).

The following example from the ''Fire in Space'' episode of the *Battlestar Galactica* series illustrates the development of this formula in terms of its beats. Starbuck and Apollo are the young heroes of the series. Adama is the older commander. Their enemies are the robot Cylons. The four acts of the hour television program are analyzed by their plot development beats.

Act 1

1. A major Cylon attack is approaching the spaceship Battlestar Galactica. Viper fighter ships are sent out to defend the Galactica.
2. Two Cylon fighters manage to evade the Vipers and ram the Galactica. Adama is seriously injured.
3. Another Cylon fighter escapes the Viper squadron and smashes into the bridge of the Galactica.
4. Some of the central characters are trapped on the damaged bridge. They include the young son of Apollo and his dog-like pet Daggit. Fire threatens the trapped characters—they must be rescued or else!

Act 2

1. Rescuers try to reach them but can't.
2. The trapped characters manage to escape into another room just as the room they were in is swept by fire.

* For clarity, three-act structure will capitalize ''Act'' and use Roman numerals for each act; a four-act division will use lower case ''act'' and use Arabic numerals. Generally, ''Acts 2 and 3'' correspond to ''Act II.''

3. They try to escape further but find they are trapped by fire (and a red hot door)!
4. Rescuers are stymied. They don't even know if those who were on the bridge are alive. If they are, the rescuers reason, they might send the pet daggit through the air duct to let them know. But not enough men can be spared to check out all air duct vents. The raging fire threatens the doom of the Galactica, and the rescuers can't stop it. Then Apollo gets the idea of loading fire extinguishing chemicals into the Vipers and, by making a strafing run, shooting the chemicals into the burning section. "Do it!"

Act 3

1. Starbuck almost crashes after shooting a chemical extinguisher at the burning section.
2. It looks as though the plan has succeeded in putting out the fire. But no; a pump fails and the fire bursts out again worse than ever.
3. Death threatens the injured Commander Adama unless he can be operated on, but failing power makes that doubtful. Still, Adama comes up with a plan—a last desperate measure—to try placing charges and blowing holes in the hull, letting the vacuum of space smother the fire. If there are any trapped persons, they would then die without oxygen, but it is doubtful that they are still alive, and it must be tried to save the ship. Apollo and Starbuck start to place charges.
4. Apollo gets the desperate idea to place mushies—a treat loved by the pet daggit—in the air vent in the hope that if the animal was sent by survivors, he would sniff out the treats. In the air vent the daggit does sniff the mushies and moves toward them, only to find flames lashing in through a vent blocking his path!

Act 4

1. Apollo and Starbuck, outside the ship, are running out of time in getting all the charges placed before they explode. A singed pet daggit comes through the air vent. Air masks are attached to him and he is sent back to his young master.
2. The fire has reached an explosive section of the ship and destruction is imminent. Outside the ship, Apollo and Starbuck have run out of handholds and must risk a dangerous gambit to place the last charge.
3. The pet daggit reaches the trapped fire victims. Apollo places the last charge on the hull, but slips and drifts into space right over the explosive charge area. He seems doomed, but his friend Starbuck won't leave him. The charges are about to blow.
4. Starbuck propels himself away from the hull, slams into Apollo and carries them both farther into space away from the explosives. There is a huge explosion. The fire is out. Apollo and Starbuck are groggy, but safely floating in space.

Tag:

Adama is recovering. Apollo and Starbuck are back. Apollo's son is worried about his pet daggit, who is missing and feared destroyed. But the pet turns up just slightly damaged. All is well.

Open Structure

On the other side from formula are the looser, more open forms of contemporary cinema. Here are the filmmakers who explore variations of traditional narrative film—Antonioni, Bergman, Buñuel, Fellini, Godard, Makavejev, Pasolini, Resnais and others.

Some avant-garde filmmakers and critics challenge the concept of narrative. Their interest is in the cinematic process itself rather than in the story. Some of their criticism is directed against the realism in film. They point out that realism is a tradition, an artistic trend. They maintain that there is no absolute justification for film's pretense of representing reality. Political filmmakers and critics apply the argument to ideology. They aver that we have a bourgeois cinema which, while pretending to present reality, actually seduces the viewer into the fantasies of a bourgeois capitalist ideology. The process by which films do this is not necessarily intentional. They think it is as much a result of the realist narrative tradition and the technical practices of film production as it is of the capitalist film industry.

These are some of the new voices that are enriching the fabric of modern cinema. How they ultimately will affect the films and television programs that we view is still uncertain. For now, our immediate concern is with practices that are more useful to the screenwriter today.

Newer approaches to structure can share any or all of the following characteristics. They are more ambiguous and oblique than the traditional Hollywood plot-dominated story film. They are less linear in their development, with less of a logical, goal-oriented narrative. In *The Passenger,* we are never quite sure of Locke's objective except that he wants to escape from himself and his past. The story that develops from this is much different from a goal-centered, external plot.

Events in the newer films often occur for reasons other than because of what they contribute to the plot. These reasons might be to create a mood, to explore character, to express a theme or simply to present an element of style to be appreciated for its own sake. The story is frequently subordinated, at least temporarily, to these other elements. (This frequently happens in a comedy when a sequence will exist solely for its humor and not because it advances the plot.) Sequences in the film assume greater independence from the plot. The development within each sequence and the interrelationships between sequences can be as important as the relationship of the sequence to the overall story.

Newer film forms are often elliptical. They leave out events that might otherwise be present. Fewer things are explained. Connections between story elements may be omitted, giving the film an episodic quality. On the other hand, intervals between story events—between beats—may assume greater significance than required by the narrative.

Fellini's *Amarcord* is a mosaic assortment of stories and incidents from an Italian village; his *Roma* is a collage of loosely connected incidents in the city. Truffaut's *Small Change* consists of a series of linked vignettes about children's experiences while growing up. *Slaughterhouse Five* repeatedly jumps back and forth in time while interweaving events from different times and places through strongly stylized transitions.

What follows are examples of techniques that characterize more open narrative structure. They include looser narrative storylines, alternative unifying devices, character exploration rather than a strong plotline, increased use of symbolic and metaphoric elements, less strict linear time sequencing, elliptical development, less traditional production techniques and surreal and presentational approaches. The chapter will conclude with examples of experimental practices from the *Monty Python's Flying Circus* television series and the film *Annie Hall*.

Looser Narrative Storylines. For some films, a clear narrative storyline may never be established (e.g., *Amarcord, Roma, Small Change*), while with other films, the primary storyline may not be established until sometime later in the film. In *Psycho,* a main character is killed halfway into the film; the storyline begun around her terminates and a new one—uncovering the murderer—begins. In *2001,* it is some time before we are clearly made aware of the storyline objective of searching for the meaning of the black monolith, while the strongly engrossing storyline based on the conflict of the astronauts versus the computer HAL doesn't appear until the second half of the film. In *Blow-Up,* it is some time before Thomas notices the crime and tries to investigate it; prior to this we are more involved with him as a character than engrossed with a strong plot line.

Alternative Unifying Devices. One important function of the basic storyline is that it unifies the total film story. Films in which a storyline is less emphatic often use other unifying techniques. *Blow-Up* begins and ends with some student mimists, whose illusory tennis game signifies much of the meaning of the film. As with so many of Antonioni's films, *Blow-Up* begins in the morning, continues through that day and night, and concludes the following morning.

There are also cyclical events in *A Clockwork Orange*. The tramp who is beaten at the film's beginning returns near the end to attack Alex. Violence against Dim in the early part of the film is repaid with a vengeance when Dim commits violence against Alex. Similarly, the attack inflicted on the inhabitants of "The Home" in the first part of the film cycles back when Alex finds himself a guest there and is violently made to suffer near the film's end.

The operating room scenes and the continual loudspeaker messages in

*M*A*S*H* help give it a certain continuity. So do the family ritual occasions and continual eating scenes in *Cousin, Cousine.*

Exploring Character. Often instead of a strong storyline we become involved with an interesting character or character relationship. Our interest in the film comes from our caring about the character and what happens to him.

Character motivations may be more ambiguous and unexplained, as with Bobby in *Five Easy Pieces,* Locke in *The Passenger* or the sailor in *Sweet Movie.* Sometimes characters are less obviously goal-oriented, as the two bikers in *Easy Rider* who are just bumming to New Orleans and around.

Films like *8½, Belle de Jour* and *Persona* explore a character's motivations and psyche, with more emphasis on this exploration than on an external story. They are structured around complex and often subtle internal storylines.

Thematic, Symbolic or Metaphoric Elements. Films may feature strongly symbolic or metaphoric elements which ask us to make meaningful connections that aren't obviously spelled out. At the end of *Blow-Up,* for example, when Thomas retrieves the imaginary ball of the mimed tennis game, he has to put down his camera to do so. The detached photographer joins their game of celebrating life and joy. Illusion is joined with reality. And on the sound track we hear the twang of rackets and the thud of the ball on the courts.

In Makavejev's wild and exciting *Sweet Movie,* the dual stories are periodically intercut with tinted old newsreel footage of German soldiers discovering the graves of Polish officers slaughtered by the Russians in the Katyn Forest Massacre. These powerful visuals are all the more striking when juxtaposed against the comic (and often violently black comic) events of the film. Then at the end of the film, we are struck by the image of the presumably dead boys stirring to life as the scene changes from black-and-white to color; it is a powerful experience.

Sometimes a strong theme will structure a film more than the story. Godard has done this with a number of Brechtian, didactic, political films (as *La Chinoise* and *Tout va Bien*).

Less Temporally Linear. Real-time progression is less important in many modern films. They can feature extensive flashbacks and flashforwards. *Slaughterhouse Five* jumps backwards and forwards in time. In *Last Year at Marienbad,* we are often uncertain of the time tense of the film. Much of *The Conformist* is presented as flashbacks within flashbacks; in one section of the film there are at least three interweaving levels of time interacting with each other.

Elliptical Development. Often there are elisions (. . . .) where we might expect story narrative. Scenes we would expect to see are omitted, while scenes which are less directly important to the story are presented. The films seem more discontinuous. Intervals assume greater importance than would be expected. Much of what is important is not shown. Events are presented, but not clearly developed. Or, an event will be built up to—then not shown. What is not shown may be more important to the meaning and development of the film than what is shown.

Cousin, Cousine is an interesting, fast-paced film of numerous short sequences. Many of these short scenes merely show characters getting into and out of cars, buses and motorcycles. While not advancing the plot, these scenes help set the pace and rhythm of the film.

In *Blow-Up,* the two scenes in the antique shop, the scenes with the painter and his wife and the guitar smashing sequence could have been omitted with no disturbance to the plot. Yet they are important to the film, in their elliptical way, in what they tell us about Thomas and his world. They are part of the mix which produces the flavor of the film.

A bit of offscreen action in Godard's *Masculine-Feminine* illustrates the experimentation typical of his films. Two young men are talking in a cafe. One goes to borrow the sugar from a girl at another table and, while reaching for it, places his arm over her body, touching her breasts. He then comes back, rejoining his friend. So the friend, the main character, goes to try it as well. But instead of the camera following him so that we see the action, we remain with the other young man at the table. We hear the offscreen dialogue as the sugar is requested. The fellow returns. All the action took place offscreen. Nor was the reaction of the person at the table important. What was absent from our view was recreated in our imagination.

Looser Production Techniques. Many of the older film conventions have been broken or at least bent to new shapes. Scene sequencing and editing often feature elliptical jumps in time and space. The once forbidden jump cut is now commonplace. So is the single-shot scene, using deep focus and mise-en-scène compositional staging (rather than intercutting within the scene). Sometimes scenes begin before we would expect them to start and continue after we would normally expect them to stop. Antonioni often does this. Ozu will end a scene by having the conversation turn to incidental topics, then lapse altogether.

Jean Luc Godard's experimentation includes the nearly eight-minute continuous tracking shot of a traffic jam and a long, slow pan shot of more than 360 degrees in *Weekend.* While his films have not greatly influenced the main stream of filmmakers, they are intelligent and provoking and should be studied by filmmakers interested in political and avant-garde feature films.

The Surreal. Many films contain elements of the surreal (in the general sense of departure from reality). Buñuel is probably the first filmmaker to come to mind when we think of surrealism. But other films also use the surreal. In the opening of *8½*, Guido is first suffocatingly trapped in his car, then floats in the sky like a tethered balloon. The later harem scene is a wild fantasy. There's a certain grotesqueness to so many Fellini films: the weird costumes of *Juliet of the Spirits,* the style of *Satyricon,* the clerical fashion show in *Roma.* In *Sweet Movie,* the sailor is killed (stabbed by his lover in their sugar bed), but then reappears later in the film. At the film's end, the supposedly dead children stir and come to life. In *Cries and Whispers,* Agnes is briefly brought to life again.

At the end of *O Lucky Man,* there is a cast party, somewhat legitimized since the main character supposedly wins a movie part; but it appears that the part he gets is in the film we've just seen, and cast members and the director appear as themselves at this last bash.

There is an intriguing surreal element in the television series *The Prisoner*. The village in which the resigned intelligence officer is held is quaint, charming. People dress as at a resort. Golf carts serve as cars and taxis. There are afternoon band concerts. Almost everyone is pleasant and polite. It would seem like a picturesque English seaside resort—except for the constant threat. There is continual electronic surveillance. We are never quite sure who are the threatening "they." One of the primary defenses against escape from the village is a large white "ball" five or six feet in diameter which pursues and engulfs those who try to get away. Episodes of the series frequently feature strange, surreal developments.

The surreal is common in comedy, where the dictates of reality are less demanding. In Jerry Lewis' *The Disorderly Orderly,* he tries to fix the "snow" on a television set and real snow—a blizzard—blasts out of the set. He snaps his fingers and his thumb shoots out a foot-long flame as though from a monstrous cigarette lighter. In an "absolute quiet" hospital area, when some characters are talking, we hear no sound but instead read subtitles of their conversation. Then, when Jerry takes a bite of an apple, the sound is hugely, disturbingly amplified. When a completely bandaged mummy-like patient in a wheelchair rolls unattended down a hill and crashes into a tree, the cast breaks apart to reveal that there is no one inside. Comedy is often footloose with reality.

Presentational Approach. Sometimes a looser approach to film reality is characterized by a presentational segment which directly acknowledges the audience, thereby "breaking the fourth wall" (as opposed to the representational approach, which purports to represent a reality to which we, through the camera, are voyeuristically witness). Godard frequently breaks filmic reality. At one point in *Weekend,* one character complains about the miserable sort of film he is in. In *Pierrot Le Fou,* Ferdinand says a line directly to the camera. Puzzled, Marianne asks to whom he's speaking. He replies, "To the audience."

Amarcord has a narrator who talks directly to the audience. At one point in *What's Up, Tiger Lily?* Two fingers appear on the screen as if grabbing the film at the projector gate. Then we cut to an office where executives ask Woody Allen if he can tell them what the film is about at this point. He replies simply, "no," and the film continues.

At various points in the Canadian film *Les Ordres,* the narrative is interrupted as the actors appear directly, introduce themselves and discuss the characters they play. Sometimes this is done voice-over, at other times they are shown talking to the camera.

In *Tom Jones,* Tom gives the camera a knowing look as we share with him the double-meaning of a lady being "Most hungry—I can vouch for it." In another scene, he places his hat over the camera to keep us from ogling a half-dressed woman whom he has just rescued from an attacker. In an argument over whether a landlady stole money from him, Tom looks at the camera and asks us, "Did you see her take that £500?"

Night Full of Rain features some "friends" who sort of introduce and narrate the film. They will break into the narrative for a moment, but then the narrative continues as if they weren't there at all. They will appear in a scene as if invisible and comment on the scene or give advice to the main characters.

Peter Watkins used a sort of presentational approach in his BBC television docu-drama *Culloden*. He treats this historic eighteenth-century battle between the British and the Scots as if it were being covered by live-television reporters who interview soldiers, generals and displaced civilians.

The television series *M*A*S*H* did a variation on a presentational approach in an episode in which the *MASH* personnel are interviewed by a war correspondent. They are permitted to talk directly to the camera as if this were a battlefield interview situation. They say hello to the folks back home, discuss their views of the war and their thoughts about the future. The episode was filmed in black-and-white to simulate a 1950 TV newsreel documentary.

Monty Python's Flying Circus

The BBC television comedy series *Monty Python's Flying Circus* provides many examples of innovative television experimentation. Characters may get mixed up about whose lines are whose and quite openly refer to scripts (all planned, of course). Characters frequently talk directly to us, the audience, from a sketch. Or they will talk to an offstage audience, or even to another scene. Sketches frequently interact with each other even though they take place at different times and places. It's possible for a particular sketch to operate within four levels of reality: the reality of the sketch itself, the reality of other sketches with which it incredibly interacts, the reality of the theater audience watching the television show being produced and the reality of the television-viewing home audience.

Sometimes a comedy sketch will stop abruptly, coming to no logical conclusion at all. Frequently a character portraying an army officer or a Scotland Yard inspector will interrupt and terminate a sketch as if he were an offended censor. Sometimes he will arrest a character/actor for taking part in such a stupid sketch. One sketch was interrupted and concluded by a supposed BBC announcer saying that it promised too much sex and violence so the BBC was putting another scene in its place. Another comic sketch was stopped by simply announcing "That sketch has been abandoned." Another was abruptly terminated when a character/actor points out that it's one o'clock and time for the actors to have lunch.

A sketch features jungle explorers who are lost and about to die. Suddenly they realize that they are not alone in the jungle. They are being filmed! There must be a camera crew somewhere. We then see them enthusiastically greeting the camera crew. But then they ask, who's filming us being filmed? They start toward this second camera and the scene ends.

An offscreen narrator setting the scene for an Icelandic saga calls it a "terrible saga." A character in the scene objects, saying it isn't all that terrible. The narrator sticks his head into the frame and says that he meant "violent," and the character accepts his correction.

One sketch brings characters to an impossibly dangerous situation. They are facing inevitable death before a firing squad, which is charging them with pointed bayonets. Then a sign flashes on the screen: "Scene omitted." Then we come up on the characters on an English country lane shaking hands and saying, "That was a narrow escape."

Annie Hall

We will conclude this discussion of more open structuring with examples from Woody Allen's *Annie Hall.* The "story" is set up in the beginning of the film when Woody, as the character Alvy, talks directly to the camera in a monologue. He tells of the trauma of turning forty, and of how the film will show how he got involved with, then separated from, his girl friend Annie Hall (thus prestructuring our expectations).

As Alvy tells us of his early school experiences, the camera trucks across nagging, nasty teachers instructing at the blackboard, then continues without a realistic break to truck past children seated at their desks in a classroom. As the classroom teacher berates Alvy (as a child) for kissing a little girl classmate, Alvy the man replaces Alvy the child in the cramped classroom desk and defends his healthy sex interest to the teacher. Then some of these same school children stand beside their desks and address the camera directly, telling, as if they were now grown up, what they have become as adults (e.g., "I own a sausage factory. . . .").

Getting to know each other, Alvy and Annie share some wine and make routine, intellectual-sounding conversation while subtitles flash on the screen showing what they are really thinking—what sort of sex partner the other would be and whether or not they are hurting the budding relationship by making a poor impression.

In one scene, a sailor and girl run by and the girl breaks the fourth wall by throwing a kiss to the camera.

Waiting in line for a movie, Alvy is irritated by the remarks of an opinionated man behind them who is pontificating to his date about films, Fellini and the ideas of Marshall McLuhan. Alvy breaks out of the reality of the scene and talks directly to us about how he can't stand the stupid things the man is saying. The man steps from the line and starts arguing with Alvy. Then Alvy goes behind a billboard in the theater lobby and brings out McLuhan, in person, who tells the other guy that he doesn't know what he is talking about.

In bed together, Alvy complains about Annie's being sexually cold. A spirit doppelgänger (double image) of Annie rises from her body on the bed and looks back at the two of them.

In a dinner scene at Annie's house, Alvy must deal with her anti-semitic grandmother (who cooked the Jewish Alvy a ham) and her critical family. At one point, he appears made up to look like an orthodox rabbi, reflecting how much they make him self-conscious of his Jewishness.

A split screen simultaneously shows this dinner and an earlier dinner with his family to point up the contrasting lifestyles. The two conversations go on simultaneously, then consecutively. The families even talk to each other across the split screen.

A split screen is also used later to show Alvy and Annie talking to their respective psychiatrists. Their conversations—each to his/her own doctor—interrelate and blend.

In a flashback to an earlier event with Annie and some guy at a party, Alvy and Annie appear in the scene as invisible viewers—as if they had been transported back in time. In another scene, with a friend of Alvy's, they go back in time to an episode in which his parents are arguing.

Talking of his childhood, Alvy says how he liked the wicked witch in *Snow White*. The film then becomes a cartoon showing a cartoon figure Alvy with the wicked witch. Then Alvy's friend enters, also as an animated cartoon figure, and says he's lined up Alvy with a date. The next scene is back in live action and we see Alvy with the date.

In a rather tender sequence, we see Alvy and Annie kiss. He directs her attention by pointing toward the camera. We cut to them in a long shot and in a different location, kissing before a setting sun. The effect is of a point-of-view shot sequence, as though Alvy was pointing to direct Annie to look at themselves in the second scene.

If done badly, the innovations of more open film forms are self-conscious, gimmicky, irritating and even infuriating. They risk being different just for the sake of being different, of being obscure under the pretense of innovation. Hopefully such obvious misuses are rare. Experimentation with the cinematic and narrative processes are inevitable in the evolving practice of film. The techniques of narrative and filmmaking are continually being shaped by those at the leading edge of the craft who are willing to take risks as they explore the media. This is what makes cinema alive and exciting. What is today's innovation will become tomorrow's formula, and in its turn it will be replaced by still newer approaches. The process, however, does not take place overnight. Innovation evolves within established tradition. We have centuries of dramatic and storytelling narrative tradition. The principles developed for narrative film structure are deeply grounded in that tradition. Within these structural principles as we have outlined them, the screenwriter has a great deal of latitude. He may use them as the formula or experiment with them in new ways. Market considerations may suggest the former, but in the latter lies the art of filmic narrative.

REFERENCES

1. Abraham Kaplan, "The Aesthetics of the Popular Arts," *The Journal of Aesthetics and Art Criticism* 24 (Spring 1966): 351–64 (a classic analysis of popular art).

Also:

Nichols, Bill, ed. *Movies and Methods*. Berkeley: University of California Press, 1976.

6

Sequences and Scenes

> Each act, a course,
> each scene, a different dish.
> —George Farquhar, *The Inconstant*

IF THE SCREENWRITER has followed the procedure outlined earlier, he has developed his story from a basic story through one or more longer narrative versions. He finally has a satisfactory narrative film story of some detail. He is now ready to go the next step and develop it in terms of its scenes and sequences.

A scene is a unit containing a single and continuous dramatic action which is unified by such means as time, space, event, theme or motif, content, concept or character. A scene is usually a cohesive series of related shots, although it may be simply a single shot. The mise-en-scène filming style tends to use long, single-take shots as scenes; a number of these appeared in *Annie Hall*. Scenes usually cover a single time period.

A sequence is a longer segment made up of a series of closely related scenes which together form a unified whole. Sequences usually aren't continuous; the narrative events are related to each other, although they may occur at different times and places.

Since what is true of a scene is often true for a sequence as well, I'll use the terms rather interchangeably in this chapter. This shouldn't cause any problems, though there seems to be a great deal of confusion among writers about the precise definition of each term. I've found three writers who claim that the number of sequences in a feature film are approximately 8, 30 and 45 respectively. One of the most conscientious attempts to categorize different types of narrative scenes was made by Christian Metz. His descriptions aren't really appropriate in our discussion, but because of the analytic value of his definitions, I've included them in the Appendix.

As he plans his scenes, a writer will want to determine how the scene functions within the overall film, how the scenes interrelate to each other and the internal structure of the scene action. He will determine a tone and setting for the scene and have an idea of the point of view of the scene.

Scene Functions

A scene functions within the script in order to accomplish the writer's purpose for that scene. The writer first determines the dominant purpose of the scene: what is it intended to do? what will the audience most get from the scene? If any scene doesn't have a useful function, question its usefulness in the script and consider eliminating it.

Some scenes advance the story; they develop a storyline by introducing or resolving a problem or by presenting some complication in the progression of the storyline. The beats, which we have previously discussed, are sequences that advance the plot. Some scenes primarily present exposition to fill us in on the backstory. A scene may be used to establish a setting, to create a particular mood or atmosphere, to express a theme or thesis or to reveal something about a character and character relationships. A scene may act as a transition from one time or place to another. Some scenes provide a pause in the action, a break from the tension so that the audience can catch its breath. Some sequences present a quick montage of action that compresses the actual time of the events into a condensed summary of shots (such as Rocky training for the big fight as shown by quick shots of his sparring, working out in the gym, jumping rope and running). Some scenes exist in the script solely because they contain interesting action; they may not directly advance the narrative (such as a comic scene that is there simply because it's funny).

While the writer will want to identify the dominant function of the scene—why he wants it there, what he wants it to do—he will also be aware that most scenes perform a number of functions, not just one. A scene that advances the story may also introduce a new character, set a mood or prepare us for a surprising plot twist to come. Characters are always revealing and defining themselves while they are on the screen. The writer will be aware that regardless of the primary purpose of a scene, if his major characters are present, they are expressing themselves, and he should insure that they are consistent and credible from scene to scene. The writer will consider everything a scene is expressing and not let it inadvertently do something he doesn't want it to; rather, he will use it to express many things he feels are important, even while it accomplishes its primary function.

In *Network,* there is a short (two to three minute) dialogue scene between Max and Diana as they have dinner in a restaurant. The dominant function of the scene is to advance the interpersonal storyline of their relationship as they are about to begin an affair. The scene also functions to reveal something about each of them. She is seen as ambitious, assertive, direct; he comes across as solid, mellow and interesting. The scene also gives us exposition; we learn that he is married and has a family, that she is work-driven, has a broken previous marriage and is a "lousy lay." The scene further acts as a lull in the build of tensions. Even though the conversation is stimulating, there is a certain relaxed feeling about the scene which provides a break from the crises we've been experiencing thus far in the film.

Scene Types

Here are some selected scene examples to illustrate scene functions. Scenes that advance the plot aren't difficult to identify. We've already seen these as the beats in our outline of the television formula story. So the three mentioned here will be a bit different in that they are all non-verbal scenes that emphasize the visual impact of the medium. They are also rather memorable. The first occurs at the end of *All Quiet on the Western Front.* The central character, a soldier, notices a butterfly on the ground in front of the trench. As he reaches to catch it, he is noticed by an enemy sniper. The scene intercuts between his hand gently reaching for the butterfly and the sniper taking aim. Then the shot. The hand jerks, slowly drops and is still. The soldier is dead. The striking and frightening shower scene in *Psycho* uses a series of short, quick shots to present the knifing death of the woman. The third example of a scene that advances the plot is equally powerful and a classic example of a suspense build. In *The Birds,* Melanie waits on a bench outside the schoolhouse. She is going to warn of the attacking birds but is waiting for the children to finish their singing lesson. As she sits, the birds assemble on the playground behind her. When she finally notices them, they are a threatening swarm.

For examples of scenes that develop character, let's again pick some memorable ones that develop without dialogue. (It's easy to find dialogue scenes that do this.) These scenes develop a strong mood, which helps us become involved with the characters and our feelings about them. One unforgettable scene is from John Ford's *The Grapes of Wrath,* when Mama Joad is seated alone in the deserted shack that the family has called home for so long but which they are now forced to leave. She is sorting through old postcards and souvenir trinkets that sum up her life over the years. She looks wistfully at each one before dropping it into the fire or the trash. Here is the pillar of the family closing a book on her life and facing an uncertain future.

Can anyone who has seen *Ikiru* forget the scene with the dying old man singing his lonely song while sitting on the swing, in the snow, alone in the park that he struggled to have built for the townspeople as his final act of meaning. Both *The Graduate* and *Swept Away* contain scenes in which characters silently introspect about themselves. These scenes are strongly influenced by the music that accompanies them and helps create the mood. These scenes aren't the most common types of scenes that reveal character—dialogue scenes more often do this—but they are some of the most striking.

While they don't occur often, we sometimes will find scenes that function primarily to present a theme or thesis which the writer feels is important to express. There's a scene like this that breaks the story development of *Seven Beauties*. As the central character is being taken to prison after being sentenced for murder, he stops at a railway station and briefly talks with a socialist who, as a political prisoner, has been given a sentence twice as long as his own. The latter's crime was opposing Mussolini and fascism.

Pauses are useful in a film because they give the audience an opportunity to evaluate their perception of previous actions and, in turn, what these actions might mean to the further development of the film. Some pause scenes merely give a breather from the narrative action. In *Butch Cassidy and the Sundance Kid,* there are three musical interludes which are identified as such in the script: while Butch and Etta ride the bicycle (to the music of "Raindrops Keep Falling on My Head"), when the three of them are in New York and during a series of South American robberies.

Comic relief scenes are useful to break the tense narrative development. They are traditional in drama. One of the best known occurs in *Macbeth*. Just after the murder of Duncan, there is an unexpected knocking at the gate and the comic porter appears. The comic relief he brings helps dispel the tension and gives us a chance to get ready for the next development.

Scenes of cars driving the streets or of characters walking from one place to another serve as transitions in space or time. Many of the scenes of spacecraft moving through space in *2001* are interesting because of their conception of what it will be like to travel in outer space. Many transition scenes have only a musical background and are shot MOS—"mit out sound."

Short transition scenes give us pauses in the action, prelude further action and help create the atmosphere of the film. John Ford cavalry films usually contain a number of scenes of the cavalry leaving the fort and riding through Monument Valley. These are often accompanied by the troop singing some spirited song. Perhaps a wife watches a husband leave who will not return.

Time transitions present a special challenge to the writer. If the transition covers a continuing action, it can be quickly developed in a condensed montage sequence, such as when a boxer trains, a bandit commits a number of robberies or a tennis player wins a series of matches. We've all seen such stereotyped time transitions as calendar pages flutter away, clock hands move quickly, candles burn down, or apples rot on a sill. The writer should try to find more interesting ways to achieve such transitions. In *A Man for All Seasons,* we see months pass as we watch the change of seasons in the view from a jail cell window. In *Slaughterhouse Five,* the passage of time is shown as leaves fall outside the house and the dog Spot is noticeably older than when we saw him previously.

Scene Continuity: Flow and Rhythm

Scenes exist within the overall formal structure of the film. In the best films, there is a flow and rhythm to the progression of scenes which contributes to the overall impact of the film. One way they do this is by increasing intensity as the film builds to a climax. Earlier parts of the film, as we get involved with characters and the beginning of the story, will have more low-key scenes. More active and exciting scenes occur as we approach the climax near the film's end. In *Straw Dogs,* there is a wild explosion of violence at the end. In *The Graduate,* Benjamin makes his desperate attempt to rescue Elaine from marriage. *The African Queen* offers us the characters' resignation to death, their attempt to sink *The Luisa,* the storm, their capture and near hanging, their marriage and finally, the destruction of the ship.

Other films, however, end on a more thoughtful note which allows us to reflect on what we have seen and what it means to us. *Midnight Cowboy* ends with Rizzo's quiet death on the bus and Buck's resigned response. *The Passenger* ends with the low-key death of Locke—almost an inevitability. The imaginary tennis game at the end of *Blow-Up* is a powerful, yet subdued ending. (We have already discussed this overall story pattern with its usual build to an intense climax. Our concern now is more with how scenes contribute to the flow and rhythm within the larger structure.)

A film needs some variety within its total structural unity. If a film is always at the same level of intensity—even a high level—it will soon lose our interest. We need novelty within the overall structure. Even a continuous build can get dull if it has no variation. A film needs a proper balance of the spacing of high and low points. Moments of crisis, confrontation and climax need to be interspersed with quieter moments, with pauses. We need those lulls when characters reveal themselves, when a mood is established, when the audience can catch its breath before being rushed to another dizzying height. Hitchcock has said that he plans his films to lull our attention at one part so that he can suddenly surprise and shock us in a following scene. He usually succeeds.

Consider how Hitchcock paces the action in his thriller *The Birds.* There is frenzied action when the birds attack, followed by lulls between the attacks when the characters take stock of the damage and discuss things among themselves, thus giving us a chance to pause before the next explosion. There are scenes of taut suspense even though the action is subdued, as when Melanie is on the park bench and the crows assemble in the playground behind her. In between such moments of high action and suspense, there are scenes of Melanie or the mother simply driving. There are interpersonal scenes between the characters—rather intimate, low-key dialogue scenes that reveal the characters, advance the love story and develop character interaction: Melanie with Annie, Melanie with Mitch, Mitch with his mother, Melanie with his mother, Melanie with the family. These provide the balance of highs and lows.

About two-thirds of the way through *The Birds* (but about in the middle of the exciting suspense/action segments), there is a long pause with the scene played in the cafe. In an interview, Hitchcock said that he felt at this point the audience needed a rest, a breather, from the tension. This pause even offers a few laughs from the drunk who keeps predicting the end of the world and from the dedicated amateur ornithologist. This pause is followed by a frantic attack from the birds.

A film needs a proper spacing—a balance—of high and low points. This provides the sawtooth build that was described when we discussed structure. A build to a climax is not a straight line rise, but a sawtooth

pattern that goes from one crisis to another with increasing intensity but with lower points between the highs. *The African Queen* doesn't jump immediately from one crisis to another. There is a crisis, then a slight lull, then another crisis. There will be time for some crises to build slowly. There will be breathing points when Rosie and Charlie enjoy each other's company and laugh at the hippos and other wildlife.

The Haunting is a frightening horror film. Its episodes of chilling suspense and terror are interspersed with pauses that are needed for our hearts to begin beating normally again. These are often dialogue scenes in which the characters talk about themselves and their situation. In films with a lot of action or suspense, dialogue scenes often serve to slow down or break the activity and tension.

This same pacing principle applies to comedy. Extremely funny scenes will be balanced—interspersed—with less comic moments. In farce, the less comic scenes are usually those that deal with a developing plot or subplot.

We've mentioned some of the most obvious contrasts that help pace a film: high and low activity, high and low intensity. Other scenic elements may be contrasted or alternated to develop scene rhythms. Dialogue scenes may be interspersed with action scenes; quiet scenes may balance those of frenzied activity. Following are contrasting elements that can be used to produce a film's rhythm:

Dialogue and non-dialogue scenes
Fast and slow tempo scenes

Light (or comic) and serious tone
Long and short time duration
Night and day
Interior and exterior
Static and dynamic activity
Intimate and expansive settings
Subjective and objective point of view
Noisy (as loud rock music) and quiet
Variations in flashbacks, flashforwards and real time
Presenting information, mood or emotion
Theme, character, mood and plot scenes

The way a writer interweaves these elements—contrasting, complementing, varying, balancing them—contributes to the overall rhythm of scenes. The writer will consider these as he plans his scenes. He will be aware that scenes do more in the overall context of the film than satisfy a story function. They also interact with each other to contribute to the formal structure—the flow and rhythm—of the film.

Internal Scene Structure

Scenes have their own internal structure. In addition to considering how the scene functions in the total film, the writer must decide how to structure each of his scenes. One helpful way to approach this is to regard each scene as having its own beginning, middle and end. This will give the writer a feeling for the pattern of the scene.

Another approach to the internal structure of a scene is to determine the objective of the scene. A scene that reveals character might have as its objective to show that a character is tender and considerate. Another scene might develop the story, its objective being to unmask the thief. Others might be: to escape the vigilantes, to recover the diamonds or to have the villains threaten the hero. However, the most effective way to approach a scene objective is perhaps by determining the objectives of the principal characters in the scene, since characters are usually the agents of action for the scene. Character objectives are best defined by the active verb form "to ———." In a scene from a typical romantic comedy, his objective might be "to seduce" while her objective might be "to resist seduction." Each character plays this objective within the scene. In most scenes at least one character (and probably other characters as well) has some objective; he is attempting to perform some action. Defining character objectives will help the writer structure the scene.

In a sequence in *The African Queen,* Charlie and Rosie attempt to sail *The Queen* past the German Fort. Their objective is clear; they want to get safely past the fort. The objective of the soldiers is to stop them. The scene demonstrates classic dramatic build. There is a problem—to get by the fort. The problem is complicated by the rifle fire coming from the fort. The difficulties increase when a bullet hits a steam line, causing them to lose headway. The soldiers gleefully continue firing as *The Queen* slowly drifts in the water. The tension increases as the German officer draws aim at Charlie, who is trying to repair the damage. The scene climaxes as the officer is about to shoot: the sun reflects in the eyepiece of his telescopic sight causing him to be temporarily blinded. When he looks again to shoot, *The Queen* rounds the bend out of sight of the fort. The primary characters' objective is achieved.

Many scenes follow this dramatic build pattern with a problem, its development and its climax. It has proven value within a narrative. Sometimes a scene will end as this one does—after its climax. At other times, the scene will conclude with a new problem or development that propels us into the continuing narrative.

The example from *The African Queen* occurred in a single scene. Here is an example of classic dramatic build in a sequence composed of a number of scenes. It is the sequence in *2001* that pits the astronauts Dave and Frank against the computer HAL. The sequence begins when HAL is suspected of malfunctioning when he reports the imminent failure of a part of the ship's antenna system that checks out okay. For the sake of the mission, the astronauts decide to disconnect HAL. They are not aware that HAL has read their lips and knows of their plans. (That we know it and they don't increases suspense. We wait to see what HAL will do to the unsuspecting astronauts.) The problem with HAL escalates into crisis as the computer causes Frank's death, cuts off life support from other astronauts who were traveling in suspended animation and locks Dave outside the spaceship. For the entire sequence, the objective of the astronauts has been to deal with the problem with HAL. Within that overall objective, separate scenes of the sequence have their objectives: to decide what to do with HAL, to replace the suspect unit. Now, with Dave trapped outside the ship, his objective in the scene is to get back inside. This scene climaxes when Dave blasts his way in. The entire sequence climaxes shortly thereafter as Dave realizes the sequence's objective and disconnects HAL in spite of the computer's pleas. Then, rather than simply fading out at this point, we are immediately thrust back into the problem of the main storyline when a prerecorded briefing message breaks in to inform Dave about the mysterious monolith and the signal it beamed at Jupiter.

Though the above sequence develops continuously through a series of scenes, a sequence need not be continuous. An early sequence in *The Bridge on the River Kwai* develops discontinuously in its opposition of Colonel Nicholson and Colonel Saito. Saito wants the captive British officers to work beside their men; Nicholson opposes this as contrary to the Geneva Convention. Saito's objective is to achieve this, Nicholson's to oppose it. Each man has the objective of besting the other. The climax of the sequence occurs when Nicholson is released from his torturous cell and the officers don't have to work. The scenes that make up this sequence are interspersed with other scenes that are involved with other things (such as the American captive).

A scene may develop by means of a number of patterns. Some scenes conclude with a climax, as we have seen. In some scenes, the climax may be implied rather than explicit. A woman is about to be attacked by a dangerous stranger and the scene concludes as he closes the door on the camera; we imagine the rest. Some scenes begin with a non-narrative element that sets the context for the scene. This might be a sound (a bird cry that sets the eerie mood for the scene), or a visual which is apart from the main focus of the scene (for example, a scene begins on a stained glass window of a church, then the camera moves away from the window and down to the characters outside the church). Beginning and ending scenes off the main focus permits accelerating other moments later in the film by not doing so. Antonioni will frequently begin or end scenes away from their main focus. Bergman does this in *The Serpent's Egg*. He begins a scene focusing on several entertainers on a stage and only later moves to the main focus of the scene. One scene simply shows a hotel doorman holding the door open for the central character to walk through, and although the doorman has no other function in the film, the camera holds an overly long time on his face before going on to the next scene. Ozu will frequently use the camera to present the spaces before and after the actions that happen there.

Comedy sometimes makes use of a "topper" at the end of a scene, that is, the scene will climax only to be followed immediately by a second climax or topper. (This will be discussed in the chapter on comedy.) Something similar occurs in dramatic material when another development crisis gives us a new problem to solve after the scene climax. In a scene in the western *The Good, The Bad and The Ugly*, some villains are sneaking up the stairs of a hotel to gun down the hero in his room. The hero lies on his bed slowly reassembling his gun after cleaning it. The sound of marching men in the street outside covers the sound of the villains' creeping footsteps. We intercut between hero and villains. Then the marching halts for a moment and the hero hears the sound of a single step. The villains pause outside the door. One slowly reaches for the doorknob. The hero hurries to insert bullets in the gun. Will he make it in time? The door is flung open—and the hero shoots them all! But then the topper—his primary antagonist appears at the window and gets the drop on him, capturing him at gunpoint. A new crisis!

Suspense

We've earlier discussed suspense as a narrative principle. Now we want to consider it as a technique in patterning scenes and sequences.

We have suspense when the audience is led to anticipate an exciting development or payoff. The expectant waiting is crucial; the apprehension of an event is often more exciting than the actual event. Suspense frequently follows a cue-delay-fulfillment pattern. The audience is cued that something is going to happen. Then it is delayed; we are kept hanging and our tension builds. Then comes the fulfillment—and hopefully it is just a bit different, a bit more surprising, than what was expected. In a scene in *The Conversation,* the central character is searching an immaculately clean apartment for evidence of a murder. He finds nothing. Looking in the bathroom, he approaches the closed shower curtain. He hesitates. We expect the worst. He flings the curtain aside to reveal . . . nothing. He looks further. Where is the evidence? Where is the body? Then comes the surprise payoff as he flushes the toilet and blood overflows from it.

If there is a grand master of film suspense, it is Alfred Hitchcock. He once defined suspense by saying that if a bomb goes off by surprise, we get a few seconds of excited response. But, if we make the audience aware that there is a bomb ticking away under the table, and then the people in the room talk about baseball for five minutes, or an important character starts to leave . . . but then returns because he forgot something. If he continues to proscrastinate and delay, if he keeps making to leave, but something always calls him back—telephone calls, a last minute memo to write—our tension is tremendous; we know about the bomb in the room about to go off, but he doesn't. This is suspense.

So one way to build suspense is to have the audience know something the character doesn't know. Then we wait for the character either to find out or to face the consequences of his ignorance. This packs a two-fold punch: suspense for us based on our privileged knowledge, surprise for the character when fulfillment comes. (And perhaps surprise for us as well if the payoff is somewhat different from what we expect.) Part of our pleasure is anticipating the character's reaction. In *The Birds,* we know of the threat from the birds before the characters do; we look forward to their realizing it.

Television crime shows often let us see the crime committed so that we know the identity of the criminal even though the detective doesn't. He has to find out. (Of course, it also works the other way, as when we don't know the criminal and find out only when the detective does in solving the case.) Sometimes we know something that some characters know but others do not. In the *Mary Tyler Moore* program analyzed earlier, some suspense is created by our learning before she does that she didn't get the job. We anticipate her finding out and look forward to observing her reaction.

In a classic suspense scene from *The Birds,* we watch Melanie seated on a bench outside the schoolhouse waiting for the children to finish singing their round. We watch crows assemble on the school playground behind her; she is unaware of them. Our suspense builds as we anticipate her discovery and the coming attack from the birds. The birds keep coming. Then she notices a solitary bird in the sky. She follows its flight path and makes the shocking discovery of the horde of crows behind her. We experience the suspense of anticipating her discovery and empathically share her surprise.

Suspense can be built by withholding a single important bit of information such as when, where, how or by whom an action will occur. Hitchcock has said that he would like to do a film about the sinking of *The Titanic*. The objection was raised that there would be no suspense since everyone knows how it comes out. Ah, said Hitchcock, but they don't know when!

The payoff should justify the suspenseful build to it. In a scene from the exciting horror film *The Haunting*, the heroine climbs a tall, shaky, circular metal staircase in a vaulted room in the mansion. Something seems to be drawing her to the top, although the platform and turret window there are empty. The staircase shakes and sways, threatening to collapse. Some men come in the room and urge her down; one even starts up after her. But she continues. She reaches the top. A shock cut shows us a trapdoor high in the wall suddenly drop open and we see a terrified face inside. This never fails to elicit screams from the audience.

The payoff from a suspense build is stronger if there is a bit of surprise to it as well—if it is somewhat different from what we expected. Imagine a comedy team such as Laurel and Hardy walking down a sidewalk; Hardy is lagging about a dozen yards behind, trying to straighten his tie. Laurel peels a banana and drops the peel on the sidewalk. We anticipate that Hardy will step on it and fall, and so he does. But as he falls, he grabs for a store awning and pulls it down. This knocks over a fruit-and-vegetable pushcart, spilling its fruit all over the intersection. Cars swerve and smash. One hits a fire hydrant, sending up a geyser. In a few seconds, the intersection is pandemonium. The payoff was much more than we expected.

In *The High Sign*, Buster Keaton did something unusual with a payoff. A man has dropped a banana peel on the sidewalk. Keaton walks around the corner. We expect him to slip, as we've seen in so many silent comedies. But Keaton passes the peel safely. Just before he swerves to leave the frame, he turns and mockingly wiggles his fingers at us. But then comes the topper as he proceeds to slip on a second banana peel!

We can see suspense develop throughout the scenes in a sequence from an *All in the Family* program in which Edith is threatened by a rapist. We suspensefully wonder whether or not Edith will escape the man, and how she will do so. The attacker enters and threatens Edith while she is alone in the house. (Archie is next door—at the Stivics—readying a surprise birthday party for Edith.) She tries to deter him but without success. He will not be talked out of his intent. With Edith's fate still hanging, we cut to next door. Archie has forgotten the punchbowl. He can't use the Stivic's bowl as they use theirs for a fishbowl. Archie is about to return home—the potential rescue—but he sees that the Stivic's fish is dead so he will wash out their punchbowl. Has Edith's chance for rescue faded? Then Archie and Mike drop and break the punchbowl, so Archie does come home. The armed attacker hides in the closet. Archie hurries in, grabs the punchbowl and leaves. He is oblivious to Edith's terror. The anticipated rescue has fizzled. Our interest has been held by the pattern: suspense, delay, twist, suspense. (Edith finally escapes by shoving a hot, charred cake from the oven at the attacker and pushing him out the kitchen door.)

Scene Mood

Each scene will have a particular tone and mood. These contribute to the overall tone of the film. Serious films often have comic relief scenes to provide a break in a tense mood. Intimate dialogue scenes often act as a change of pace in an otherwise tense narrative. The alternation of relaxed and tense moments or of other mood contrasts help develop the pacing of the film. (See the discussion of tone and mood in Chapter 3.)

Scene Point of View

Everything we discussed in Chapter 3 about point of view applies when we consider choosing the point of view for a particular scene. One decision for the writer is the extent to which a particular character's presence dominates the scene. Should the scene emphasize this character's presence and thereby let his point of view pervade the scene? Or should the character be more objectively observed, being just another character among many in the scene? The writer also indicates camera placement. Will the camera be subjective—as if the eyes of a character—or quasi-subjective, with the camera placed just off the line of sight, or completely objective, with no character identification? The writer also chooses how near or far to place the viewer in the scene. Should the camera be in the middle of the scene so that the viewer feels he is in the center of the scene action? Or should the camera be distanced back from the scene for a different perspective? Distance can also be achieved by other means, such as placing foreground material between the camera (viewer) and the scene or by using internal framing, such as shooting through a doorway.

Subjective shots can be striking. In Dryer's *Vampyr,* there is a subjective shot as the corpse would see the world from his position laid out in a coffin—and then he starts to move! In *Spellbound,* there is one shot in which the camera is in the subjective position of a man sighting over a revolver he holds on a woman. She talks him out of killing her in cold blood. We follow her over the sights of the revolver as she goes to the door and exits. The gun slowly turns around until it directly faces the camera—the man—and then is fired.

Some interesting effects result when an event is seen through the eyes of an external observer. We tend to interpret the activity as it is seen by the observer. In one scene in *Paper Moon,* we observe the con man pulling his Bible-selling scam through the eyes of the young girl he has started traveling with. She is learning that he is a con man. We identify with her as we watch the scene from her point of view. An exciting moment in *2001* occurs when Dave and Frank sit in the pod discussing how they must disconnect HAL and we cut to HAL's point of view as he reads their lips and we know that he knows their plans.

Point of view is one of the exciting considerations in planning a scene. A scene will frequently be made up of many points of view mixed together and shifting according to the design of the writer (and director). Imagine a scene in which a woman walks down a crowded city street. First there is a distant, objective establishing shot showing her and the street. Then, a subjective camera shows the shop windows as if through her eyes. Her perception colors what we see in the windows. We may also see her reflection in the window as a sort of mirror subjective-objective view. Then we see her in a medium shot or close-up as if we were beside her; this is a privileged shot. Voyeuristically, we can observe her without embarrassment. Someone calls to her and we observe her reaction. Then we see the one who calls in a shot that is nearly a subjective point of view shot (being her view), but is really a bit off to the side and thus quasi-subjective. Then, as she and the friend meet, we are back in the position of a more distant, more neutral, more objective long shot. This is how a disinterested observer might see them. Finally, there is an extreme long shot that shows them dwarfed among the buildings and engulfed in the madding crowd of shoppers.

Shifting a point of view can produce surprise and suspense. Imagine shots of a couple talking intimately, the scene building until they finally embrace and kiss. Cut to a shot of the kiss in a very long shot, as through some bushes. Then establish that this is the point of view of her jealous husband.

Once Upon a Time in the West opens on a trainman writing on a small blackboard. We concentrate on him in the opening shots and his presence establishes his point of view. He nervously watches three gunslingers who await the train. The point of view—the focus of the scene—shifts to the three characters. Titles appear superimposed over their waiting. We stay close on these three men. The train arrives as we shift to longer shots. The train leaves. We hear the sound of a harmonica. We then include the point of view of the new character who is playing the harmonica. He kills the three who were waiting to ambush him. We have watched the focus of the scene shift from a lesser character to the three ambushers to the central character. The sequence has built through three different points of view.

Scene Transitions

The bridges between scenes help stylize the film by contributing to the flow and impact of the scenes. These bridges usually involve some transition in time and space. A standard approach is to have a character say that he is going somewhere, then cut to the place and his presence. Many times we've seen one character tell another that he's to be in London tomorrow, and we cut to a stock shot of a plane, then Big Ben and then show the character in London. It works, but it isn't very imaginative. The standard filmic devices for transitions are the cut (direct, quick), the dissolve (a smooth transition, often used for a change in location) and the fade (a more definite transition, usually in both time and space, and representing a major punctuation between sequences). Special effects can use superimpositions or optical wipes for transitions. While a director chooses many of a film's transitions, there is no reason why a knowledgeable writer couldn't indicate the effect he desires. Interesting transitions can use visuals, dialogue, sound, music and narrative logic. Following are some especially challenging examples.

There is a striking visual transition in Lester's *The Three Musketeers*. We leave one scene on an insert extreme close-up of two diamond studs in the black-gloved hand of the Cardinal's cohort. Then we go to an extreme close-up of the Queen, in which we see her eyes in the exact position of the diamond studs. The visual replacement is extraordinary; at the same time, the link between her missing diamonds and her conflict is underscored.

Dialogue can provide continuity from one scene to the next by matching words or by continuing dialogue over two discontinuous scenes. In *Last Year at Marienbad,* the man and woman are looking at a baroque sconce or sculpture frieze. The man points out something on it to her. He: "Hadn't you ever noticed all this?" She: "I never had such a good guide." He: "There are lots of other things to see here if you want to." There is then an abrupt cut to the characters in a similar composition on the screen, but now they are dancing. The jump is in both time and place, yet the conversation continues as though there were no break. She: "I'd love to. Does this hotel contain so many secrets?" He: "An enormous number." And so on.

In a scene in *The Wilby Conspiracy,* a character is telling his fellow conspirators what equipment they will need to recover some diamonds from a deep sump hole. As he continues talking, the scene shifts to sometime later when they are assembling the materials. His voice continues describing what is needed as if from the first scene. When his description finishes, the scene of their activity continues with music behind it, until they are finally at the hole and involved in the recovery process.

In *Citizen Kane,* there is a scene in which the banker Thatcher wishes the young boy Kane a "Merry Christmas." Kane replies, "Merry Christmas." Then we cut to the next scene fifteen years later as Thatcher continues, "And a happy New Year." In the same film, there is a scene during Kane's gubernatorial campaign when Leland tells a street crowd: "Charles Foster Kane . . . entered upon this campaign . . ." and we cut to Kane in Madison Square Garden extolling ". . . with one purpose only . . ."

There is a word match transition in an episode from the television series *McCloud*. A criminal is telling his cohorts how they can rob a rich New York jewelry store "by the making of a movie." We then cut to officer McCloud exclaiming, "A movie?!" as he gets instructions from his chief about his new assignment handling crowd control for a movie being filmed in the city.

Sound can also serve as a transition device to help maintain the continuity of the transition. In *Citizen Kane,* Kane's applause for Susan's singing segues into supporters' applause for Kane at a political rally. There's a similar transition from a scene in Susan's seedy apartment where Kane is listening to her singing (before she becomes his mistress). The film then dissolves to a scene at a later time in which Kane, in the fancier apartment he has given her, listens to a richly dressed Susan conclude the song.

Another common transition is to bring in early the sound or dialogue from the next scene so that it is heard over the tail-end visual of the current scene. In *Taxi Driver*, there is a scene in which the pimp is doing a slow dance with the young whore, persuading her to stay with him. At the end of this scene, the sound of gunshots is heard, which leads us into the next scene, in which Travis is shooting at target practice. This also foreshadows Travis' later shooting of the pimp.

An interesting transition occurs in *The Passenger*. Locke is switching identities with the dead Robertson. He is playing a tape recording of an earlier conversation between him and Robertson. Robertson's voice on the tape asks a question of Locke. Locke in present time looks toward the window, and we see two figures standing there, their backs to us; they are Locke and Robertson at an earlier time. Locke answers in the time of the flashback and they continue to play the scene in flashback.

Transitions that depend on the logic of the narrative don't have to be as simple as "I'm flying to London"—cut to London street. In *Kelly's Heroes*, the story, which takes place during the Second World War, centers around the attempts of several American soldiers to loot enemy gold from behind the German lines and keep it for themselves. After much scheming and conniving, they are facing one of their last hurdles—a powerful German tank guards the village bank where the gold is hidden. The Americans have fought their way into enemy territory, taken the town and destroyed two enemy tanks; this one now, however, blocks them. Assuming that the German sergeant commanding the tank doesn't know about the $16 million in gold, three of the soldiers approach him to try to make a deal. The sergeant gets out of the tank and hears them. They make him the offer—all he has to do for an equal share of the gold is to leave. The sergeant turns his head and looks toward the locked outside door of the bank. Cut to his point of view of the door as the door suddenly explodes. His tank has shot open the door of the bank. The transition is a momentary jar, since the cut makes a jump in time that we don't expect, but it is logical within the cause-effect pattern of the action.

There are a number of unusual scene transitions in *Slaughterhouse Five*, a film that puts them to good use as it jumps back and forth in space and time. Billy Pilgrim's wife calling him—"Billy, Billy"—segues into a voice calling him when he was in the army—"Billy." As a child, Billy is thrown into a swimming pool to either sink or swim; he sinks. From his envelopment in the depths of the water we go to his being under anesthetic in a hospital where he is receiving shock treatments. Billy nominates an army friend for POW leader and the subsequent applause from the men leads into the applause that Billy receives as he accepts the presidency of his town's Lion's Club later in his life.

Billy walking upstairs with his dog in his arms is intercut with his walking up the bomb shelter stairs in wartime Dresden. On the planet Tralfamadore, Billy asks its unseen inhabitants: "What will I do?" and we cut back to Dresden where, as if in reply, a German officer tells him and his fellow POWs to pick up the dead bodies from the air raid.

Interesting transitions between scenes can add to the tone, rhythm and style of the film. A writer will think of the sort of effect he wants in a transition and then come up with it. (But he will avoid getting so carried away with unusual transitions that they seem gimmicky.)

Writing the Scene Outline

By now the writer has his narrative story written out satisfactorily. If he is writing a feature film, he may have written as many as thirty pages of narrative story outline. He has taken a basic story and expanded it through all its complexity until he has accurately laid out the story. (For a shorter television program, his narrative would range from three to twenty pages, depending on how long and how involved the story. Many television writers quickly proceed to a scene outline to sketch out their narrative story, since it reflects the act structure which commercial breaks impose on television.) Since narrative film is constructed around sequences and acts, the next step is to prepare a scene outline that lists the scenes in chronological order and gives special attention to scene beginnings and endings, scene development and transitions. It is still written as narrative, excluding all but the most flavoring snatches of dialogue and camera directions. (We shall use the expression "scene outline"; other terms for this process are: step sheet, step outline, continuity outline, master scene outline, scene breakdown and treatment.)

In doing a scene outline, the writer describes the action and substance of each scene in a clear, brief manner. He gives special attention to the beginning and end of each scene. Since the outline will be used to check the progression of the scenes—the balance of high and low moments, of peaks and valleys, of the rhythm of the scenes—many writers like to do their initial scene outline on index cards (3 x 5, 4 x 6 or 5 x 7). These cards can be tacked to corkboard or spread out on the floor so that they can be easily studied, shuffled around, switched or have changes inserted.

The following example shows what the first page of a scene outline for the *Battlestar Galactica* episode might look like. Another popular alternate form of scene outline includes a descriptive slug line for each scene that gives useful production information, such as interior or exterior, location, day or night. If the writer chooses to use this form, the first few scenes of the example might appear as:

1. INT. REJUVENATION CENTER (GALACTICA) - DAY

    Athena and Boxey are playing compartment billyarks...

2. INT. BRIDGE (GALACTICA) - DAY

    Tigh and Adama watch blips on the scanner. Tigh believes...

BATTLESTAR GALACTICA

"Fire in Space"

ACT ONE

1. In the rejuvenation center of the Galactica, Athena and Boxey are playing compartment billyarks, a billiards-like game using multi-patterned balls and bumpers that light up in colors and give off harmonic sounds when hit. Other crew members play other futuristic games in the background. Boxey is winning. Muffy sits watching. Boomer enters and greets them. He has a surprise for Boxey, but the boy guesses that it's a mushie from the way that Muffy is sniffing Boomer's pocket. Boxey tells them how he's trained Muffy to sniff out mushies. Suddenly a blaring klaxon and flashing red lights signal a red alert.

2. Inside the bridge of The Galactica, Tigh and Adama watch blips on the scanner. Tigh believes it's a Cylon combat probe. Adama orders Blue Squadron launched to intercept.

3. Various shots of vipers being launched and flying in formation.

4. The bridge again. Two large blips appear on the scanner--Cylon base ships! It's a major attack! Adama orders all squadrons launched and The Galactica prepared for attack. Tigh hits the button which secures all compartments.

5. Various angles show bulkhead doors sliding shut. The siren sounds and flashing lights continue.

The writer chooses the form he feels most comfortable with unless he is going to submit the scene outline, in which case he conforms with the preferred form of the producing company.

Once the scene outline is drafted, here is how a writer will use it. He will notice his most important scenes—if using index cards, he has indicated these by some mark placed on the card—and he will check how they are spaced over the length of the film. These are the beats, the highlights of the story. He will ask if the progression of scenes moves the story forward at an effective pace. Is the overall dramatic suspense of the story maintained? Are there enough surprise elements—the unexpected twists and turns which hold interest—to keep the audience involved? Do story crises occur at reasonably spaced intervals over the film rather than being bunched together? (Some bunching may occur near the climax as is typical of dramatic structure.) Are relief-pause scenes used when needed? With the scenes laid out before him, the writer will get a sense of the rhythm and flow of the scenes and how they interrelate with the other scenes.

The writer will also know the function of each scene, its purpose in the script. And he will note other things it is doing. He will notice when the different characters appear. Are the characters credibly and consistently presented through what they say and do? Do characters appear appropriately throughout the script, or does one or another get "lost" for too long a time? The writer will know the characters' objectives from the scene descriptions.

The writer will check the scene outline for weak spots which he can correct. He might find that action high points are bunched too closely together and he might correct this by inserting a break, such as a dialogue scene in which we get to know more about the characters, a mood scene or some delay in a suspense build. On the other hand, if the script seems to drag, with not enough exciting highs, he may want to insert some additional crises, build suspense more carefully to keep us involved or add some surprising twists. If the script seems too active or too melodramatic, he may want to add more scenes that reveal character or the relationships between characters. This will give us time to get to know the characters instead of simply giving us scene after scene that accentuates the high points of the plot.

The writer will be conscious that each scene has an internal structure appropriate to its development; he will give careful attention to the internal structure of his scenes. If a scene isn't right, is he clear about its beginning, middle and end? If the scene builds, is the high point—the payoff—appropriate? Are the actions and characters in the scene credible? Will the audience believe that the characters would act the way they do given the circumstances of the scene? Is the tone appropriate to the scene? Is the scene basically interesting? Is the scene really necessary to the story?

The film writer has a rich variety of materials from which to concoct his magic. There are many elements of expression in a scene—organization, characters, relationships, setting, tone, point of view, camera angle, props, clothing, dialogue, sound effects, music and so on. He won't overlook the use of any of these in constructing his scene.

The writer will think visually while writing the scene outline, as he did with the narrative versions and as he will with the screenplay. Images rather than words are the screenwriter's basic unit. While he works, he will visualize the location and action of the scene.

The Screenplay

Once the scene outline is set, the writer will begin the first draft screenplay. This will be primarily written in master scenes, with only a general indication of camera shots. A writer's attempts to "direct on paper" are usually ignored, not only because the director prefers to choose his own shots, but because excess camera directions make the screenplay harder to read. (Television directors are more likely to follow a writer's shots than film directors.) However, a writer should present his descriptions of scenes in such a way that what he has visualized is readily apparent even though he hasn't spelled it out in shot description shorthand. The Appendix contains both sample script pages, showing proper script format and typewriter spacing, and a glossary of film terms, shot abbreviations and descriptions.

Example Scene Breakdowns

The following two examples will be useful for a sense of the progression of scenes in each film. They are presented in abbreviated form, not like a scene outline. Doing your own scene breakdowns from films or film scripts is a useful way to learn something about the pattern of scenes in a film.

Scene Breakdown: Antonioni's Blow-Up

1. Morning, exterior. Student mimists in a jeep soliciting contributions. Thomas comes out of a down-and-outers hostel, gets into Rolls Royce. (Introduces Thomas and the mimists. The contrast between his appearance and the car intrigues us about him.)
2. Driving. (A transition as he moves to another aspect of his lifestyle.)
3. Photography studio. Thomas photographs an erotic model, then other models.

   (This fast-moving, exciting sequence characterizes Thomas, shows him at work.)
4. Thomas visits the painter and his wife (who live by the studio.)

   (A more intimate scene. Introduces an aspect of the theme when the painter talks about finding a clue in his painting.)

5. The studio. Two young girls want their pictures taken but he's too busy. He leaves his models stranded in their poses.

   (A fast-paced scene. Characterizes Thomas. Introduces the young girls.)
6. Driving in car. (A transition break.)
7. Antique shop. Thomas checks out the antique shop, talks with an unfriendly old man working there.

   (A short, quieter, interior scene.)
8. The park. Thomas takes pictures. The woman tries to get the pictures from him.

   (Exterior. Introduces conflict and the plotline gets underway.)
9. Antique shop. Thomas talks with the girl owner, buys propeller.

   (Interior. Short scene shows Thomas's interpersonal ease. A bit of a break from the previous tension.)
10. Driving in car. (Another transition break. Note how so many driving scenes seem to punctuate—set apart—aspects of Thomas's life.)
11. Interior, restaurant. Thomas lunches with a writer friend who is writing the commentary for his book of photographs. Then Thomas discovers that a stranger who had been watching them is trying to break into his car.

    (The first part of this scene shows us more about Thomas. We understand the reason he was photographing in the hostel. Then the scene ends on a suspense point, developing the storyline.)
12. Driving. He is followed by another car.

    (Another driving break, but also a further story development as he is being followed.)
13. The studio, Thomas's private quarters. The woman comes trying to get the pictures, even offering sex for them. The propeller is delivered. Thomas gives her a blank roll of film.

    (A strongly interpersonal scene which reveals character through the way Thomas plays around with her, and advances the storyline and our interest in what is happening.)
14. Thomas develops the film and from enlargements discovers the gun. He believes he's prevented a murder. He calls his friend Ron to tell him.

    (A very personal scene in which we are alone with Thomas. A quiet scene, yet one which builds strong suspense. Advances the storyline.)
15. The two young girls return, interrupting his phone conversation. They have sex.

    (A very active sequence in contrast to the previous one. An interruption in the plot.)
16. Alone, Thomas again studies the photographs. He does another enlargement and discovers the corpse.

(Another scene alone with Thomas. Quiet, but engrossing, suspenseful. The new crisis furthers the storyline.)

17. Night, driving. (A brief scene as Thomas drives to the park.)
18. Night, Thomas in the deserted park. He finds the corpse.

    (Exterior, quiet, Thomas again alone. This is still another crisis development in the plot.)
19. The house of the painter and his wife. Thomas goes to talk with them, sees them making love. Patricia, the wife, looks up at him imploringly.

    (An unusual scene. A sort of pause, yet with a strong interpersonal touch. A strong contact between Thomas and Patricia.)
20. His quarters in the studio. Thomas discovers that all the photographs are stolen except for one blow-up.

    (A new complication in the storyline.)
21. Patricia comes to visit. They talk abstractly of the possibility of her leaving the painter. He tells her of the murder. She can't get involved in it. She leaves. Thomas tries to call Ron.

    (A dialogue scene and a sort of brief, interpersonal interlude. It touches on the theme when Patricia says the blow-up enlargement looks like one of Bill's paintings, tying back to Bill's earlier remark.)
22. Driving in central London. (Another driving transition break. Thomas leaves the studio, goes to London.)
23. In London, Thomas sees the woman by the shop window. He rushes after her but loses her. He ends up in a club in which a rock group is playing. A guitar gives trouble, so one of the group smashes it. The audience rushes for the pieces. Thomas grabs a large chunk and runs off, pursued by others. Outside on the street, he tosses it away.

    (A new plot crisis when Thomas sees the girl, but then we move away from this. An active scene contrasting with previous ones. Takes us away from the storyline.)
24. Interior, a party. Thomas meets the erotic model whom he photographed earlier, then finds Ron to tell him about the murder. But Ron is too stoned to understand. Thomas stays at the party and gets high.

    (A different sort of activity characterizes this scene. Very different atmosphere. Reflects the dead end Thomas has reached.)
25. Morning, the park. Thomas has returned, but the corpse is gone. At the tennis courts, the student mimists mime a tennis match. Thomas is drawn into their illusion as he recovers an imaginary ball. Camera pulls up and out.

    (A quiet, personal, symbolic ending scene which underscores the theme of illusion. The morning and the mimists complete the circular pattern of the film.)

Scene Breakdown: Kubrick's A Clockwork Orange

1. Alex and his droogs act out violence. They beat a tramp, fight with other droogs, drive the highway aggressively, forcing others off the road, and beat and rape in "The Home" house.

   (Establishes the violent character of Alex and the droogs. Establishes the main storyline—the problem of excess violence. Very active scenes. Also a plant as Alex sings "Singing in the Rain" while committing violence in The Home.)

2. At the Milk Bar. Alex shows his extreme appreciation of Beethoven's *Ninth Symphony*. Alex clashes with and strikes Dim (one of his droogs).

   (Some contrast with the previous violence scenes. Establishes the conflict storyline of Alex vs. droogs.)

3. Alex alone at home, plays Beethoven's *Ninth,* fantasies violence.

   (Reveals Alex alone. Symbolically relates Beethoven's *Ninth* and violence. Emphasizes the main line by showing Alex reveling in violent images.)

4. Morning. His parents try to awaken Alex for school, but he sleeps in. They express mild concern about him.

   (Characterize parents, establish them for later role in the film.)

5. Interior, the apartment. Mr. Deltoid, Alex's sort of probation officer, warns him to change his ways or else.

   (Complicates main storyline with Alex facing prison.)

6. Alex visits mod record store, picks up two girls, comes back to apartment and has sex with them (in fast motion).

   (A sort of interlude, although also emphasizes the role of sex in Alex's life.)

7. The droogs meet Alex and challenge his authority. He violently reasserts his control, cutting Dim with a knife in the process. They plan new violence.

   (Furthers the main storyline—Alex is heading for trouble. Also furthers the secondary line of Alex vs. Dim and the droogs.)

8. The "Health Farm." Alex breaks in and assults the woman living there. He kills her when he hits her with a piece of abstract sculpture. As he leaves, the droogs knock him out, leaving him for the police.

   (An active, violent scene. Develops both storylines of Alex's violence and his clash with the droogs.)

9. Police headquarters. Alex is roughly interrogated by the police and Mr. Deltoid.

   (A more confined scene. Concludes Mr. Deltoid's involvement in the film.)

10. Prison. Alex checks in. He assists the prison chaplin and fantasies religious sex and violence. He inveigles the chance to get out of prison by trying a new rehabilitation treatment.

    (A series of scenes move Alex into prison, show him polite and courteous although still with his violent and sexual fantasies, and get him into the new treatment.)

11. Medical facility. Alex is given aversive conditioning, and in the process is accidentally conditioned against Beethoven's *Ninth*.

    (Close-ups of Alex and film clips of sex and violence are prominent.)

12. In a public demonstration, Alex is shown to be conditioned to become ill when tempted to violence or sex. He is "cured."

13. His parents' apartment. Alex is rejected by his parents and becomes sick when he attempts violence.

14. Alex runs into the tramps, including the one he beat earlier. They beat him, and he can't fight back since he becomes ill if he tries. He is rescued by two policemen, who turn out to be his former droogs—Alex and Georgie. They take him into the countryside and beat him badly.

    (This concludes the subline of Alex vs. Dim and the droogs. It leaves Alex in bad condition.)

15. Alex is taken in and helped by the man in "The Home," who is now crippled from the earlier beating he received from Alex and the droogs. The man sees the chance to use Alex to discredit the government political party, which advocated the conditioning treatment. Alex's singing in the bathtub—"Singing in the Rain"—clues the man to Alex's identity. Alex is tormented by being locked in a second-story room and forced to listen to Beethoven's *Ninth*. He jumps from the window.

    (Suspense comes when we see that the man recognizes Alex from the singing. We watch to see what revenge the man will take on the unsuspecting Alex.)

16. Hospital. A bedridden Alex is deconditioned, since the government minister accused of inhuman brainwashing wants Alex back to his "normal" self again. His parents offer to take him back. Alex is able to hear the *Ninth* without reacting and is back with his fantasies of sex and violence.

    (The ending ironically concludes the main line, and makes a statement about governmental hypocrisy.)

7

Theme

> These Stories are magical Teachers in this way. They are Flowers of Truth whose petals can be unfolded by the Seeker without end.[1]
>
> —H. Storm

A THEME IS AN IDEA presented in the film; it is an idea about life and its meaning, about the human condition. It is the underlying truth signified by the film—universal, enduring, significant, expressive and eloquent. A theme is the writer's thesis or "message." It springs from the writer's view of the way the world is and his sense of morality of the way the world should be.

Themes deal with such universals as love, courage, greed, freedom, death, the dehumanization of modern society, the corrupting power of ambition and the nature of our responsibilities to ourselves and to others. A concise paraphrase of a film's theme will often yield statements such as: love conquers all, my country right or wrong, all men are brothers, crime does not pay, war is hell. Some classic themes have been expressed in the form of something leading to something else: jealousy leads to its own destruction (*Othello*), ruthless ambition leads to its own destruction (*Macbeth*), excess pride leads to a fall. These capsulizations are perhaps useful in some cases; however, they risk becoming simplifications. An effective presentation of a theme is inextricably bound to the unique way in which it's expressed in the total film. Rather than simply saying "war is hell," a film shows us that war is a particular form of hell. The effect of war on human lives has been shown powerfully in such films as *All Quiet on the Western Front, The Harp of Burma* and *La Grande Illusion*.

Themes are probably inevitable, since it would be difficult to imagine a film from which one couldn't get some meaning. However, a film doesn't need a strong, consciously chosen theme; it can be quite entertaining without one. But it is doubtful that a film will ever be considered "great" without the universal sense of significance of a powerful theme.

Themes are best handled implicitely as part of the total fabric of the film. It is dangerous for a writer to try to impose a theme on his work. If he is too obvious with the theme and allows it to dominate the story, the film can appear stiff, preachy and pretentious. It becomes propaganda. An old Hollywood bromide says, "If you want to send a message, use Western Union." As restricted as this is, it reflects a kernel of truth: it is risky to write from a theme. A theme is best expressed by the story rather than the other way around. A theme may be a good point of departure for a story idea, but it shouldn't dominate to the extent that the result is heavily moralistic or propagandistic.

Films such as *Billy Jack* and *The Trial of Billy Jack,* which are aimed largely at a younger audience, contain anti-war messages, push experimental education and present aspects of Eastern and American Indian philosophies. Unfortunately they are too obvious and direct in that effort. Television has been in a period of the relevant series which tries to be meaningful by dealing with strong themes. This is a far cry from its earlier days when Jack Parr walked off NBC because he wasn't permitted to say WC (for water closet) or when a large car manufacturer tried to eliminate a segment in a variety show in which a white woman entertainer (Petula Clark) placed her hand on the arm of a black entertainer (Harry Belafonte). The petty censorship is still around; however, now the base level has shifted. *All in the Family* has given us shows that featured Edith almost raped; Edith suspecting she has breast cancer and facing a possible mastectomy; Archie and Mike quarreling about Nixon, Vietnam, Ford—almost any issue. Archie and Edith almost get involved in a swinging sex orgy; Mike has an impotency problem and a vasectomy; Archie meets a transvestite, a homosexual, a draft deserter. In addition to these themes, situation comedies have dealt with all sorts of issues, including abortion, mental illness and death. When done well, they are honest, tasteful and subtle. Too often, however, the message seems imposed on the program. The theme is too strong for the program to sustain and seems pretentious. Dramatic programs have similarly tried to be "relevant." Their success ranges from the excellent work done on such programs as *Lou Grant* and in television movies such as *Dummy,* which dramatizes problems of the deaf and deaf mutes, and *Like Normal People,* which presents the problems of a marginally retarded couple seeking love and marriage. On the other end of the spectrum are the life and death themes of "comic book" adventure programs, wherein superheroes save the world from destruction.

Themes can be presented through many aspects of the film: storyline and problem, character, setting, story digressions. The two television films mentioned present their themes as part of the story. It's the idea of a black sheriff who has to prove himself in dealing with the Black-White issue in a small southern town. The theme may appear as a sort of secondary storyline, as it did in one television program that argued for the value of holistic medicine by presenting one doctor's opposition to another doctor's holistic approach. This was secondary to the main storyline but formed part of an interpersonal line that was related to the plot. Characters frequently embody a theme. Frank Capra's "Capracorn" combined a blend of idealism, sentiment, and social comment in such films as *It's A Wonderful Life, Meet John Doe* and *Mr. Smith Goes to Washington*. These films each featured a strong, typal character who represented the value and worth of the individual and showed that the common man—the little man—can battle and defeat the big, powerful capitalists. *Red Desert* makes us aware of pollution by showing it in the environment rather than pretentiously inveighing against it. One of the least effective ways of presenting a theme is to have it spoken in the script. An effective theme is not a lecture on life but an interpretation of it.

Theme is sort of an elusive concept. We can speak of the dominant theme of a film and be on reasonably safe ground. But when a theme is considered as the meaning found in a film, we have opened a Pandora's Box, since meaning is a complex and ubiquitous topic. It is embodied in all aspects of a film, including the ideology of its production. Many radical filmmakers and critics question whether traditional cinema can reflect the interests of feminist, political and third-world filmmakers. They are asking if traditional narrative techniques can sustain these new cinemas or if the form of their film has to be equally radical and innovative. Much of their concern relates to the covert meanings which infiltrate the traditional narrative film. Many of our films exalt the macho hero and his violence. They present a man's world in which little real power is given to women. Woman is often the sex object for males. Guns, cars, trucks and ships are phallic power symbols. The hero is glorified and rewarded, while the average person is expendable (just another member of the posse who didn't survive); if you aren't a hero, you don't seem to count for much.

Many film messages are quite subtle even as they are pervasive. McLuhan claimed that the most important message of media is the medium itself and the way in which it is changing our society and reality. One questionable message from television is that human problems aren't as complex and difficult as most of us experience them; after all, can't most everything be cleared up in the half-hour or hour time period? *Patton* seems to tell us that it takes bullies to win battles, and in a similar vein, the original *Baa Baa Blacksheep* television series was telling us that the best pilots are hard-drinking womanizers. *Marcus Welby, MD* and similar programs imply that there are some select, all-wise professionals who will help us with our problems if we just give them our trust and confidence. The hidden meaning may well be supporting authoritarianism and acquiescence. These are difficult messages to deal with since they are intrinsic to our culture. The writer should at least try to be aware that his work will contain such messages—even if they aren't conscious on his part. He should try to raise his consciousness to become aware of them and to listen to voices of the likes of the feminists, who point out just how destructive these cultural stereotypes are.

Our concern is with the more overt meaning which the writer adds to his film. It's convenient to talk of four types of thematic elements. The *theme* is a meaning that is embodied in the story or characters of the film. A *thesis* is a more direct statement about a salient and significant issue, such as pollution or ecology. It is often presented directly. A thesis is often the starting point of a documentary. *Symbols* or *metaphors* convey meaning through their associations. *Motifs* are meanings that run through a film or through many of a filmmaker's films.

Theme

Themes can range from the personal and interpersonal to the social and cultural and to the philosophical. Following are some examples of themes.

The old daytime radio serials often led off with the theme stated as a question: "Can a woman over thirty-five still find romance?" (*Helen Trent*) "Can this girl from a mining town in the West find happiness as the wife of a wealthy and titled Englishman?" (*Our Gal Sunday*)

Rocky tells us of the victory of the underdog, that achievement can come from hard work and drive even if against difficult odds. The theme of the television series *The Prisoner* has been called the unrelenting struggle of the man of conscience to be free. The question of what it's like to be old is handled with respect, care and entertaining filmmaking in *Harry and Tonto*.

The typical theme of Howard Hawks' films is that man must test himself against his environment and prove himself to his peers. *Who's Afraid of Virginia Woolf* explores the theme of truth and illusion in human relationships and shows how interpersonal game-playing may produce a difficult moment when the games end.

Swept Away and *The Admirable Crichton* make the point that given the right circumstances, social status is an artificiality that yields to survival needs. The films also point out that love is fickle and depends on social circumstances. *One Flew Over the Cuckoo's Nest* shows us that absolute authority can squash individualism and force conformity. *The China Syndrome* raises the issue of the danger of nuclear power.

A *Twilight Zone* episode some years ago was built around an ironic theme. It made the point that beauty was in the eye of the beholder. We saw an attractive girl horrified at her appearance, which was the result of some mutation. We couldn't understand her concern since she was so beautiful. We never really saw the faces of her doctors and nurses until the end, when we saw that they were deformed—what we might call ugly. Yet, to this alien culture, they were beautiful, while what we consider beautiful was a deformed mutation to them.

Westerns are frequently a restatement of the mythical good vs. evil theme.

Star Wars is a fairy tale-level epic with a message of hope and of good triumphing over evil. It shows that simple, ordinary people can triumph over seemingly impossible odds. *Close Encounters of the Third Kind* says that the universe is friendly and that we can share much, including the appreciation of beauty, with alien life-forms. *2001* holds out the fantasy that the leap from ape to man was no less dramatic than the coming leap from man to starchild.

The theme of many vampire and frankenstein stories (*The Golem, Nosferatu*), like the Faust legend, warns that we shouldn't seek knowledge beyond that given to human beings.

Slaughterhouse Five expresses many messages: about the horror of war and the inhumanity of the allies' bombing of Dresden, the value of living each moment to the fullest—of being in the eternal *now*—and that nice guys can finish first.

Thesis or Issue

An issue is often a challenging starting point for a script. A writer might be eager to expose corruption or to promote energy conservation and ecology. However, he should moderate his zeal to avoid being too obvious and preachy. Young writers sometimes overlook the fact that there are more sides to a problem than the one they want to espouse. Still, there is no reason that a thesis or issue shouldn't be expressed in a film if it can be done smoothly. *Seven Beauties* makes a point about the oppression of fascism in the scene with the imprisoned socialist. In *The Grapes of Wrath,* Casey the preacher gives a direct message about social change, but it is an integral part of the theme of the film. A subtle point about our bureaucratic society is made in *Harry and Tonto,* when Harry meets an Indian in jail who cures his bursitis by prayers and ceremonies. The Indian is in jail for practicing medicine without a license.

Both *The China Syndrome* and *Alien* make a point about the ruthlessness and heartlessness of corporations. The nuclear power company chairman takes action which leads to the death of the engineer, while in *Alien* the corporation makes the crew expendable in order to bring the alien creature back.

The writer who wants to express a message directly in his film should try to do so subtly and to make it natural to the context of the drama. He doesn't want us to read it as a separate message that is laid over the film and hits us on the head.

Symbol, Metaphor, Archetype

Symbols create a meaning beyond the literal image—as a lonely, whining dog signifying its owner's death. Symbols can enrich the fabric of meaning of the film; however, they run the risk of calling undue attention to themselves. An extraordinary film, Jodorowsky's *El Topo* almost becomes swamped under its massive symbolism. At times symbols are too obvious and simplistic, as with the white-hatted hero and black-hatted, mustached villain in B-westerns. The western is itself an archetype of man conquering evil and the wilderness. A character frequently conveys a symbolic message, as does the peripatetic lover Don Juan. The comedian Harold Lloyd has been called the image of the 1920s' American virtues of aggression, innocence and moral earnestness.

Following are some examples from film and television. They give some idea of the range of use of symbols, metaphors and archetypes.

The vampire is a symbol of evil vanquished by the forces of goodness and religion. *Planet of the Apes* is an extended metaphor of the rigid, dogmatic aspects of civilization. The huge background flag that dwarfs the general at the beginning of *Patton* suggests his hyperpatriotic views. The bleak, barren, rocky island in the opening of *L'Avventura* suggests the alienation and isolation of the characters. In *The Grapes of Wrath,* the Joads leave their dust-bowl farm for California in a rickety old truck piled high with belongings and precariously tottering down the road. It is representative of the uncertain condition in which the family finds itself. Clothing, too, can be a symbol: Fonzie's jacket in *Happy Days;* Brando's jackets in *On the Waterfront* and *The Wild One;* the hippie costumes in *Easy Rider*.

Animals have been used symbolically in many films. A horse appears mysteriously in so many Fellini films; it is a personal idiosyncrasy of the director. Zapata's horse in *Viva Zapata!* stands for the leadership of the man. The dog in *Shane* leaves the room when the villain (Jack Palance) enters. The stray dog at the end of *Alfie* symbolizes the condition of the hero. There seems to be an extended dog metaphor in *Yojimbo,* reflecting the dog-eat-dog world presented in the film. Dogs bark intermittently on the sound track. In one scene a dog runs by, holding a human hand in its mouth. There are frequent references to dogs in the dialogue: "The smell of blood brings the hungry dogs." "Not even a dog fight" describes a peaceful moment; "lucky dog" characterizes an escaped enemy.

Music becomes symbolic in *A Clockwork Orange* when the central character is aversively conditioned to Beethoven's *Ninth Symphony*. It is his singing of "Singing in the Rain" that identifies him as the earlier attacker in The Home. The tuba in *Mr. Deeds Goes to Town* is linked to goodness, integrity and honest rural values. The cryptic neon sign in *Blow-Up* seems to suggest the elusive truth that evades Thomas. In *The Graduate,* water is used as a metaphor of isolation and drowning. Benjamin sinks to the bottom of the swimming pool in his diving gear, and he floats on the pool reflecting on his affair.

Other representative symbols include the "No Trespassing" sign at the beginning of *Citizen Kane;* the guard's mirrored sunglasses in *Cool Hand Luke;* the stuffed birds in *Psycho;* the baby carriage in the Odessa Steps sequence of *The Battleship Potemkin;* the bridge in *The Bridge on the River Kwai;* the act of touching as a symbolic gesture in *Cries and Whispers;* Archie Bunker's chair; the assembly line machine in *Modern Times;* the pietà likeness in *Cries and Whispers;* the devilfish at the end of *La Dolce Vita;* the "innocent girl" in the latter film and in *8½*; and Chinatown as a symbol of all that is corrupt, unfathomable and frustrating in the film *Chinatown:* "Forget it, Jake, it's Chinatown."

Motifs

One sense of motif is as a recurring element internal to a film, such as the use of clocks to show time running out for the sheriff in *High Noon*. Motif is also used to define a thematic element that recurs throughout a filmmaker's work. Such motifs have been the study of structuralist and auteur critical analyses.

Although there is some controversy about their appropriateness, here are some of the motifs that have been identified in the films of director John Ford:[2] wilderness vs. the garden, the wandering nomad, strangers in another land (such as displaced Indians), mature and effective old people vs. less effective young people, characters imprisoned by society, East vs. West, European vs. Indian, ploughshare vs. saber, book vs. gun, married vs. unmarried, settler vs. nomad, civilized vs. savage, and themes of cultural dislocation: sexual dislocation (rape, miscegenation, fear of the purity of one's own culture), technology—the forces of change that can't be stopped (railroad, printing press, telegraph), and language—as writing replaces the more direct spoken word.

The analysis of motifs is more the domain of the film scholar (with his penchant for over-analysis) than for the practical writer. What a study of motifs can tell us is that all of us have certain personal themes which we may not be able to consciously articulate—we may not even be aware of them—but they will find their way into our work as we write. They will continue to enrich what we do if we do it authentically.

A meaningful and significant theme can add an important dimension to what we write. But not if it appears as an imposed message—preachy and pretentious. The theme is most effective if it is embodied in the drama or comedy of our script.

REFERENCES

1. Hyemeyohsts Storm, *Seven Arrows* (New York: Harper & Row, 1972), p. 10.
2. See Peter Wollen, *Signs and Meanings in the Cinema,* 2d ed. (Bloomington, Indiana: Indiana University Press, 1972) and William Luhr and Peter Lehman, *Authorship and Narrative in the Cinema* (New York: Capricorn/Putnam's Sons, 1977).

Also:

Newcomb, Horace, ed. *Television: The Critical View,* 2d ed. New York: Oxford University Press, 1979.

8

Setting

> Spring too, very soon!
> They are setting the scene for it—
> plum tree and moon.[1]
>
> —Basho

THE ENVIRONMENT created by the film, the context in which the story unfolds, is a dynamic factor which contributes to the meaning of the film. The camera photographs places—an environment—as well as characters. The setting of a film is more than just a stage for the actors, it is an interactive element of the narrative. In this chapter we will consider setting (or location) as well as props, lighting and make-up. The latter contribute to the image in the frame and are part of the "setting." A useful term for this is mise-en-scène, the total contribution of all these factors to the space within the frame. (The term mise-en-scène also includes the placement of actors and their movements and behavior and camera perspective.)

The setting can activate the story by providing a stimulus for character action and interaction. It can help define the style of the film. It can be a scenic metaphor of meaning in the film. Mood, tone and atmosphere are all created to some extent by this environmental context of the film.

We see that settings—environments—express meaning. Regions have characteristic modes of architecture. Cities, neighborhoods and houses say something about those who live in them. The rooms we inhabit, the furniture we have, the decorations and arrangements we give them, as well as our clothes and adornments, reflect who we are. So it is with the setting of a film.

A writer should attune himself to his surroundings. Contact them, listen to them, let them speak their meanings. How does the immediate environment reflect and affect those who live in it? If your room, your house, were viewed by a stranger for the first time, how would this stranger imagine you from what they express? The writer who is in touch with the messages of the environment is better able to use the setting expressively in his film.

A film is often intimately connected with a setting. *Roma* reflects that city. *Amarcord* is about remembered life in an Italian village. *Taxi Driver, Mean Streets* and *Manhattan* are New York City films in style and atmosphere. *Annie Hall* humorously contrasts the New York City that Woody Allen loves with the Los Angeles he doesn't. Western films so often reflect the wide open spaces of the frontier; Monument Valley, Utah, has been called another character in the films of John Ford. The many versions of the shootout at the OK Corral are closely tied to that historic place. The old South lives again perpetually in *Gone With the Wind. Murder by Decree* recreates the Victorian London of Sherlock Holmes.

Cooley High presents life in a Chicago ghetto; *Walkabout* moves through the Australian bush; *Short Eyes* takes place in the Tombs, a New York City detention center. The set of *All the President's Men* was a complete re-creation of the *Washington Post* newsroom. *The Last Picture Show* presents life in a small, dying Texas town in the 1950s. *American Graffiti* re-creates both a time and place as it presents adolescent life in a typical California town in the early 1960s.

Historical films (*Tom Jones, Joseph Andrews, Barry Lyndon, A Man for All Seasons, Romeo and Juliet*) depend heavily on the successfully authentic re-creation of the period in settings, costumes and atmosphere.

If the story takes place in a distinctive setting, the writer will need to be thoroughly familiar with the location to give the script the feeling of authenticity. This is even more important if the film takes place in a different culture or historical period. The writer of such scripts will do extensive research on locations, cultures and epochs. If possible, he will visit a location. If his film takes place in San Francisco and he wants that city to be an important element in the film, he will try to go there and absorb its ethos. Some writers find that it helps to play music from a culture or a period while working on a story from that time or place. It helps them get in the mood.

One decision that the writer will want to make early in his writing is to what extent he wants the setting to play a part in the film. In some films the setting is an integral part, functioning almost as another character. Live television series are somewhat restricted in setting. The set may be an important element, but it tends to remain constant from episode to episode and so offers little opportunity for change.

The film writer will decide on the scope of the setting. Some subjects need a grand-scale treatment: *War and Peace, Lawrence of Arabia, Dr. Zhivago, Giant, Birth of a Nation, Spartacus*. Such films call for open settings with broad outdoor landscapes and expansive environments. To try to restrict such material to a few tight rooms would be difficult. Other stories need a closed setting which encompasses the characters in several rooms or a similarly restricted space. Live television has such restrictions, of course. Beginning writers sometimes err in writing films as though they were doing theatrical plays, with all the action in enclosed sets, rooms and offices. The mobile film camera makes this unnecessary; it can go out and film the world. The scope of the setting should fit the material and the visual rhythms of the film.

Just as there are rhythms developed by temporal elements, there are also spatial rhythms created by contrasts and harmonies in the chosen settings. These rhythms may develop from a balance of interiors and exteriors or of open and closed settings, or they may stem from the more complex interactions of the various visual components of the setting.

Unusual and imaginative settings contribute to the overall effect of the film. Hitchcock has used a number of exciting locations. *North by Northwest* features a crop-dusting plane chasing the hero over an open field, with a later chase on the huge sculptured stone faces of Mt. Rushmore. *Lifeboat* takes place almost exclusively in a lifeboat. *Saboteur* features a chase on the Statue of Liberty. *Psycho* locates its gruesome murder in a shower.

The restricted, forced intimacy of a sailboat contributes to the tense interaction in *Knife in the Water*. *Brief Encounter* shows a love affair developing amid the hustle and bustle of a railway station. Strange, unique sand pits are the setting for *The Woman in the Dunes*.

Remote, desolate islands reflect the lives of the characters in Antonioni's opening of *L'Avventura,* as they do in some of Bergman's films (*Through a Glass Darkly, Hour of the Wolf*).

There is the ornate, formal, baroque chateau of *Last Year at Marienbad;* the theatrical exuberance of the house next door in *Juliet of the Spirits;* the surreal extravagance of the spa in *8½*.

The love nest in *Last Tango in Paris* is a bare apartment. An idyllic green park is the scene of murder in *Blow-Up*. Factory pollution suffuses *Red Desert*. *Five Easy Pieces* sets up a contrast between the pop-culture Los Angeles scene (with its country and western music, mobile homes, freeway traffic jams and bowling alleys) and a cultured, isolated family home in the Pacific Northwest (with its lush foliage, sophistication, classical music and illusionary detachment from the outside world).

In *Rocky,* there is a scene in a large cold-storage locker of a meat packing company in which Rocky plays around punching the hanging beef carcasses. A strongly interactive dialogue scene between the three friends in *Husbands* is played in the toilet stall of a public lounge during a drinking party. *The Third Man* features a notable scene staged in a large ferris wheel compartment high in the air; the exciting climax chase of this film occurs in the sewers of Vienna. Rooftop chases and amusement park shootout climaxes are almost clichés by now. One of the best is in Welles' *The Lady from Shanghai;* it takes place in the fun house mirror maze of an amusement park.

At the end of *Roma,* we see much of Rome at night—fountains, the lighted Colosseum and other sights—with the camera on dozens of motorcycles as they travel, en masse, through the streets.

Horror films revel in expressive settings—lonely, foggy moors; old mansions with hidden rooms and secret panels; dingy castles with massive pseudo-scientific equipment; and forests in which the trees seem menacing demons. The old house in *The Haunting* is presented as though it is a living thing. Doors seem to breathe; they pulse as if they have lungs and a heartbeat. Viewed from the outside grounds, the tower windows seem to be watchful eyes. The hallways of the house twist and turn in confusing, convoluted patterns. The shaky spiral metal staircase in the library seems alive and ready to hurt those who risk climbing it.

Television Settings

Expansive settings are less effective on television due to the smaller screen size and the sense of intimacy of the medium. Live television, including many of the situation comedies, uses standing sets and a more theatrical approach to staging than do film shows. The Bunker's house in *All in the Family* is an easy set to move around in with its connecting kitchen and living room and the outside porch and separate upstairs bedroom. Its furnishings and decor reflect the blue-collar socio-economic status of the Bunkers.

Props

Properties—objects that are handled and carried by the characters—can individualize and characterize a character or can be important elements in the plot. In *The Caine Mutiny* courtroom scene, Captain Queeg shows his instability by nervously clicking steel balls in his hand. Kojak uses a lollipop as an identifying prop. The laser swords of *Star Wars* have a special technological appeal. Woody Allen makes marvelous use of turn-on metal spheres in *Sleeper*. The gun has long been a symbol in westerns. Sometimes it is a special gun, as is the very powerful rifle of the bounty hunter in *The Missouri Breaks* or the long pistol of Wyatt Earp. The gun assumes special significance in *Yojimbo;* the film takes place at a time in Japan when guns were just being introduced. The sword was still the honorable weapon, but the gun was devastating.

Costumes

Costumes say something about the characters who wear them—about their social status, their taste, their sophistication. Costumes should fit the characters, the culture and the historical period. Think of Columbo's raincoat; of the gaudy, bizarre costumes of *Juliet of the Spirits;* or of Chaplin's tramp outfit, which beautifully reflects his poverty and social alienation, yet also conveys a sense of pseudo-aristocracy by virtue of his derby and cane.

In *A Clockwork Orange,* Alex and his droogs dress in white costumes. So do the storm troopers in *Star Wars*—in contrast to the black outfit of the arch-villain Darth Vader. Mirrored dark glasses are an important symbol of anonymity, separation and authority in *Cool Hand Luke.* The silent film comic Harold Lloyd never really became effective until he hit on the idea of wearing the frames of glasses for his character (no lenses, just the frames).

An interesting use of costume and color combine in *Track of the Cat.* This film concerns the internal entanglements of a family and the external threat of a killer mountain lion. The film is set in a cabin and its surroundings in a snow-covered, isolated wilderness. Dingy grays and blacks predominate in both the setting and the dress of the characters, with the exception of the central character, who wears a red plaid coat and thus stands out. The coat isn't that colorful, but it contrasts with the drabness of things around it.

There's a similar symbolic use of costume and color in Zeffirelli's *Romeo and Juliet.* The Capulets are dressed in reds, yellows and oranges—loud, aggressive colors which reflect the family's aggressive position. In contrast, the Montagues, a more established, perhaps declining, family, appear in blues, deep greens and purples. Both spectrums of color reflect the character of each family and help us identify them in the duel scenes.

The writer is not always concerned about the costumes of the film. The director and producer, working with the designer, will do that. However, if there is a particular effect that he wishes, he should describe in the script what he wants.

Color

If it is important that a scene or setting contain a certain color quality, it should be described as part of the description for that scene. *Red Desert* is one film that is interesting to study for its use of color.

Lighting

The same that is true for color is true for lighting. If the quality of light is important to the image of the scene, describe it. Do so with the economy characteristic of script descriptions, but do so. Is the set semi-dark? Is a scene shot in silhouette? Are there strong lighting contrasts in the scene? What special lighting effects are important to the staging of the scene?

Make-up

If there is a special make-up effect to be achieved, it should be mentioned in the script. Alex, for example in the opening of *A Clockwork Orange,* wears a single long eyelash.

Other Environmental Elements

The writer has even more to work with than what we've described. There is *time of day*. Day and night are obviously different. But so are evening, the bewitching hour of midnight, the mysterious "hour of the wolf" and the moment just before daybreak. So, too, are morning, noon, afternoon and evening. Each carry connotations that the writer can use. Antonioni has begun many of his films in the morning; he carries them through that day and night and into the following morning.

Time of year is important. Each of the seasons has its own feeling. Holidays can provide a special ethos, a fact to which many Christmas films attest. Nor should the writer forget that he can use *temperature* and *weather* conditions.

The aforementioned *mise-en-scène* refers to the use of visual space within the frame. It may be that for a particular scene the writer senses a feeling of *depth*. He may want the action to develop in a tunnel, alley or hallway, providing a strong feeling of depth, as with using a wide-angle lens. Or he may want the effect of compression of depth that is achieved with a long focal-length lens—as when a character runs toward the camera but seems to be going nowhere. In *Weekend,* Godard deliberately flattens many of the shots, destroying the sense of depth. His moving camera is 90 degrees to its subject. Characters move from side to side, parallel to the camera. They are often posed against shallow walls. This flattening may well be an ideological statement to distance the viewer from the material instead of involving him; it has been called a non-bourgeois camera style.[2]

While such choices are often the prerogative of the director and cameraman, there is no reason why the filmically sophisticated writer shouldn't completely describe the image he envisions.

A writer shouldn't over-describe in his script, but he should as concisely as possible mention whatever he feels is important with respect to setting, costume, light, color and mise-en-scène.

REFERENCES

1. Matsuo Basho as tr. by Harold G. Henderson in his *An Introduction to Haiku* (Garden City, N.Y.: Doubleday Anchor, 1958), p. 46.
2. Brian Henderson, "Toward a Non-Bourgeois Camera Style," *Film Quarterly* 28 (Winter 1970–1971). Also in Bill Nichols, ed., *Movies and Methods* (Berkeley: University of California Press, 1976), pp. 422–38.

9

Dialogue/Sound/Music

> Who are you?
> I am number two.
> Who is number one?
> You are number six.
> I am not a number, I am a free man.
> Ha, ha, ha. (mocking laugh) [1]
>
> —*The Prisoner*

THIS CHAPTER IS largely concerned with the writing of dialogue, the words that the characters speak. Before getting to that, it's appropriate to remember that film is primarily a visual medium. Images, not words, are the basic unit of the film writer. It is usually preferable to show something rather than to tell it. The best advice for the screenwriter is to think visually.

Television is not quite as visual as film. It is more dependent on the audio because of the smaller screen and less-resolved visual picture. The viewing situation is also a factor; it's been said that we "attend to" television rather than look at it. But this is a difference of degree. The television writer should still conceive his script visually.

Thinking visually includes realizing that both film and television express much through behavioral details. Body language is important in media communication. Such non-verbal actions as gestures, pratfalls, reactions, looks, shrugs, touches, poses and other bits of business speak very loudly and should be visualized by the writer even as he conceives his dialogue. Characters don't just stand or sit and talk back and forth. They interact. They touch and assume expressive positions and react with facial and body gestures. In real life, people subtly communicate by intonations, movements and gestures that are ordinarily unconscious and involuntary. The writer should consciously be aware of these as he develops character interaction and dialogue. With this in mind, we turn to dialogue as spoken lines.

Dialogue does a number of things. It provides information and advances the story. It defines characters by reflecting their background, education, occupation, social status, individuality and attitudes. It reveals emotion, mood, feelings and intent. Perhaps even more important than the spoken words, we "hear" the intent and feelings that underlie the words. Dialogue adds to the rhythm and pace of the script. It contributes to the ambience of each scene. It can connect shots and scenes through providing a continuity. Offscreen dialogue and sound can suggest the presence of objects, events and persons which aren't seen.

Effective film and television dialogue sounds natural. It conveys the sense of real speech even while it is more structured than the meanderings of daily speech. Effective dialogue has more economy and directness than real-life conversation. The television special *Blind Ambition,* based on John Dean's account of Watergate, featured the characters at times actually speaking lines from the Presidential tapes transcript. But it didn't work. It sounded artificial. The rhythm sounded strange.

The tone of dialogue is conversational, non-literary. As in conversation, effective film dialogue is essentially oblique. The term conversation is a good description of film dialogue. Compared with theater, film dialogue is more conversational. Its rhythms and diction seem more naturalistic than stage dialogue. It has been said that while we listen in theater, we eavesdrop in film.

Screen dialogue uses all the indirection, pauses and hesitations that we use in everyday speech, though it is condensed. Sentences will be incomplete and interrupted. Characters can mumble, evade and exaggerate.

Film writing is typically lean and economic. Effective dialogue is written sparsely, with short sentences of simple construction using simple, informal words. Speeches are brief and crisp. Both dialogue and narration should be easily comprehended by the audience, since a missed segment can't be turned back to and reread as with a novel. Dialogue and narration are written for the ear, not for the eye; written to be listened to, not to be read.

In film, words are used more for their implicit rather than explicit meaning. What is important in dialogue is the meaning that is being conveyed in the circumstances of the scene, not the literal meaning of the words used. What is not said or what is left unsaid can be as important as what is said. Ernest Hemingway compared writing words to an iceberg—there are only a few visible on top but many more implied underneath.

Dialogue should fit the character and his mood and emotions in the particular situation. It should have the rhythm and individual form of expression typical of the character. The dialogue should sound like the character and not like the writer. This is often difficult to accomplish since we tend to write our character's dialogue as we ourselves sound. Characters' speech should also differentiate them from each other so all characters don't sound alike; however, this shouldn't be overdone to the extreme that it seems unnatural. Your characters will sound individualized if you know them. Listen to them. Attune yourself to their individual ways of expression. Get in touch with their dialogue style and rhythms, their voice patterns, their favorite words and expressions and their non-verbal means of communicating.

One test is to see if the speeches of different characters can be switched with each other with no evident distinction. If they can be, then the characters and their dialogue haven't been effectively individualized.

One way to individualize characters is to give them favorite expressions and dialogue styles. (Although a writer will be wary of trying to write slang and jargon. Unless he knows it very well, the result may sound phony.) Archie Bunker has his "stifle it," and "jeez, Edith." Kojak says "what can I tell ya?" Rocky, from the film of that name, has a characteristic way of expression based on who he is and on his Philadelphia working-class background. He makes continual use of punctuating expressions: Ya know. Ya know what I mean. You understand. Wha'd'ya mean? Wha'd'ya think? I dunno.

We all have unique ways of expressing ourselves. It's an interesting exercise to list characteristic expressions that you use or hear your friends use. Some that have come from writing students are:

Know what I mean
And blah, blah, blah
O-kee-doh-kee
If you know what I mean
You're kidding me
What can I say
Oh wow!
Then he goes . . . then she goes . . .
Are you ready for that!
So what else is new?
So tell me about it
No way
Just blows me away
I hear you
I can relate
Really!
Far out
What's happening?
Apropos of nothing
Let's get the show on the road
No kidding, sports fans
Girl, would you believe
I'm gonna tell ya something
Cause like I say
I'm tellin' ya
You understand what I mean?

Dialogue also fits the situation and emotion. In a time of emotional stress, we will be less coherent, less able to speak in concise, formal prose. A beginning writer's script illustrates the problem of being too verbal when it doesn't fit the condition of the character. An old woman has fallen and hit her head; she had passed out from lifting heavy crates of vegetables outside her small New York City store. Her collapse is sudden and unexpected. A young woman rushes up to help and asks what happened. The old woman replies: "I don't know. First I got dizzy. Then I broke out in a cold sweat. My hands felt clammy. And then I blacked out. The next thing I knew was that I was flat on my face in the street." It is difficult to believe that anyone would talk so coherently under the circumstances.

Meaning in dialogue is dependent on both the context in which it is spoken and the speaker's intent behind the words. Consider the words, "I love you." Depending on the way they are said, to whom and in what circumstances, they can mean: I care for you. I worship you. I want you sexually. I feel protective of you. I want to control you. I want to make you feel guilty. I like you. I don't want to be bothered by you. I hate you.

Dialogue is best when underwritten and understated. A writer avoids having his characters spout platitudes or the excessive emotion of the melodramatic. He doesn't let the words express more feeling and intensity than we have seen the characters can handle. If a dialogue scene is strongly emotional, he will be sure that we have been adequately prepared for it and therefore won't be turned off by its heaviness. This is even more important when the material and emotions are potentially embarrassing because of either the content or the intensity. A writer tries to avoid tired truisms and clichés. (Sometimes a character speaks clichés as part of his personality, as does Ted Baxter, the pompous newscaster on *Mary Tyler Moore*. In such cases the audience realizes that the clichés are meant to be seen as clichés and not as serious expression.)

It doesn't take too many hours of television watching before one can spot a sizable number of clichés and examples of overwritten dialogue. Here are just a few: "Being a cop is a thirty-hour-day job." "In my department, you're a cop first, a person second." "I know what it means to die." "Even a single life matters." "You've given me more than any wife has a right to expect." "Now I'm left to live my life in a living hell, why didn't you let me die." "Why do I get the feeling that deep down inside you're lonely?" Or, as the lovers tearfully part, with tender violin music in the background, one says to the other: "Nothing lasts forever." Or the teenagers parked in their car making out, and: She: "Don't." He: "I have to, I can't help myself." These are the sorts of things that a writer will avoid.

To learn to write good dialogue, learn to listen. Listen to what people say—to the expressions they use—and to how they say it. Listen and observe how meaning is expressed, both verbally and non-verbally. Listen to the meaning beneath the overt sense of the words. Listen in the way of an impressionist who is planning to imitate a person's voice, gestures and expressions.

Above all, listen to your characters. If you know them well enough, if they have developed a reality and presence of their own, they will write their own dialogue. They will talk through you.

It is a good idea to read your dialogue aloud for the feel of it. Try doing this with one hand cupped by your ear as radio announcers have done so as to better hear the sounds of the words. It may also help to have others read your dialogue to you. Listen to it as if you were hearing it for the first time, blocking out all the privileged information about the scene and characters which you know as the writer. Listen as if you were a first-time audience. Some writers find it helpful to use a tape recorder to tape passages and then listen to them.

When viewing films and television, try listening to the spoken dialogue as though it were written dialogue; imagine it appearing typed on the script page. This can help connect what is typed and what is spoken on the screen.

Subtext

What is important in dialogue is what's being communicated—the meaning expressed. This is frequently not what is literally being spoken. In film dialogue, as in life, the actual meaning often lies beneath the ostensible surface meaning. The expression used to describe this is *subtext*—what is being said beneath the text lines. The subtext is the real meaning being conveyed, the real intent—conscious or unconscious—of the character. Subtext is found in the mannered discourse of diplomacy and in the conventions of social manners when it is considered polite to have a proper overt expression convey a different underlying meaning. Subtext expresses the hidden agenda of a character. A revealing metaphor describes an interpersonal dialogue scene as one in which the text words bounce back and forth like ping-pong balls while the true meaning resounds like bowling balls rolling under the table.

Subtext is the actual meaning underlying the apparent surface meaning. It is the emotion, thought or intent underneath both the overt words and actions, for subtext applies to action as well as words. Recall the wonderful eating scene in *Tom Jones* when Tom and Mrs. Waters are eating a meal in the tavern. Their action is to eat, but what is actually going on is a rather obvious mutual seduction.

Subtext often occurs in interpersonal "games." If the game is an unconscious one, unknown to the participants, it can be destructive and keep them from authentic involvement. But if both are party to the game, as often happens in a seduction, the results can be pleasurable. Eric Berne describes a flirtation game which takes place at a suburban party. A man and woman meet. He mentions to her that their hosts have done a good job restoring the old barn, would she like to go out and look at it? What he really is saying—the subtext—is that he finds her interesting and sexually attractive. Would she like to explore the possibility of a romance? She replies that she loves old barns and would like to see it: let's go. Her subtext is that she finds him attractive as well and would like to see what they might get on together.[2]

Sometimes subtext is part of a deception. A character says one thing but means another. Another character might not read this subtextual meaning although he may sense it. The audience is aware of the subtext even if the characters aren't. A writer considers not only how characters in a scene read (understand) what is said and done but also how the audience reads it. The "silver cord" mother tells her son that she only wishes the best for him and that the girl he brings home is "nice"—but is he sure that he's ready for marriage? Read this as "Don't get involved with her, stay with me."

In the short film *Doubletalk,* the actors speak the text while their voice-over commentary speaks the subtext. Subtext is given a novel treatment in *Annie Hall:* In a scene just after Alvy and Annie have met, they are talking non-committally and intellectually about art; at the same time, subtitles flash on the screen letting us read what they are really thinking—wondering how she looks naked, concerned for how they are coming on to each other and the like.

A frequent comedy subtext, too often overdone on television comedies, is the sexual innuendo played for laughs. In *Little Big Man,* young man Jack is being bathed by Mrs. Pendrake who, along with her stuffy husband the Reverend Pendrake, are going to take him in and raise him properly. Throughout the bathing and subsequent drying, her words are telling Jack about Jesus and the need for purity and resisting temptation, while her tone and actions express her obvious sexual arousal and interest.

The Servant has a great deal more going on with the character of the servant Barrett than is overtly apparent. Gradually he ruins his employer and takes control of the house. While the employer isn't aware of this intention, his fiancée is. She and Barrett clash from the beginning. At one point, Barrett interrupts an intimate romantic scene between the employer and the fiancée. She expresses her annoyance by authoritatively prohibiting him from removing some flowers from the employer's sickroom. The tension of the scene leads to an emotional clash between the employer and his fiancée. Later, as Barrett shows her out, he addresses her with a startling comment which viciously refers, subtextually, to her spat with her fiancée. He says, "I'm afraid it's not very encouraging, Miss." She looks astonished, shocked. "—the weather forecast," Barrett adds with feigned innocence.

The television special series *Washington Behind Closed Doors* presents many examples of subtextual meaning. As it is concerned with the behind-the-scenes intrigue of a White House not unlike that of Nixon's Watergate period, we hear implications, innuendoes, suggested meanings and veiled threats. Characters constantly protect themselves by saying what would seem innocent if reproduced in print but which, given the context and intonations of their machinations, has quite different meanings. We hear a character urge another to commit an illegal act, without actually committing himself to the given order or to the potential incrimination connected with it. Yet the message is conveyed. The bowling balls roll under the table. We see the President asking his top aides to quietly prepare a strategy just in case he wants to get the Twenty-Second Amendment changed so that he can succeed himself. Not that he would even seriously consider it, he demurs, but still . . . .

Dialogue Models

Dialogue and sound lend themselves to much innovative use. The following illustrate some of what can be done with dialogue.

Sometimes an intimate dialogue conversation will sound as though the speaking characters are nearby, as in a medium shot, but the actual accompanying visual is in very long shot. There is a scene in *Annie Hall* in which two characters walk toward the camera from an extreme long shot in which they are so distant that they are almost out of sight. Yet their voices are close and remain so as they approach. In *The Goodbye Girl*, a scene begins outside the window of the house and the camera slowly moves in and through the closed window to the scene inside. Yet the dialogue, even when outside the house, sounds intimately close, as though we were inside.

We usually think of dialogue as alternating between characters, but dialogue can also overlap, producing rhythmic and realistic effects, or a comic feel. This happens in *The Magnificent Ambersons* as the guests leave the Amberson's ball. Dialogue of one group of characters overlaps that of another, and then another. Each group has its own verbal quality—young people speaking rapidly at normal levels, a middle-aged couple talking softly and slowly, the family members shouting. All blend into a harmonious sound montage. Quarrels among the Ambersons are similarly treated, with the shouting and accusations overlapping as they do in reality.

In the film *M*A*S*H,* Radar and the Colonel often talk simultaneously, since Radar anticipates everything the Colonel wants and expresses it even as the Colonel does (although not quite identically).

Many things can be done with offscreen dialogue. At its simplest, it conveys the presence of another character. Sometimes it is used in a more stylistic way. Near the opening of *Mr. Klein,* Klein is buying a painting from a Jew fleeing Paris during the Second World War. We hear the dialogue of this transaction over the visual of a woman—Klein's mistress—in the next room getting out of bed, putting on lipstick and so on. The moving camera stays with her as we hear Klein buy the painting for much less than it is really worth.

In the television movie *Dark Victory,* a woman is being operated on for a brain tumor. An older specialist is doing the operation. Her younger doctor, who has romantic feelings for her (they later marry), is waiting outside in the hall. He talks with nurses and a colleague and moves around the hospital corridors. All of his action is shot MOS (mit out sound), while on the sound track we hear the sounds from the operating room—the surgeon describing what he's doing during the operation and so on. The scene continues at some length like this.

Films frequently contain scenes shot MOS (mit out sound). This is typical of mood scenes or travel scenes. Such scenes often feature a musical background. A more unusual use of MOS is when we would ordinarily expect to hear the sound but don't. In *Cries and Whispers,* there is a scene in which the two estranged sisters briefly reconcile. We see a series of MOS shots linked by dissolves in which the women urgently say to each other all that they have been unable to say for so long; all that they have stored up to say is coming out now as they contact. But we hear none of it; it is all MOS.

There is a scene in *Mr. Klein* in which Klein goes into a cafe, orders a coffee and then makes a phone call. While this goes on, the camera remains outside, looking in through the window. We don't hear any of what he says. All the while he talks on the phone, there are only the sounds of traffic.

The sudden introduction of sound—dialogue or narration—over silence can have a strong effect if the silence has been dominant. The only spoken word in *Silent Movie* is said with comic irony by the Mime Marcel Marceau: "No!!!"

One of the two stories in Pasolini's *Pigpen* (*Pigsty*) develops without dialogue up to the execution of the savage brigand for his vicious crimes. The words then spoken are the intoned statement of the charges against him, but they are accompanied by a loud tolling bell which obliterates the meaning and hearing of the words.

In television situation comedy, entrances and exits are usually accompanied by comic lines. A character often says something funny as he comes in and leaves.

Tag lines (which close a scene) and curtain lines (which close an act) are frequently climax lines that carry some impact and project us into the next scene. A television adventure program curtain line might be: "It wasn't an accident, it's murder!" And we go to the commercial break. In *The Sting*, Johnny Hooker is asked why he wants to pull the big con on the racketeer who had his friend murdered. He replies: " 'Cause I don't know enough about killing to kill him!" This powerful line helps him win the respect and help of his con artist colleague. The line is followed by a non-dialogue scene backed by music and the sound of machinery. This gives the line even more of a chance to register with the audience.

Tone and voice quality are important not only with human characters, but also with their mechanical counterparts. Much of the impact of HAL, the computer in *2001*, comes from the soothing, calm, unmechanical texture of his voice. There's an individuality, too, in the fussy, "auntie" quality of C-3PO in *Star Wars*.

Narration is sometimes used in films to set the story and illuminate it. It can supply a certain objectivity if the narrator is not a character (*Tom Jones, Joseph Andrews*) or a personal touch if the narrator is a character (*Little Big Man, Diary of a Country Priest, A Clockwork Orange*). Some stories need a narrator to supply a different perspective or a unifying structure to the story. Fellini narrates certain parts of *Roma*. In the beginning he tells us that this is a film without a story, a film of a city. *Sunset Boulevard* is narrated by a dead man, whom we see killed at the conclusion of the film.

Written legends are frequently seen at the beginning of films to set the situation. They have also been used effectively at the end to sum up and provide a final impact greater than that possible without such a change in format. In *How Tasty Was My Little Frenchman,* we have just seen the Latin American Indian tribe kill—and eat—the Frenchman who had been living with them. The end legend hits us hard when we read that in retribution the entire Indian tribe was destroyed. Powerful, too, is the dramatic printed conclusion of *Z,* as a list unrolls on the screen of all the activities and literature barred by the despotic government, ending with "and the letter Z, which means he is alive."

Sometimes dialogue is not prescripted but is developed with the actors through improvisation. When effective, this can produce an exciting touch of authenticity, as in the taxi cab scene in *On the Waterfront* when Brando mutters, "Oh Charlie . . . it wasn't him, Charlie, it was you . . . you was my brother . . . it was you, Charlie." John Cassavetes has evolved an improvisational technique with his near-ensemble group of actors in which he writes out the basic plot outline with character development and suggestions for motivation. Then, after discussion, he and the actors have an extended session of dialogue brainstorming, making an audio recording of what develops. Cassavetes uses this tape as a source from which to write additional new dialogue patterned after that developed by the actors and taking the form of a script.

Improvisation may produce exciting results, but it is not without difficulties, which suggests that it has limited use. Many film actors can't handle the demands of improvisation. Attempts at totally improvised dialogue frequently produce long, talky scenes as the actors struggle to reach the point of the scene. The demands of film continuity, rhythm and pacing require tighter control than improvisation permits. Cassavetes has been able to work well with his modified improvisational technique, yet sequences in his films sometimes stretch interminably and are without the focused development that guides audience involvement. Still, experiments with ensemble improvisation are exciting and worthwhile.

Dialogue Mechanics

These suggestions about the composition of dialogue should be taken with caution. Followed too rigidly, they will give your dialogue a mechanical, artificial feeling. They represent some general principles that should be used quite judiciously. They cannot take the place of dialogue that sounds natural to the characters. As your characters become increasingly real, they will make their own dialogue.

Dialogue Hook

Dialogue has a certain flow and continuity. A speech smoothly follows the one preceding it. Usually the flow of ideas and character involvement insures this, but there are some dialogue techniques that can help supply this continuity. These are known as dialogue hooks, reflecting the idea that each speech somehow acknowledges or "hooks" the one preceding it. Used sparingly, these devices make for a smooth dialogue progression; overused, they make dialogue seem artificial and constructed. Commonly used hook techniques are: question-answer, agreement-disagreement, repeated or matched words, parallel structures of repeated lines (with or without variation) and a unified progression.

Question-Answer is rather obvious and hardly needs illustration. One character asks a question and another supplies the answer. An interesting variation occurs when the answer isn't what is expected, especially if it is not a verbal reply. In a western, when the fast gun is asked "How good are you?" he may well reply with a sudden demonstration, as in *Butch Cassidy and The Sundance Kid* when the Kid is trying out for a job as mine payroll guard. With his gun in hand, he shoots at the tobacco plug target and misses. Sundance: "Can I move?" Garris (confused): "Move? What the hell you mean, move?" Hardly are his words out when Sundance draws from his holster and fires, hitting the target. Sundance (explaining, simply): "I'm better when I move."

In *Network,* Max and Diana first meet. He asks her what she's doing for dinner tonight. Instead of answering him directly, she picks up the phone, taps out a number and tells the person on the other end that she can't make it tonight and to call her tomorrow. Max has his answer.

Then, there is a wonderful bit in the third film of Inagaki's *The Samurai Trilogy*. The famous Samurai swordsman Miyamoto Musashi—the greatest swordsman in Japan—is staying at a humble inn. A crowd of men outside his room are very noisy. The lad who has been traveling with Musashi goes out and asks them to be quieter. The leader of the group, a tough horsetrader, comes into the room and challenges Mushashi, not knowing who he is. Musashi does not wish any trouble and pays him no attention. But the man insists, drawing his knife. As if in reply, Musashi pauses from eating his noodles and plucks a fly from the air with his chopsticks! He flicks it away, then plucks two more off his kimono, then some from the bowl of noodles, all with the tips of his chopsticks. This fantastically deft display of skill awes the horsetrader and answers his challenge; the astonished man hurriedly backs out of the room.

Agreement-disagreement is another way of relating to a previous line by either expressing agreement with it or by disagreeing with it. Disagreement can also be expressed by contradiction, evasion or sometimes by no answer when one is expected. Here are some examples.

Peter, a young industrial filmmaker, is talking with Curry. He has just denied making sex films. Unknown to Peter, a young woman, Shade, has entered the room. She is angry with him for making a clumsy sexual overture to her earlier in the day.

CURRY: Are you sure? You look like you make dirty movies.

PETER: I don't make dirty movies!

SHADE (interrupting): —But you'd love to, wouldn't you!

In *Butch Cassidy and the Sundance Kid,* the pair are trying to escape the posse.

BUTCH: I think we lost 'em. Do you think we lost 'em?

SUNDANCE: No.

BUTCH: Neither do I.

In the following example from *Network,* Max and Diana are breaking off their relationship. They disagree (in rather excessive prose).

DIANA: I don't want your pain! I don't want your menopausal decay and death! I don't need you, Max.

MAX: You need me badly! I'm your last contact with human reality! I love you, and that painful decaying menopausal love is the only thing between you and the shrieking nothingness you live the rest of the day!

DIANA: Then don't leave me!

MAX: It's too late, Diana! There's nothing left in you that I can live with!

Repeated or Matched words. Continuity can be developed by hooking repeated or matched words from one speech to another (but don't overdo it). From *Network:*

DIANA: —Well, Max, here we are—middle-aged man reaffirming his middle-aged manhood and a terrified young woman with a father complex. What sort of script do you think we can make out of this?

MAX: Terrified, are you?

DIANA: Terrified out of my skull, man.

From *A Clockwork Orange:*

DIM: What did you do that for?

ALEX: For being a bastard with no manners. . . .

* *

ALEX: To what do I owe this extreme pleasure, sir? Anything wrong, sir?

MR. DELTOID: Wrong? Why should you think of anything being wrong?

* *

GEORGIE: All right, no more picking on Dim, brother. That's part of the new way.

ALEX: New way? What's this about a new way?

Parallel Structures of Repeated Lines. A similar device uses parallel construction of consecutive lines or the repetition of a line.

PETER: Uh, hello, Shade. I bet you didn't expect to see me!

SHADE: I bet you don't expect me to talk to you!

* *

SHADE: Apologize and I'll *think* about working for you!

PETER: Awright, I'll apologize *if* you come and work for me!

Butterfly, an older homosexual, is asked about his party.

BUTTERFLY: Oh . . . it was alright. But it broke up early. Really there's something depressing about a group of aging queens reminiscing about the past and celebrating a birthday.

WALT (a retired man): Really, there's something depressing about a group of aging anything celebrating a birthday.

Police are concerned about a possible criminal threat and what they might do to prevent it.

FIRST POLICEMAN: What are we going to do?

SECOND POLICEMAN: What are *they* going to do?

Sharing a Progression. A smooth continuity is achieved when speakers are sharing a progression. This might be an interrupted build:

HAL: There'll be music and grass and—

ANDREA: —and wine and dancing—

HAL: —and we'll have a ball!

Or there might be a building progression:

PETER: I want you to take the job!

SHADE: I already told you what you could do with your job.

PETER: I know, I read my door!

SHADE: Was there anything there you didn't understand? I'll gladly show you graphically the area I had in mind!

PETER: I want you to have the job because you are highly qualified—

SHADE: —not for what you have in mind!

PETER: To make films! You're a good cameraman. I want to hire you.

SHADE: It's camera*person,* and I'm waiting for your apology.

PETER: That's not why I came!

SHADE: But that's why you're staying!

These are useful devices for smoothing dialogue, but their obviousness or overuse will call attention to itself and the dialogue will appear artificial and unnatural.

Dialogue Examples

The following are examples of effective screen dialogue.

The first is an example of a rapid interchange of short, interrupted dialogue from *Butch Cassidy and the Sundance Kid.* Butch and Sundance are trapped on the top of a fifty-foot cliff by the posse trailing them. Below them is a rushing river.

BUTCH: We'll jump!

SUNDANCE: Like hell we will.

BUTCH: No, no, it's gonna be okay—just so it's deep enough we don't get squished to death—they'll never follow us—

SUNDANCE: —How do you know?—

BUTCH: —Would you make that jump if you didn't have to?—

SUNDANCE: —I have to and I'm not gonna—

BUTCH: —It's the only way. Otherwise we're dead. They'll have to go all the way back down the way we came. Come on—

SUNDANCE: —Just a couple decent shots—that's all I want—

BUTCH: *—Come on—*

SUNDANCE: —No—

BUTCH: —We got to—

SUNDANCE: *—No—*

BUTCH: —Yes—

SUNDANCE: —Get away from me—

BUTCH: —Why?—

SUNDANCE: —I wanna fight 'em—

BUTCH: —They'll kill us—

SUNDANCE: —Maybe—

BUTCH: —You wanna die?—

SUNDANCE: —Don't you?

BUTCH: I'll jump first—

SUNDANCE: —No—

BUTCH: —Okay, you jump first—

SUNDANCE: *—No,* I said—

BUTCH (big): *What'sa matter with you?*

SUNDANCE (bigger): *I can't swim!!*

BUTCH: You stupid fool, the fall'll probably kill you.

They laugh, then jump together.

The dialogue of *A Clockwork Orange* is unique in its rhythm and in its use of an idiosyncratic jargon of invented words. We can often guess at their meaning, but their role in stylizing the dialogue is more important than a precise denotative meaning. We understand what is being expressed even if certain specific words escape us.

At one point near the beginning of the film, Alex and his droogs come across Billyboy and his gang in the act of a rape. Alex challenges them to a fight after first introducing us to the situation as follows:

ALEX (voice over): It was around by the derelict casino that we came across Billyboy and his four droogs. They were getting ready to perform a little of the old in-out, in-out on a weepy young devotchka they had there.

ALEX (on camera): Ho, Ho, Ho. Well, if it isn't fat stinking Billygoat Billyboy in poison. How art thou, thou globby bottle of cheap, stinking chip oil? Come and get one in the yarbles, if you have any yarbles, you eunuch jelly thou.

After Alex and his droogs beat up and rape a couple, they go to a milk bar for refreshment, and Alex hears a woman singing a phrase from Beethoven's *Ninth*, a favorite composition of his. Dim, one of the droogs, gives the singer a raspberry, so Alex smashes Dim across the legs with his stick.

DIM: What did you do that for?

ALEX: For being a bastard with no manners and not a dook of an idea how to comport yourself publicwise, o my brother.

DIM: I don't like you should do what you done. And I'm not your brother no more and wouldn't want to be.

ALEX: Watch that . . . Do watch that, O Dim, if to continue to be on live thou dost wish.

DIM: Yarbles, great bolshy yarblockos to you. I'll meet you with chain or nozh or britva anytime. Not having you aiming tolchocks at me reasonless, it stands to reason I won't have it.

ALEX: A nozh scrap any time you say.

(Dim slowly backs down.)

DIM: Doobidoob. A bit tired maybe. Best not to say more. Bedways is right ways now, so best we go homeways and get a bit of spatchka. Righty, right?

PETE/GEORGIE: Righty, right.

ALEX: Right, right.

Some of the most effective film dialogue is that from the films of Michelangelo Antonioni. It reflects an oblique, elliptical and ambiguous quality that invites audience involvement.

This selection is from *The Passenger*. Locke is in a Spanish palace, a tourist tour is passing through. An attractive girl sits on a bench near him. Locke goes up to her, sits beside her.

LOCKE: Excuse me. I'm trying to remember something.

GIRL (very naturally): Is it important?

LOCKE: No. Do you know what it is? I came in by accident.

GIRL: The man who built it was hit by a train.

LOCKE: Who was he?

GIRL: Gaudi. He built this house for a corduroy manufacturer.

(She gets up.)

GIRL: Come.

(They enter a big room.)

GIRL: They used this room for concerts. Wagner.

LOCKE: Do you think he was crazy?

GIRL: What do you think?

LOCKE: No, he wasn't.

(She laughs easily.)

GIRL: How could you come in here by accident?

LOCKE: I was escaping.

GIRL: Wow . . . From what?

LOCKE: I thought there was someone following me, somebody who might recognize me.

GIRL: Why?

LOCKE: I don't know.

GIRL: Well, I can't recognize you. Who are you?

LOCKE: I used to be someone else. But I traded him in. What about you?

GIRL (smiles ironically): I'm in Barcelona. I'm talking to a man.

(Locke smiles at her.)

GIRL: I was with those people but I'm going to see the other Gaudi buildings alone.

LOCKE: All of them?

GIRL: It depends how much time you've got. They're all good for hiding in.

LOCKE: I must leave today—this afternoon.

GIRL: I hope you make it. People disappear every day.

LOCKE: Whenever they leave the room.

GIRL: Goodbye.

In *Blow-Up,* Thomas, the photographer, visits Bill, a painter, and his wife, Patricia, in their house beyond Thomas' yard. As Thomas enters, Bill is studying a painting on the easel, which he describes.

BILL: That must be five or six years old. They don't mean anything when I do them—just a mess. Afterwards I find something to hang onto—like that—like—like . . . that leg. And then it sorts itself out. It adds up. It's like finding a clue in a detective story.

(Bill and Thomas look at a picture lying on the floor.)

BILL: Ha . . . Don't ask me about this one. I don't know yet.

THOMAS: Can I buy it?

BILL: No.

THOMAS: Will you give it to me?

(Bill shakes his head. Patricia brings Thomas a beer.)

PATRICIA: Here you are.

THOMAS: Hmm. Thank you.

(She begins ruffling his hair.)

THOMAS: Tight-faced bastard. (grinning) He won't sell me one of his crappy paintings. Hmm. I'll creep down one night and knock it off.

(Patricia stops ruffling his hair.)

THOMAS: Don't stop. It's lovely.

PATRICIA: You look tired . . .

THOMAS: Mmmm . . . I've been all night in the doss house.

Later in the film, Thomas goes to tell Bill and Patricia about seeing a gun in a blown-up photograph, but finds that they are making love. Patricia looks separated, uninvolved with Bill, as she watches Thomas. Thomas then returns to restudy his blow-ups and discovers the corpse. Patricia comes in.

PATRICIA (perfectly normal voice): Were you looking for something just now?

THOMAS: No.

PATRICIA: Oh.

THOMAS: Do you ever think of leaving him?

PATRICIA: No, I don't think so.

(Pause.)

THOMAS: I saw a man killed this morning.

PATRICIA: Where?

THOMAS: Shot. In some sort of park.

(He studies photograph.)

PATRICIA: Are you sure?

THOMAS: He's still there.

PATRICIA: Who was he?

THOMAS: Someone.

PATRICIA: How did it happen?

THOMAS: I don't know. I didn't see.

PATRICIA: You didn't see?

THOMAS: No.

PATRICIA: Shouldn't you call the police?

THOMAS: That's the body.

PATRICIA: It looks like one of Bill's paintings.

THOMAS: Yes.

PATRICIA (thinks, then): Will you help me? I don't know what to do.

THOMAS: What is it? Huh?

PATRICIA: I wonder why they shot him . . .

THOMAS: I didn't ask.

(She smiles, leaves.)

There is a sequence in which the woman in the park who figured in the killing comes to the studio to get the film (before Thomas has examined it). They meet outside his home/studio.

GIRL: I . . . I've come . . . I've come for the photographs.

THOMAS: Well, how did you manage to find me?

GIRL: Do you live here?

THOMAS: Mmm.

(They enter, go to the upper studio. Thomas switches on a few scattered lights and some music.)

THOMAS: Drink? (sets drinks) What's so important about my bloody pictures?

GIRL: That's my business.

THOMAS: The light was very beautiful in the park this morning. Those shots should be very good. Anyway, I need them.

GIRL: My private life's already in a mess. It would be a disaster if . . .

THOMAS: So what—nothing like a little disaster for sorting things out.

(Girl paces, Thomas watches her.)

THOMAS: Have you ever done any modeling? Fashion stuff, I mean? You've got it.

(He pulls down a backdrop, stands her in front of it.)

THOMAS: Hold that. Not many girls stand as well as that . . .

GIRL: No thanks, I'm in a hurry.

THOMAS: You'll get your pictures. I promise. I always keep my word.

(He falls onto the couch.)

THOMAS: Come here. Show me how you sit.

(Telephone rings. He ignores it, suddenly dives and digs around to find it.)

THOMAS (into phone): Who is it? Oh yes, that's right. Hold on a second.

(He holds receiver out to girl.)

GIRL (shocked): Is it for me?

(She hesitantly picks up receiver.)

THOMAS: It's my wife.

(Girl hurriedly puts receiver down.)

GIRL: Why should I speak to her?

THOMAS (takes phone, says into it): Sorry, love, the bird I'm with won't talk to you. (hangs up)

(Girl is impatient.)

THOMAS: She isn't my wife really. We just have some kids . . . no . . . no kids. Not even kids. Sometimes, though, it . . . it feels as if we had kids. She isn't beautiful, she's . . . easy to live with.

(He sits down, lights a cigarette.)

THOMAS: No, she isn't. That's why I don't live with her.

(Girl shows first sign of interest in him.)

THOMAS: But even with beautiful girls you . . . you look at them and . . . that's that. That's why they always end up by . . . (sighs) . . . well, I'm stuck with them all day long.

GIRL: It would be the same with men.

(Fast beat music track starts playing.)

THOMAS: Have a listen to this.

(He turns up volume.)

(Girl starts to sway rhythmically.)

THOMAS: No, keep still. Keep still! Listen. Keep still.

(He hands her cigarette he's been smoking.)

THOMAS: You can smoke if you like.

(Girl takes it, keeps swaying.)

THOMAS: Slowly, slowly. Against the beat. That's it.

(Girl returns cigarette. He draws on it. Offers it again. Girl jumps up.)

GIRL: Ohhh . . . I can't stand it. I'm nervous enough as it is.

(Girl sits, rummages in bag.)

GIRL: Can I have some water.

THOMAS: Sure. (goes to kitchen)

(Girl glances after him, grabs his camera, rushes out. He surprises her at the door.)

THOMAS: And I am not a fool, love.

(Girl returns the camera.)

GIRL: Can I have the photographs?

(Pause.)

THOMAS: Of course. Later.

(They start toward the stairs.)

THOMAS: Your boyfriend's a bit past it.

(Upstairs, she looks directly at him.)

GIRL: Why don't you say what you want?

(Girl removes her blouse; she wears no bra. Thomas admires her, looks at her, then:)

THOMAS: Get dressed. I'll cut out the negatives you want.

Sound

Sound is one of a filmmaker's most useful resources and one of the most neglected. Sound is pervasive; it gives the impression of filling the screen. It has no specific direction (except for special stereophonic and multi-speaker systems for special films). Perhaps because it is less specific than visuals, sound can be strongly suggestive and connotative. And sound can make its contribution without slowing the action; because it is added on top of the visual, sound doesn't take up extra space.

As you visualize your scenes, listen to their sounds as well. What special sounds are there in your scenes? How can sound complement or counterpoint other scene elements?

Perhaps the most common use of added sound is as a background contribution to the ambience of the film to help establish a locale or set an atmosphere. Such sounds include birds, crickets, clocks, traffic, the surf, city noises, village festival sounds and the sounds of war.

The level of sound is a factor in its use. *A Clockwork Orange* has a consistently loud sound track. The noise assaulting the audience reflects the violence of the film. At the end of *The Bridge on the River Kwai,* the sound of the approaching train with its screeching whistle is over-modulated; this is soon followed by the explosion as the bridge is blown. All the sounds contribute to a cacophonous climax. Sound amplified beyond the normal is frequently used for creating a feeling of suspense or terror, as increasing the level of a ticking clock or of a train or plane.

Increasing or decreasing sound volume can convey the effect of movement toward or away from the camera. Bresson's *Lancelot du Lac* opens with the sound of galloping knights riding into and out of frame; they are barely visible in the darkness of the night. Much of the striking effect of their appearance and disappearance comes from the increasing and disappearing of the sound of the galloping hoofs. The scene is repeated a number of times intercut with other static scenes. It is a strong opening.

The fast tempo of a sound can produce excitement. The chase sequence of *The French Connection* gains much of its impact from the acceleration of the screeching auto tires and the clatter of the rushing subway train. These grow louder and higher in pitch and increase in velocity, producing a very exciting effect.

Offscreen sound can be used to expand the frame or to signify an event that we don't see, as when the villain takes the girl into a room and closes the door after them and we hear her scream! Trains are frequently evoked by the sound of their whistle.Their wail can mean many things—an opportunity missed, a separation, loneliness or adventure. In *One Flew Over the Cuckoo's Nest,* instead of escaping to Canada, McMurphy waits in the mental hospital in order to give Billy, a shy person, the experience of one of the whores. As he waits, we hear the sound of a distant train whistle over a close-up shot of his face. He never does get away.

In *Paths of Glory,* the pervasive sounds of gun and cannon fire both enlarge the limits of the trenches and reflect the constant danger under which the soldiers exist. In *Mary, Queen of Scots,* at Mary's execution, we see an extreme close-up of Elizabeth's eyes and hear the swing of the axe. It signifies the deed is done.

An offscreen crash can substitute for staging the real thing. In *The Pink Panther,* a bystander has been watching the wild chase of cars. At the end of the chase sequence, we hear the loud sound of a terrific offscreen crash. The camera follows the man over to where he discovers all the cars piled up.

In *The Parallax View,* an airliner returns to the airport because of what the pilot announces as technical difficulties. It is really because of a possible bomb on board. The camera follows a main character, who wasn't a passenger, as he walks along a runway. We hear loudspeakers instruct the departing passengers to report to security guards. (We do not see the plane.) The message is repeated as the character continues walking. Then there is the sound of a large explosion offscreen. We know it is the plane.

Sound seems to have a special ability, along with music, to evoke emotion. Consider the effect of a wailing wind and a creaking door in horror films. The sounds of birds screeching are terrifying in Hitchcock's *The Birds*. Before some of the frenzied attack scenes, a few preliminary screeches and wing flaps cue us to suspensefully expect the terror-filled moments to follow. When the birds do attack, the sounds are overpowering.

At the end of *Duel,* the personified tractor-trailer truck that has been trying to destroy the central character is forced over a hill. In slow motion, it falls to its destruction. As it falls, it is accompanied by a strange sound, an almost animal cry like an elephant call. The truck "dies" like some huge animal.

There's a tense scene in *The Godfather* when Michael, planning to kill Sollozzo and the crooked police captain, goes to a rendezvous at a restaurant. As the car pulls up outside the restaurant, the sound track contains the ambient sound of the elevated train, which is so much a part of the background that we don't pay much attention to it. Later, as Michael leaves the men's room where he picked up the concealed gun, the sound of the elevated train is brought in again. Then, as he is sitting at the table deciding to make his move and shoot, we again hear the train noise and the hiss of the car doors opening and closing. The sound effectively punctuates the scene.

In *Star Wars,* the archvillain Darth Vader is all the more menacing because of the snorkle-like sound of his heavy breathing through his breath mask. The whirring and humming of the small droid, R2D2, and the whistling way in which he communicates to the other robot is a clever way to characterize him. The sound of the laser swords in this film helps to give the dueling scenes much of their attraction.

Sound may be used to build suspense, as with the sound of footsteps in the night, or to shock, as with a suddenly banging shutter. Both suspense and shock combine in a sequence from *Cat People*. The film has suggested that a woman may be pursued by a leopard. While walking at night, her tapping heels alternate with periods of silence during which the camera is on shadows and quietly rustling leaves, strongly suggesting—by the absence of sound—the padded silent footsteps of the leopard. The parallel editing of the two effects accelerates. Suddenly there is a loud, frightening screech—which turns out to be caused by a bus, whose huge form suddenly fills the screen.

We have already discussed how sound can help make a transition between scenes. Sometimes this can be done with sharp segues. The classic example is Hitchcock's *The 39 Steps,* in which a cleaning woman enters a room and discovers a dead body. Her scream segues into the screech of a train whistle and a shot of the train tearing along the countryside. A similar effect occurs in *The Godfather* when the screaming of a woman being beaten segues into the sound of a baby crying as we go to the next scene.

Much can be done with the absence of sound. Unexpected silence has a way of directing attention, perhaps because when we become attentive we quiet down and become aware of the slightest stimuli. A moving camera shot seems especially suspenseful when accompanied by silence, as though it is the hush before the expected payoff.

At the conclusion of *Bonnie and Clyde,* there is a moment of quiet as they stop their car to help someone who has presumably had car trouble. The relative silence is then broken by extensive submachine gun fire as they are killed.

In *Ikiru,* Watanabe has been told, in effect, that he is dying of cancer. As he leaves the doctor's office, there is silence on the sound track. He goes out onto the busy street, but there are still no sounds. Only when he just misses being hit by a passing car does the sound track burst into the reality of city traffic noises.

In *Kwaidan,* a Samurai is riding a galloping horse and shooting arrows at a target. A close-up of the horse's hoofs is accompanied by the loud sound of their pounding on the ground. Suddenly the hoof beats are silent even though they continue visually. The effect is striking.

The horrible massacre of peaceful Indians in *Little Big Man* is accompanied by noisy gunshots, screams and the cries of frightened horses as well as music. Then Little Big Man's Indian wife is killed. We go to silence. The massacre continues. Indians are shot. Horses mill wildly in the dust thrown up by the carnage. The screen is very active. But there is no sound. Then, fading up gradually, is the sound of "Garry Owen" played on flutes and drums. There is no other sound. It's an eerie scene.

Much of the violent destruction in the gym in *Carrie* and the incidents leading up to it are played MOS. There are some dialogue lines in the sequence—we can even read the lips of a boy who says something like "What the hell's going on?!"—but we don't hear the words. There is only the music background.

Sound can have symbolic use. In *Chinatown,* Jake responds to a call about a woman, goes to her place, enters and finds her dead. As he moves around, we hear the sound of a dripping faucet, which is ironic since she was killed because of the Los Angeles water scandal.

In Buñuel's *The Discreet Charm of the Bourgeoisie,* sound is used to obliterate dialogue. A jet plane noise drowns out an explanation of why characters are to be released from prison. This happens each of the three times that the explanation is repeated. We never do hear it. In *Don't Go Near the Water,* a Navy PR group picks a "sailor of the year," only to discover that every other word said by their sailor is an offensive obscene expression. But it is always blocked out by some sound, such as a boat whistle, which acts like a "bleep."

Sergio Leone makes effective use of sound, especially in the openings of his films where there is little dialogue. At the beginning of *Once Upon a Time in the West,* we hear a squeeking windmill sound, bird sounds, sounds of a telegraph key, a buzzing fly, a man cracking his knuckles, a train whistle, and then, finally, the sound of a harmonica (which becomes the signature of a main character). These sounds, isolated and amplified as they are, help create an atmosphere of tension and apprehension suitable to the impending ambush.

My Name is Nobody opens to a tolling bell. A main character enters a barber shop for a shave, unaware that the regular barber has been replaced by one of the men waiting to ambush him. As he gets his face lathered, we hear the ticking of a clock. The straight razor is stropped on the pseudo-barber's hand to amplified scraping sound. The main character shoves his gun in the man's stomach as the shaving starts. We hear a fly buzzing and chickens clucking outside. The clock sounds start again. There is an exaggerated sound of the razor shaving. The clock. The scrape of the razor on the cheek. The shave is finished. The central character gets up, checks himself in the mirror. One of the bushwhackers outside shoots the image in the mirror. The central character shoots them all. This is done in slight slow motion, and the sound of the last shot is drawn out, echoing like the sound of thunder.

Music

Music is one of those important elements in film which we think of as added during or after production by someone other than the screenwriter. However, a writer can suggest the use of music in his script and describe how he feels it can be used to augment or counterpoint the effect of a scene.

Music has the ability to create mood and emotion from a love theme (*Dr. Zhivago, Romeo and Juliet, The Way We Were*) to the feeling of adventure and grandness (*Exodus, Gone With the Wind, Lawrence of Arabia, Star Wars*). A Strauss waltz accompanies the space vehicles and astronomical bodies floating across the screen in *2001*. The theme song of *High Noon* explains the concern of the main character. The haunting, animal-like theme music of Leone westerns sets the mood for the tense action (e.g., *The Good, the Bad and the Ugly*).

Mood sequences depend heavily on music to create the proper atmosphere and tone. Music can reinforce the intent or emotion of a scene or it can serve as counterpoint. In *The Birds,* the children's round sung in the schoolhouse as the birds assemble outside contrasts to the mounting danger and increases our tension through the irony. The banjo music of *Bonnie and Clyde* is an ironic contrast to the activities of the gangsters, though appropriate to the rather light tone of the film—which it helps create. As the computer HAL is being disconnected in *2001,* he reverts back to singing the song he learned when being first programmed: "Daisy, Daisy."

Through its ability to reinforce or counterpoint, music can strengthen a weak scene or moderate a scene that is too strong. Music can help build a scene and climax it—it's almost an essential in chase sequences. It can reinforce a suspense build or surprise and shock with a sting chord. Film composers usually avoid the heightened intensification known as "Mickeymousing," which overscores each move of the film.

Music can evoke emotion and feeling so successfully because it works beneath our conscious level. It can cue us as to how to respond to the film or to a particular scene of the film without taking up additional screen time or space. The type of music helps lead us to expect a light, comic action or a romantic one, a stirring adventure or a serious drama. Music can also set a time period or a location and suggest socio-economic and ethnic groups: Indian drums in a western; the folk tunes of John Ford westerns; the rock music of *Easy Rider,* suggesting the drug culture of the 1960s; the pop tunes that catch the atmosphere of the 1950s and early 1960s in *The Last Picture Show* and *American Graffiti;* the music from 1968 that backgrounds *Coming Home;* the juxtaposing of country and western songs and classic pieces in *Five Easy Pieces;* and the radio programs and music from 1936 that help create the atmosphere in *Paper Moon*.

Music can identify characters. In *M,* the psychopathic killer is identified by a blind man from the Grieg melody he whistles when planning a killing. In *Dr.*

Zhivago, when Zhivago longs for Lara and determines to search for her in a Russia torn by civil strife and revolution, we realize his intention by hearing Lara's theme played on the sound track. A certain musical quality can help a characterization, as does the melancholy trumpet played by Gelsomina in *La Strada* or the harmonica in *Once Upon a Time in the West,* which serves as the signature for a character. Music can suggest a character's emotion by joining with the actor's expressiveness and the film's context, thus further enabling us to understand the feeling.

The presence of music, with all its tone, color and evoked feeling, can add so much to the meaning of the film. So, also, can the absence of music within music-informed sequences. If we are hearing music, and the music stops, we know something new or different is about to happen. The climax gunfight showdown of *Once Upon a Time in the West* builds with music behind it as the men take their positions, but then there's a moment of silence as the camera moves in on the central character's face and we enter a memory flashback. The music begins again in the flashback as we see that the men he is confronting were those who cruelly hanged his brother. The music stops as we come out of the flashback and into the quick shooting. Later, the character and his friend leave town—to music accompaniment—but the music stops momentarily as the friend dies. We didn't even know he was wounded, but now his unsentimental death happens offscreen with a groan and the sound of his body falling to the ground. The music begins again as the film concludes. As shown by this tight climax sequence, knowing when to leave out music is as important as using it.

Music may well be most effective when it is used sparingly, at selected, significant moments, as is the solo cello playing Bach in Bergman's *Through a Glass Darkly*.

Music can originate in a film—plot music—as well as be added as "background music." In John Ford westerns, the cavalry frequently sings some of the folk songs or army songs that are also used as the background music of the film. Sam plays again "As time goes by" in *Casablanca*. There's an exciting banjo duel in *Deliverance*. *A Clockwork Orange* features Beethoven's *Ninth* throughout. The "Colonel Bogey March" is whistled by the British troops in *The Bridge on the River Kwai*. As the main character falls dead in *Public Enemy,* a phonograph playing "I'm forever blowing bubbles" gets stuck in a groove.

Television series use theme songs as well both to identify the series and to establish the situation and characters.

The musical score of a film is usually the responsibility of the composer, director and producer, yet the impact of music on the meaning of a scene is so important that a writer shouldn't ignore this potential when writing. He should allow for the use of music in the script and describe it when he thinks it's important for a scene.

REFERENCES

1. From the opening teaser of *The Prisoner,* a television series created by Patrick McGoohan.
2. Eric Berne, *Games People Play* (New York: Grove Press, 1964).

Also:

Antonioni, Michelangelo. *Blow-Up*. New York: Simon and Schuster, 1971.

Chayefsky, Paddy. *Network*. Unpublished screenplay, *c*. 1976.

Goldman, William. *Butch Cassidy and the Sundance Kid*. Unpublished screenplay, 15 July 1968.

Kubrick, Stanley. *A Clockwork Orange*. New York: Ballantine Books, 1972.

Peploe, Mark, Peter Wollen and Michelangelo Antonioni. *The Passenger*. New York: Grove Press, 1975.

10

Comedy

> Give me a number from one to ten.
> Eleven.
> Right.[1]
>
> —The Marx Brothers

IS COMEDY WRITING a gift? Perhaps more than any other writing, comedy writing is visceral, and a sense of timing, which is so important to comedy, is, perhaps, a gift of sorts. On the other hand, comedy writing is a skill that can be acquired through practice. In this chapter, we'll look at comedy and some techniques of comedy writing.

Man (with perhaps a few higher primates) is a laughing animal. If we are apparently the only animal aware of non-existence—the starting point of tragedy—we are also the only animal aware of our imperfections and of the deviation between life as it is and as it ought to be. This self-consciousness is the starting point of comedy. For comedy is a mirror of our human absurdities. It shows us our weaknesses in an easy, tolerant way, arousing laughter rather than anger. Comedy shows us our pretentions. It says: all men are fools.

A certain detachment operates in comedy—the comic distance. We know that it is not real and so are reassured by the comic approach. Even in broad, low, slapstick comedy, no permanent harm results no matter how brutal the physical pounding. So Ben Turpin can get a foot caught in a rope attached to a car and have to hop down the road after it at fifty miles an hour. Or silent film comic Larry Semon, setting out to rescue the ingenue, can rush at a locked door behind which the villain holds her captive only to have the villain throw it open as he approaches. Semon rushes through it, across the room, out the window on the other side, dives down three stories and lands on his head! Immediately, in the next scene he's into some other adventure! There's a strong element of play in comedy; it's not serious but only kidding.

So, too, there is less empathy in comedy. We identify less with comic characters (at least to the extent that they are consistently comic). It wouldn't be so funny if we identified too closely with the character who takes a smashing slip on a banana peel.

Comedy involves our having an attitude of superiority. We feel superior to the comedy and the comic character. They are the ones doing the stupid things, falling prey to the embarrassing and ridiculous situations and looking foolish. In much comedy we are laughing at the characters (although in more sentimental or sophisticated comedy we may be laughing with them). There is an aggressive quality in our response to the comic.

As with suspense, one aspect of our comic superiority occurs when we know something that the character doesn't know. In an *All in the Family* episode, Archie believes he has saved a woman's life by giving her mouth-to-mouth resuscitation. However, we know that the recipient was not a woman at all but a transvestite. We wait expectantly with our superior knowledge for the moment when Archie finds out. Then we enjoy his abashed reaction. Comedy operates like suspense in other ways, too, but the expected payoff we build to is laughter and amusement.

There is a cruel element to comedy, which is permitted by the not-for-real aspect of it. It contains an element of derision. We enjoy the misfortune of others—the pie in the face, the hapless cuckold, the violence of Punch and Judy, Laurel hit by Hardy or Costello picked on by Abbott. There is a certain pleasurable superiority in seeing it happen to someone else (all the while knowing it is comically "safe"). It's funny when in *The General* Buster Keaton loads and lights the fuse of a mortar on his train tender only to find that the movement of the train joggles the barrel down until it is pointed at him; at the same time, his foot is caught on a chain which anchors him as the helpless target.

Similarly, we enjoy seeing a narrow escape and our enjoyment is heightened if the character doesn't realize it until afterwards, or if he never realizes it and we laugh as well at his stupidity or naiveté.

We enjoy destructiveness in comedy—car crashes; pie throwing, leaving the bakery in shambles; or complete demolition, as shown in *Big Business*—one of the funniest of the Laurel and Hardy short comedies—wherein the comic duo wreck a house while their adversary, the home owner, destroys their curbside car.

Comedy is often iconoclastic, destructive of aspects of our culture and society. Comedy is by nature impolite, impious and sacrilegious, as with the great comedy of Chaplin, Tati, Sennett, Fields, Keaton, the Marx Brothers and Lenny Bruce.

Comedy is exaggeration. Characters and events are overdrawn for comic effect. It is incongruous. Comedy has been defined as, in part, frustrated expectation. The laugh comes from the shock of an unresolved contradiction (along with the reassurance that this is not real or serious). We see this with the incongruous punch line when one reality is replaced with another. The punch line is consistent with the development of the joke, yet it isn't. It "fits," yet departs from expectation. In *Sleeper,* Woody Allen finds a two-hundred-year-old Volkswagen in a cave and it starts instantly. Volkswagens are supposed to start, so it is consistent, yet it is incongruous as it shouldn't start after two hundred years. He also tries to avoid a dangerous assignment by making the point about how helpless he is when he says, "As a kid I was beaten up by Quakers." We expect to hear of someone violent who beats up others. Quakers are connected with violence by being anti-violence pacifists. By some convoluted logic, the punch line "fits" even though by another reality it is incongruous. It is this juxtaposition of two related but incongruous contexts that gives rise to this theory of comedy.

We are the incongruity. We are capable of such transcendence yet incapable of controlling ourselves. And this, Walter Kerr feels, is the basic joke. Kerr points out that comedy frequently occurs when the situation is hopeless. He quotes James Agee, who describes the comic situation as Laurel and Hardy trying to move a piano across a narrow suspension bridge hanging over a deep chasm in the Alps and midway across they meet a gorilla.[2]

Laughter has been frequently called a tension release, and so it is. But this is not necessarily so. Psychological studies of laughter to jokes show there may be increased arousal which can persist even after the punch line.[3]

There is a broad range of comic styles extending from the farcical slapstick of the Keystone Kops through television situation comedies to the reality of sophisticated, sentimental comedy, such as that of Neil Simon, Billy Wilder and George Cukor. Subject matter for comedy is as broad as human experience and often concentrates on human foibles (miserliness, clumsiness, stupidity), forbidden feelings and wishes and hidden attitudes (sex, romance, death) and social conventions and institutions (marriage, hospitals, the police).

When writing comedy, it's important to establish the comic climate early in the film. Cue us, the audience, that it's a comedy. (This will be helped by the film's titles, the actors, the subject matter, music, dialogue and initial action.)

Comedy is fast-paced. It should be kept moving. If a certain funny bit or joke is holding up the scene, consider dropping it.

Comedy seems most effective when the audience is not aware that it is so obviously trying to be funny. The comedy should seem to flow naturally no matter how weird it is. A frequent problem with television comedy is that a comic line or action is too obviously set up. We are too aware that the writer is now making a joke, rather than that the characters are (comically) expressing themselves.

Remember to allow for the laugh when writing comedy. Give some time after a joke or comic bit before giving an important bit of subsequent action or information because the audience may still be laughing. We want to keep comedy moving, but if it moves too fast after something very funny, it steps on the laugh and loses some of what follows. This is part of that all-important matter of comic timing. Another part of it is knowing just when to deliver the comedy. The latter may well be a gift.

Through *comic relief,* humor serves important functions in serious drama. By providing a break in the tension, it gives the audience a moment's breather before starting to build the tension again. A mixture of the very serious and the comic can have a powerful impact, as in the tragicomic (or serio-comic), where the serious seems all the more striking because of its contrast to the comic. We see this in a film such as *One Flew over the Cuckoo's Nest,* which contrasts McMurphy's zany behavior with his final tragic end. This happens, too, in Makavejev's very exciting *Sweet Movie,* in which much of the wild sex farce is contrasted with the interjected newsreel clips of the unearthing of the bodies of massacred Polish officers.

Another mixture of the serious and the light occurs in films that treat normally serious matters or characters in a humorous, light way, as with *Bonnie and Clyde* or *Butch Cassidy and the Sundance Kid.* For example, at the end of the latter film, the two men are surrounded by over a hundred Bolivian troops. Wounded and facing certain death, Butch says: "—Wait a minute—" Sundance: "What?" Butch: "You didn't see Lefors out there?" (Lefors is a well-known marshal who had been chasing them.) Sundance: "Lefors? No." Butch: "Good. For a minute I thought we were in trouble."

A similar light tone often pervades television shows and characters, as in *The Rockford Files, Quincy, McMillan and Wife* and *McCloud.*

Just as serious drama often has scenes of comic relief, so comedy has the serious break. In Marx Brothers comedies, Harpo plays a serious harp solo or Chico does a piano piece. In *Harold and Maude,* there is the moment when we see a concentration camp number on Maude's arm.

The comic character is all important to comedy. Just as effective characters form the story in a drama, comedy, too, often grows out of a comic character. Type characters are more common in comedy, for we don't want them so realistic that we empathize too much with them. (However, realistic characters are found in the more sophisticated comedy.) Comic characters can appear comically in basically unfunny situations (*M*A*S*H*), or comic characters can act seriously in a comic situation which we know is not to be taken seriously. In Woody Allen's *Take the Money and Run,* there is a sequence in which Virgil is trying to rob a bank. After patiently standing in line, he hands his hold-up note to the teller. However, the teller can't make out the writing. He interprets it as "I have a gub. Abt natural." The bank manager can't figure it out either. They all get involved in a seemingly serious discussion over the meaning of the note. In a television special, Bob and Ray did a sketch underscored with a strong, pounding music beat that suggested a tense adventure program crisis high point. This was further accentuated by the camera work—low angles and intense intercutting. The actors, too, played their roles with serious intensity. But the action is simply the trivial and ordinary activities of Bob and Ray leaving their homes, getting into their cars and driving into traffic.

The Comic Situation and Comic Premise

Much comedy develops out of a situation that has obvious comic potential. A comic premise may serve for an entire film or for a segment within the film. Archie Bunker's giving mouth-to-mouth resuscitation to a transvestite is a very funny premise for an *All in the Family* episode. So is the idea in *Sleeper* of cloning a person from his nose. In a more sophisticated comedy, a situation can presage the happy ending, as in *The Goodbye Girl,* wherein an attractive man and woman are forced by circumstances to share an apartment. Even though they start out disliking each other (it seems), we know they'll get together at the film's end.

The film *M*A*S*H* develops a number of comic situations or premises. In one, a microphone planted near the lovemaking cot of Major Burns and Hot Lips (the nurse) broadcasts a moment by moment live account of their lovemaking over the camp's public address system. Another episode is built around the idea of a hugely endowed army dentist who contemplates suicide when he experiences a single case of temporary impotency.

One of the main characters in *Some Like It Hot* is impersonating a female in order to escape from a gangster. He is pursued by an aroused millionaire with lascivious intentions. This develops to where the millionaire is so persuasive that when he finally proposes marriage the character forgets himself and consents. Only when they are about to begin a honeymoon on the millionaire's yacht does the character remember and says he isn't a woman. To which his ardent suitor cavalierly responds, "Nobody's perfect."

The rather sophisticated film comedy *A Touch of Class* develops much of its comedy around the difficulties of a married man consumating a love affair. As the romantic pair fly to Spain, a friend of the man turns up on the plane, so they have to sit separately. After a spat in which they throw clothes and furniture around their room, they start to make passionate love, but his pants' zipper sticks. Finally it appears they are going to make it, but he suffers a back spasm. The complications to the basic comic premise keep developing.

In *The President's Analyst,* there's a very clever premise that doesn't emerge until near the end. In the plot, all sorts of foreign agents are trying to kidnap the President's analyst because of what he knows about the President. The analyst flees from the pressure he's under; even the FBR and the CEA are after him—to kill him if necessary. He is alternately captured by different agents until finally a congenial Russian gets him. As they drive along, the camera dollies back to reveal that they are being watched by someone on a television monitor. Soon the analyst is snatched by this new adversary, the most dangerous of all—The Phone Company! After some wild adventures, he finally shoots his way free of the guards and the smiling, human-like robots of The Phone Company. The film ends with a celebration Christmas party only to have the camera pull back to reveal that they are being observed on TV by many robots from The Phone Company. A clever idea for a comedy.

Comic Prop or Device

Film comedy has always had an affinity for the malfunctioning gadgetry of our modern world. Just about any machine can go beserk. Almost any object can serve as a comic prop. Comedians have interacted with furniture, pianos, cars, escalators, paint cans and pets. A hand becomes stuck in a jar, an elevator door closes on a character, machinery goes haywire (like the assembly line feeding machine in *Modern Times*). The Tin Lizzies of the Keystone Kops did all sorts of weird tricks. W.C. Fields did very funny things with a pool cue.

Charlie Chaplin did much with comic props. In his Keystone comedy *Dough and Dynamite,* he uses dough as bracelets, boxing gloves, quicksand, a slingshot, a discus, a mallet and a chair. Chaplin could make props into anything. Empty pie tins and a pair of ham bones become a xylophone. A pair of beer bottles become binoculars. He shoots dice as though he were a pitcher delivering a hard-breaking curve ball. He passes out dinner plates as though he were dealing cards. In *The Pawnshop,* Charlie is given a clock to inspect by a customer. He applies a stethoscope to it. He cuts open the lid with a can opener. He examines it with a jeweler's eyepiece, a dentist's forceps and a hammer. He takes an oil can to it. He finally returns to the customer just a collection of parts.

In *The Return of the Pink Panther,* Inspector Clouseau struggles with an enormously powerful vacuum cleaner that sucks a painting, clothing, a slipper and the chest of a hefty masseuse. It sucks a parrot into its canister and when Clouseau removes the top to release the bird, he gets sucked in. The freed parrot rewards him by defecating on him. The beserk vacuum cleaner was a device much explored by silent film comedians such as Billy Bevan.

In *Midnight Cowboy,* there is a lovemaking scene during which the lovers roll back and forth on a TV remote-control unit laying on the bed, changing channels to all sorts of programming, including an exercise program ("up-down, up-down"), a Japanese monster movie and a Catholic theologian.

In *Take the Money and Run,* Virgil tries to play his cello in the school marching band, but since it is necessary to be seated to play the cello, he plays a few notes but then must stop and get up to move his chair to keep up with the band.

One comic sequence in *The Return of the Pink Panther* serves no plot function but is there just to make us laugh. Inspector Clouseau is carrying a suitcase which he maintains "never leaves my hand." It gets caught opposite him in a revolving door and the comic interaction develops from this. Clouseau gets whacked by the door, constantly misses retrieving the bag, gets pushed around by others using the door and is bounced around inside the door. A revolving door seems to invite comic use.

Physical Comedy

Entanglements with props and objects are effective in film because they fit the visual quality of the medium; physical comedy works well on film. Pies in the face, buckets of water on the head and trips on banana peels were hallmarks of the silent comics. From the zany chase sequences of the Keystone Kops to the physical humor of Woody Allen, Peter Sellers, *Monty Python's Flying Circus,* Jerry Lewis and Mel Brooks, there have been unlimited opportunities with visual comedy.

Comedy has always had a special affinity for the physical. If tragedy rarely shows a commode, comedy has a fondness for such and for all the body functions and weaknesses our flesh is heir to. Comedy enjoys outhouses, body itches and scratches (Chaplin made marvelous use of his cane to do an itch here, a scratch there), toothaches, bellyaches, gout, ice packs, mummy-like bandages, sneezes, fingers stuck in holes, feet caught in doors or wastebaskets, kicks in the pants, farts (the cowboy bean-eaters in Mel Brooks' *Blazing Saddles*), enormously endowed women (Mae West) and men (the dentist in *M*A*S*H*), toupees, smashed hats, long underwear and fallen trousers.

Within a film, an entire *sequence* may be given to a comic situation or sketch (as Clouseau pursuing his suitcase in the revolving door). A shorter comic segment is a *comic bit,* such as a pesky fly which keeps returning during an attempted seduction or someone in a similar scene that calls for seriousness or decorum trying to get gum from his shoe or his foot from a wastepaper basket. A *visual joke,* such as a pratfall, is a short action similar to a verbal wisecrack or one-liner. It happens quickly and gets the laugh. The *comic reaction* is a special kind of visual joke; it is very important in comedy, especially television comedy. Jack Benny and Archie Bunker are well-known for their reactions.

Ernie Kovacs was a television comedy innovator. He once presented the Swan Lake ballet beautifully danced—by a company in gorilla costume. Perhaps his best-known sketch is the Nairobi Trio, featuring three musicians in gorilla costumes—a conductor, a pianist seated at a small piano and a percussionist. They move slowly and mechanically, something like metal wind-up toys. At one point—when the conductor isn't watching—the percussionist gorilla slowly turns and knocks the conductor on the head with his mallets. As the conductor slowly turns to question what happened, the percussionist equally slowly resumes his regular position as if nothing had happened. In the pause after the hit, we project into their reactions even though it is difficult to read expressions through their gorilla masks. The action repeats a number of times, culminating with the conductor smashing a vase over the percussionist's head. The steady beat of the music, the slow, mechanical movements, the sustained reactions, the timing of each action—all are impeccably done.

A familiar visual comic piece is the mirror bit. It usually happens when the comic character is trying to hide from detection and when seemingly discovered pretends he is the mirrored reflection of the person chasing him. The comic imitates the movements and actions of the other. Soon the antagonist gets suspicious and tries to expose the comic by quick and unusual gestures, but the "reflection" adroitly continues—up to some point of discovery. This technique was probably first introduced to films by early silent comedian Max Linder in a variation in which his servant breaks his mirror at the moment he is about to shave, so the servant impersonates Linder in the empty frame, faithfully duplicating his shaving gestures. The mirror bit has been done by Harpo Marx, Lucille Ball and Danny Kaye.

A similar bit was used by Kaye in *Knock on Wood.* He is hiding under a desk where his two antagonists sit down to talk. The two men start reaching down and scratching, slapping and patting their legs under the desk. Instead of doing it to their legs, however, they do it to Kaye's. So he must match what they do on their legs to avoid discovery. Naturally, it gets more and more involved as it continues.

A funny visual bit, with pathetic overtones, occurs in *The Gold Rush;* Chaplin's Little Tramp celebrates Thanksgiving in a desolated arctic cabin by boiling a shoe for dinner, basting it as might a professional chef, sucking flavor from the nails, and twirling the laces on a fork as if they were spaghetti.

Chase sequences can be marvelously comic. There's a fine one in *What's Up, Doc?* Several cars are chasing a pedal wagon down San Francisco streets. At an intersection part-way down one hill, workmen are crossing the street with a large plate glass window, while overhead, another workman on a tall ladder is trying to hang a large banner over the street. The workmen carrying the glass pane frantically dodge back and forth as the cars just miss them on either side—something so improbable in itself that it is funny. Just when they believe they're safe on the sidewalk, a car turns around and knocks over the ladder causing the workman hanging the banner to grab onto it for support. The banner breaks loose on one end. He swings on it and hits and breaks the window pane. (This is also an example of the comic delay.)

Comedy Techniques

Comedy uses a variety of techniques. Those I've observed are exaggeration, absurdity, incongruity, the comic build, the topper, the reversal, the Rule of Three, the recall, the delay, running gags, the misunderstanding, jokes, one-liners, word-play, satire, suggestive humor, insult and deflating the pompous. These may not exhaust the possibilities, but they will give you some ideas. I suggest you watch film and television comedy to see how they get comic effects. Listen for the laughs—your own and those of the audience (not the laugh track)—then determine what produced the laughs.

Exaggeration, Absurdity, the Incongruous and the Outrageous

Exaggeration is basic to so much comedy for what is exaggerated, in reality, is the human comedy which we all live. Comedy often exaggerates to the absurd. There is a scene in *The Geisha Boy* in which Jerry Lewis's character is being chased by a huge Japanese. Jerry is in a communal bath when the man bursts in, trips and belly flops into the pool. A reasonable splash results. Cut to the hall outside as Jerry is trying to get away, with a thigh-deep wave of water pursuing him down the corridor. Cut to outside in the street: as Jerry runs out of the building, a huge wave of water bursts through the door and windows of the building. (This not only exaggerates the splash, but follows the Rule of Three to be discussed later.)

We've already mentioned the absurd, surreal events in *The Disorderly Orderly*—when Jerry's character is trying to fix the "snow" on a television set and a real blizzard blasts out from the screen or when he snaps his fingers and a large flame shoots from his thumb.

In one episode, Archie Bunker goes on a TV show and advocates that the way to solve airplane hijackings is to arm all the passengers, to pass pistols out to them when they get on the plane.

What is exaggerated is often incongruous as well. In the short film *The Boat,* Buster Keaton throws the anchor out of a boat—and it floats! While in *Steamboat Bill, Jr.,* Keaton, on shipboard, knocks a life preserver into the water—it immediately sinks! In *Take the Money and Run,* Virgil, imprisoned on a chain gang, is punished by being locked in a sweatbox with an insurance salesman. In *The Pink Panther Strikes Again,* a woman is tortured by a gloved hand with steel nails which is drawn down a blackboard with a screech.

On the BBC radio program *The Goon Show,* a voice says: "I must ask you to parade your men." Second man: "Why?" First man: "I'm looking for a criminal." Second man: "Find your own, it took me years to get this lot."

Monty Python's Flying Circus is filled with the exaggerated, the absurd and the incongruous. One sketch features gangs of little old ladies (Hell's Grannies) who run around tripping people, stealing and beating up leather-jacketed motorcyclists. In another sketch, all the citizens are supermen (complete with costume). When one has a bicycle accident, we discover who their hero is—Bicycle Repairman! Another *Monty Python* sketch features a man on television reading nursery stories to children. Each story begins as a rather typical fairy tale, then to his astonishment quickly takes a blatantly realistic sexual twist.

In *Dr. Strangelove,* the survival kit check on the bomber reveals that the kit contains vitamin, pep, sleeping and tranquilizer pills, a combination Russian phrase book and Bible—postage-stamp size—nine packs of chewing gum, three pairs of nylon stockings and three lipsticks. At one point in the film, the British officer is trying to phone the President at the Pentagon to warn him of the unauthorized attack on Russia. He doesn't have enough change for the phone. He tries to call collect, but they refuse the call. Later, with the Third World War threatening, the President calls the Russian Premier and finds him drunk at a love nest. The dialogue is silly and childish. "I'm fine too . . . I'm glad you're fine . . . did a silly thing . . . ordered his planes to attack your country . . . of course I like to say hello . . ." They argue about who's sorrier while war threatens.

Understatement is almost a form of reverse exaggeration. Very serious subjects are treated lightly or trivially, as with the last example from *Dr. Strangelove*. Or, exaggeration can come from overplaying the trivial. In a *Monty Python* sketch in an English courtroom, the judge asks the defendant if he has anything to say prior to sentencing. The defendant begins humbly, but his plea swells until he ends giving an eloquent oration on the blessing of freedom and the need for mercy. When he's finally finished, the judge replies perplexed: "It's only a bloody parking offense."

Exaggeration is one way to add comedy to serious situations. The Little Tramp having to eat his shoe in *The Gold Rush* is a pathetic case, but the comic way in which it's done produces humor. The same is true of murder, death, suffering or even torture. If done in the comic spirit, with some exaggeration, they can be funny. The many duel scenes in Lester's *The Three Musketeers* are comic because they include pratfalls, blows that backfire, comic relief from a drunk who keeps getting bashed by a stray thrown bottle every time he tries to get up, and the comic reactions of those involved—plus the fact that we know it's a comedy and are prepared to respond as such. The same is true of the killing of the agents in *The President's Analyst*. It is done as humor and taken as such. In the disposal of the body in *Seven Beauties*, the character's reactions, his bumbling inefficiency in removing the dismembered body and the increasing difficulties he endures (e.g., a too-curious dog)—all produce laughter.

The Comic Build

Comedy often contains a build to a payoff climax—the punch line. This can climax a visual build, as does the surprise epiphany of nurse Hot Lips in the shower in *M*A*S*H* when the canvas of the shower tent is jerked away to reveal her in the altogether. Or it can be the punch line to a verbal build, as in this example from a *Rhoda* show when Rhoda is querying her very sexually active work partner, Myrna, about the "dating" of the clients that Myrna has been doing (which has helped business). Rhoda asks how many Myrna has been "dating."

MYRNA: How many do we have?

RHODA: Fourteen.

MYRNA: Fourteen? It seemed like more.

RHODA: What about Phil . . . he's gay.

MYRNA: Not anymore!

In Harold Lloyd's *The Freshman,* Harold is wearing a tuxedo which the tailor has had time only to baste, not sew securely. At the big college dance, Harold keeps ripping parts of the suit, which the tailor, who came along, quickly repairs while trying to stay hidden. One comic development follows another from this. At the end of the sequence, when his girl accepts his marriage proposal, Harold's chest so swells with pride that the buttons on his suspenders pop, culminating in his pants falling down. (Lloyd originally didn't want to use the familiar pants-falling-down gag, but put it in when he discovered that the scene needed some climactic event.)

A punch line often has a quality of the unexpected about it—a surprise twist that fits the context but in a new and unexpected way. In *Take the Money and Run,* Virgil carefully cuts a square of glass from a jewelry story window, but instead of stealing jewelry, he steals the pane of glass.

In a *Welcome Back, Kotter* episode, the principal of the school comes into the classroom and insults an old wino whom the class is trying to help get on his feet. Kotter reproves the principal by saying, "What do you do on Christmas Eve, go door to door telling kids there's no Santa Claus?" The principal shrugs and replies, "Well, someone has to do it."

On a *Maude* show, the housekeeper doesn't want Walter, Maude's husband and an ex-alcoholic, to taste one of her bourbon cookies for fear he'll revert. To counter Maude's dissent, the housekeeper tells of a teetotaler relative of hers who took a bite of fruitcake and became hooked. "He'd go to the worst parts of town. I'd have to pull him out of—bakeries."

In many of his early Sennett films, Chaplin would frequently take someone's, anyone's, pulse, as sort of a running bit. Later, in *The Bank,* he adds the twist that makes it a true joke. As a custodian in the bank, he gratuitously takes the pulse of a waiting customer, then, showing great concern, asks the man to stick out his tongue. Chaplin promptly wets a postage stamp on the man's tongue and sticks it on a letter. The twist payoff completes the joke.[4]

There is a funny build to a payoff in *Sex and the Single Girl.* Four cars full of people are racing after each other in an effort to properly unite the various lovers. The cars come to a tollgate serviced by a sad-funny attendant, who is waiting with extended palm to collect the toll. The speeding cars zip through without slowing down. As the first car passes, we cut to an insert of the hand as the attendant looks and sees a quarter in his palm. The second car races by—two quarters. The third car—three quarters. The fourth car zooms through—and in the attendant's hand is a dollar bill and the three quarters are gone.

The Topper

Often a punch line is itself ''topped'' with another punch line, the topper (for which the first punch line may be the straight line leading into the second). Just as the laugh to the original punch line is beginning to diminish, you hit them with another joke line. They have exhaled with the previous laugh and just as they are inhaling the new breath in, hit them with the laugh.

In an *All in the Family* episode, Mike appears wearing a shoulder bag. Archie gives a disagreeable reaction and Mike asks him what's wrong with it. Archie replies: ''If you don't know, I'll spell it out for you.'' Archie makes a faggy face and minces: ''F-a-g.'' (This gets a laugh.) ''Fruit!'' (This gets a bigger laugh.)

In an episode of *Taxi,* a somewhat drunk Jim volunteers to join Latka in fighting for his country's revolution. Jim: ''The tyrannical despot will soon learn the name of Jim—uh—'' (as he can't recall his last name). Alex: ''Ignakowski.'' Jim: ''Right, see, already it's spreading.''

In one of his films, Chaplin is shown being very polite and considerate to an elderly drunk in a flophouse. He makes up the man's bed, then hits him on the head with a mallet to put him to sleep. Then he kisses him goodnight.

The Reverse or Switch

There's often a laugh in the twist reverse on a developed expectation or a consistent action. We see it as the comic boastfully says, ''I'm not scared, I'm not scared,'' and then, when the hidden passage opens: ''I'm scared.'' Or Lucy in the *Peanuts* comic strip repeatedly assuring Charlie Brown that she won't pull the football away this time but will let him kick it, then pulling it away at the last minute.

In one episode of *Mary Hartman, Mary Hartman,* Mary has a sexual relationship with the policeman, Dennis Foley, while he is in the hospital recuperating from a heart attack. She feels terribly guilty about it since it could have had harmful effects. She talks to a social worker about this terrible ''thing'' that she did. He keeps assuring her that he is a professional social worker and has heard everything. Nothing bothers him; she can tell him. So she does. ''Oh, my God!'' he strongly overreacts.

In a *Maude* show, Walter has a disturbing dream which he's embarrassed to share with Maude, for he's certain she'll laugh. She swears she won't laugh. This builds back and forth for a while, with her steadfastly maintaining she won't laugh. Then he tells her that he dreamed he kissed someone. What's so bad about that? It was Arthur. And Maude laughs.

In *Little Big Man,* Jack and his wife Olga have just lost their business. Up rides General Custer, proudly seated on his horse. Go out west, he advises them, that's where things are happening. Olga gives out a wail. Jack explains that she's afraid of Indians. General Custer assures them that there is nothing to fear from Indians—"I give you my word." Cut to Olga screaming against Jack as the stagecoach in which they are riding is under wild Indian attack.

A type of reversal occurs in an Ernie Kovac show in which we watch a man at a shooting gallery shooting down wooden ducks that pop up as targets. Then another duck flips up and a toy cannon behind the duck fires at the man.

A switch occurs on *All in the Family* when an angry Edith caps her argument with Archie by shouting back at him *his* favorite expression: "Stifle!" It gets a big laugh. (In part, I'm sure, from our seeing him get an overdue censure and seeing Edith asserting herself.)

It may be a type of reverse that occurred on a *Happy Days* episode. A street gang is threatening a fight, and one of the show's regulars tries to break a pop bottle to use as a protective weapon against the gang. But it won't break. Each time he tries to smash it, it just bangs. Later, after the danger is over, he takes a drink from the bottle, sets it down on the table—and it breaks.

The "Rule of Three"

Not a rule, of course, but a guiding principle which states that when building a joke, it is usually effective to use two builds and then the punch line—a total of three. Two seems too few, four too many. I first heard of this from a magician colleague who mentioned it as a way of handling sleight of hand. Set up twice, then deliver the payoff; do the trick "properly" to mislead the audience, then do it again; the third time do the sleight of hand trick. It is used in a great many verbal and physical comic bits. As in a *M*A*S*H* episode when a general is trying to persuade Hawkeye to become his personal physician. "Do you know what this could mean to you?" he asks. Hawkeye replies, "Sure—the moon, the stars, and your high school letterman sweater."

One of the running bits on the *Barney Miller* television series was the gentle sarcasm that Fish, one of the series' regulars, expressed when talking about his wife. In one episode, Barney comments to Fish after the latter has just made another crack about his wife.

BARNEY: You should be happy you've got a wife who is gentle—

FISH: —Uh-huh—

BARNEY: —Considerate—

FISH: —Uh-huh—

BARNEY: —Attractive—

FISH: Let's not go too far.

A similar progression of three occurs in a bit from a *Nancy Walker* television show. An actor is pretending to threaten a producer in order to show the man that he can play the role of a psychotic killer in a film.

ACTOR: This afternoon I wanted to commit suicide.

PRODUCER: So what do I care. That's not my problem.

ACTOR: And I'm still feeling so bad about it that I may well kill myself.

PRODUCER: That's not my problem.

ACTOR: And take you with me.

PRODUCER: That's my problem!

This is also an example of the reverse.

In *Duck Soup,* the Marx Brothers are choosing from among themselves a volunteer who will sacrifice his life for his country. Chico counts around the four of them with some strange round designed to come up with an odd man out. But it ends up on himself. "I did it wrong." He does it again, with the same result. He does it the third time and it ends up on Harpo.

The Recall

A comic bit that is used in a film and then used again in a different context or with variation later in the film is all the funnier when we remember back to its original use. In a *Monty Python* episode, a secretary tells her boss a very poor joke. It is so bad that he has to comment on it by telling her how horrible it is. She bursts into tears and says, "But it's my only line." Later in the program, there's a comic sketch about a newly married couple who are shopping for a mattress. But they are advised not to say the word "mattress" to the salesman, because when he hears the word, he puts a paper bag over his head and then others in the store must go through an elaborate (and ridiculous) ritual to get him to remove it. The husband, however, slips and says it. They go through the ritual. Then the husband mistakenly says "mattress" again. The ritual is performed again, and everyone is aghast that someone should say it to the salesman twice. Then the wife says, "We'd like a mattress." How could she?! She replies, "But its my only line!" This is all the funnier since it refers us back to the earlier sketch.

In the *M*A*S*H* episode in which Hawkeye turns down becoming a general's personal physician, he at one point expresses what being a doctor means to him. He flashes his lapel to show his medical insignia, but it isn't there, it's missing. (He jokes about leaving it in a patient.) Near the end of the show, in a comic situation, he makes to flash it again. "I'm a doctor, see." Of course, there's nothing there. We laugh in part because we recall the previous reference.

There's a sort of recall in another *M*A*S*H* episode when an unexploded bomb lies buried in the MASH compound and all the personnel fear they are facing imminent death. This gives the shy Radar the courage to approach a nurse and score with her by saying how he's always admired her and always wanted to tell her so and now with death near he can—and so on. It works for him. In the tag, after the bomb has proved to be filled with leaflets, Radar sees another skirted nurse (he thinks) hanging up her clothes. So he tries the same line on her. But "she" turns around and proves to be Corporal Klinger (the male who wears female clothes in an effort to get a medical discharge).

In *A Wedding,* a mother with half a dozen children is trying to find the bathroom. In the dressing room, she opens a number of mirrored doors before finding the one that leads to the bathroom. Later in the film, a security guard helps an aged, senile bishop upstairs to the bathroom. After the slow ascent, the guard leaves him in the dressing room—"Have a good day." The bishop opens the nearest door and looks puzzled staring into a linen closet.

The Delay

A delay occurs when we are set up for a joke or punch line, but then it's delayed a beat (pause) or longer before it hits. In Lester's *The Three Musketeers,* a man is seen carrying a large basket of eggs while a fight is occurring nearby. The fight knocks over some barrels which roll toward the man. He watches them coming, but the barrels stop just as they reach him. The expected fall doesn't occur. The man walks a few steps—and *then* he trips and falls into the basket of eggs.

In an *All in the Family* episode, Archie's visiting favorite niece Linda goes on a date with Lionel, a black neighbor. She leaves behind in the house a picture of her and Lionel together. The bigoted Archie comes in and sits down. Although Edith tries to keep Archie from seeing the picture, she can't manage it indefinitely. Archie leans over in his chair, casually glances at the picture, then settles back with his paper. There is a delay as the camera holds on his expressionless face. (And we wait in pleasurable anticipation.) Then suddenly it dawns on him, and we see the expected comic reaction. The *delayed reaction* is a common comic device. (The *double take* is similar, except there is a second comic reaction that occurs right after the first.)

The Running Gag

The running gag is a visual or verbal comic bit repeated a number of times throughout the film, sometimes with variation, sometimes with some build to it. A classic running gag occurs in the film (and stage show) *Hellzapoppin*. In the beginning, a deliveryman appears carrying a small plant and calling for "Mrs. Jones." He reappears periodically throughout the film trying to make his delivery, and each time the plant grows larger until it is a small tree that he is carrying around. At the end of the film, he comes in driving a large truck containing a huge tree, still looking for "Mrs. Jones."

In *Young Frankenstein,* Igor's humped back keeps shifting from left to right and back throughout the film. And in a parody of a typical motif in horror pictures, each time the name "Frau Brooker" is mentioned, the horses violently act up (handled comically, of course). The tourists are so concerned about his antics in *Mr. Hulot's Holiday* that each time he does something disruptive all the hotel windows suddenly light up. In *A Wedding,* the doctor is always brushing imaginary ashes off the breasts of the nurse, a young woman and others.

In *The Pure Hell of St. Trinians,* the wild girls from this madcap girl's school cause panic in the hearts of the bureaucrats who have to deal with the problem of the school and the girls. Early in the film, one man suddenly stops his normal routine and puts on a record of pastoral music and begins dancing around his office. His psychiatrist advised him to do so. Later, as threats and pressures from the girls increase, he is joined by his supervisor. Still later in the film, another superior takes up the comic dancing in the face of a new problem. At one point, a telephone call about a problem features the pastoral music heard on the other end of the line and we then imagine the dancing. The end titles of the film come over shots of the different characters, each in his own locale, doing this clumsy, tranquilizing ballet.

A variation of the running gag is comic bits that occur over many episodes of a television series. These might be typical gestures or expressions (Archie's abashed look, the upstairs offscreen toilet flush, his "Stifle;" J.J.'s "Dyn-o-mite" from *Good Times;* or Maude's "God will get you for that, Walter.") The Bing Crosby-Bob Hope road pictures featured a well-known bit when in a tight spot they would play pat-a-cake and end up punching their curious antagonists and usually escaping from a dangerous situation.

The Misunderstanding

A misunderstanding is a frequent source of comedy. Comic plots have been built around cases of mistaken identity. Romantic comedies frequently revolve around one partner mistakenly believing the other is involved with someone else. Disguised as a woman, one of the characters in *Some Like It Hot* is taken for a woman, made a proposal of marriage and almost follows through with it. In a classic sequence from *Modern Times,* Chaplin tries to return a red warning flag to the truck that dropped it and unknowingly becomes the flag-waving leader of a revolutionary parade.

In *Sleeper,* Miles and Lura are mistaken for expert doctors and find themselves in a hospital amphitheater operating room expected to clone the entire person of the Leader from his nose remnant.

A gun that is really a cigarette lighter gets confused with a real gun in *The Return of the Pink Panther,* with comic consequences. The Chief Inspector gets so angry with Clouseau that he shoots him—only it's with the lighter. The chief confuses the guns and in lighting a cigarette wounds himself at one point; later he accidentally shoots his assistant.

Humor can come from misread communication between characters as in a *Taxi* episode when a loaded and bewildered Jim asks help while taking a written test for a driver's license. Reading a question, he asks his friends, "What does a yellow light mean?" "Slow down" the answer comes back. So Jim repeats his request more slowly.

Jokes, One-liners, Gags, Wisecracks and Funny Stories

These are traditional comic standbys. Of the many varieties of jokes, here are a few. Groucho Marx was good with gag lines, as with his reply to being told that the garbage man is here: "Tell him we don't want any." Or, in response to "Mind if I join you?": "Why? Am I coming apart?" In *Young Frankenstein,* Dr. Frankenstein's future wife arrives to be met by him and his young female assistant. He tells his other assistant, Igor, to "grab the bags." Igor's reply is pure Groucho: "You take the blond and I'll take the one with the turban."

At one point in *Dr. Strangelove,* the air force general and the Russian ambassador are scuffling, so the President says, "You can't fight in here, this is a war room."

On a *Saturday Night Live,* Milton Berle points out that "Sex after seventy is terrific—especially the one in the winter."

In the beginning of Preston Sturges's *Sullivan's Travels,* the idealistic director is talking with his producers about a film. The dialogue, in part, is as follows.

It died in Pittsburgh.
What do they know in Pittsburgh?
They know what they like.
Then why do they live in Pittsburgh?

Redd Foxx frequently dropped one-liners on *Sanford and Son,* such as, "Tell him to take castor oil and run for office."

The story was told on the *Two Ronnies* (a BBC television program) about a man who had been in prison for twenty years and, having just come out, found at home a stub for a pair of shoes he was having repaired twenty years earlier. Out of curiosity, he stops by the cobbler's shop to check on them, telling his story to the cobbler: "I have this stub. . . ." Cobbler: "Heels and toes, and stitches around?" Man: "That's right." Cobbler: "They'll be ready Wednesday."

Word Play: Puns, Malapropisms, Goldwynisms and Allusions

Humor can come from how we use words: from misuse of words (a gross, absurd misuse is often called a malapropism after Mrs. Malaprop, who, in Sheridan's play *The Rivals,* constantly misused words); from puns (in which words with similar sounds but different meanings are used, or where there are two different, rather incongruous, meanings for a word); from allusions to meaning beyond that intended in the words; and from Goldwynisms (malapropisms credited, often apocryphally, to Samuel Goldwyn, the film producer).

Groucho Marx was rich with puns. "One morning I shot an elephant in my pajamas. How he got in my pajamas, I don't know. But that's entirely irrelephant." When, in *Monkey Business,* a woman tells Groucho that he's awfully shy for a lawyer, he replies: "You're right I'm shy. I'm a shyster lawyer." In *A Night at the Opera,* during a shipboard celebration, the band starts up with a rumba. Groucho invitingly asks the woman seated across from him: "Do you rumba?" She eagerly replies that she does, to which Groucho says, "Then take a rumba from one to ten."

A Night at the Opera also features the well-known bit between Groucho and Chico: the "Party of the First Part." Groucho is trying to get Chico to approve a contract. As the scene develops, they keep tearing off and throwing away the pieces of the contract that Chico doesn't like. Finally, Groucho reads the segment about the contract being void if one party proves to be insane. Chico objects. Groucho says that this is a standard part of all contracts: "It's the sanity clause." Chico replies: "You can't fool me, there is no 'sanity clause'."

Here are some more of Groucho's classics. "I used the past tense. But we're past tents now, we're living in bungalows." "You go Uruguay and I'll go mine." "I bagged six tigers . . . I bagged them to go away." "That's three quotes—add another quote and make it a gallon." "You can leave in a huff—if that's too soon, you can leave in a minute and a huff." "If you run out of gas, get ethyl—if you run out of Ethyl, get Mabel." In *Animal Crackers* he offers to marry two women. One objects: "But that's bigamy." He replies, "Yes, that's big of me, too." In *The Cocoanuts,* Groucho is giving a spiel selling Florida land lots. "You can even get stucco—oh yes, you can get stucko." This film also features a classic exchange as Groucho tries to explain to Chico his plans for building up the area. When he describes levees along the river, Chico asks if that's the Jewish neighborhood. Groucho points out the location of the viaduct leading over to the mainland and Chico asks "Why a duck?" They go on with this for a while. Groucho finally mentions a wire fence, and when Chico asks, "Why a fence?" Groucho calls it quits.

Archie Bunker frequently misuses words, such as saying "groinocology" for "gynecology." In one episode, Archie almost has a romantic entanglement with a woman but doesn't. As they part, Archie says they had better not see each other anymore; they'll be "like two sheeps that pass in the night." Once, when Archie and Mike are arguing about baseball, Archie comments about the change in the game when in 1947 Jackie Robinson broke the color barrier of the major leagues, which Archie says "changed the complexion of the game." (In this case, it was a deliberate pun.)

A classic play on words is the Abbott and Costello "Who's on first" sketch, featuring a baseball team of players with such names as Who, What and I Don't Know.

In an Aunt Flabby sketch on *Johnny Carson,* she mentions a recipe she makes for shish kebab on toast. She calls it "shish on a shingle." On a *Sanford and Son,* Fred responds to a Puerto Rican "buenas dias" greeting with, "Yeah, beans and disease to you, too."

The television program *Mork and Mindy* offers a number of opportunities for word play; because Mork comes from another planet, he can take our expressions literally. When someone asks if he and Mindy are close, he replies, "Sometimes we stand right next to each other." When going on a picnic, Mork brings a jar of ants, since Mindy said picnics and ants go together. Her father responds, "Those ants are revolting." Mork replies, "No, they're happy with their form of government." Once, as he walks into the apartment, he catches Mindy by surprise. "Oh, Mork, I didn't hear you come in." He replies, "Oh, shall I go out and do it again noisier?" Mork is entertaining Susan. She says "I'd like a little wine." So Mork obliges by whining for her.

Sometimes a joke derives its humor from its allusion to an outside reference that we will presumably understand. When the Egyptian leader Sadat went to Israel, Johnny Carson mentioned that there was some antagonism to his going as he found a camel's head in his bed (an allusion to the horse's head in the bed in *The Godfather*). In response to a warning that it might be dangerous to tape record a bribe attempt, a politician on the *Phyllis* television show naively answers, "What politician ever got in trouble taping conversations?"—alluding, of course, to Nixon and Watergate. A *Welcome Back, Kotter* television sit com episode features his students role-playing a sociodrama about married life while trying to persuade two engaged students that they are not prepared for marriage. Arnold Epstein, one of the role-playing students, plays the part of a child. Afterwards, Arnold says to Kotter: "You know, I just became an orphan. Little Orphan Arnold!"—alluding to the comic strip "Little Orphan Annie."

Some Goldwynisms include: Gentlemen, include me out. We're overpaying him, but he's worth it. If I want your opinion, I'll tell it to you. A verbal contract isn't worth the paper it's written on.

Satire, Irony, Parody and Burlesque

These are frequent forms of comedy and are often used for social comment. Burlesque and parody are the broad comic imitation of another film, television program or literary work. A spoof makes fun of its target by playing an exaggeration of it seriously. Satire is similar but not played so broadly. Irony exists when the communicated meaning is the opposite of what is actually said or done. Ironic devices include contrast, understatement, imitation, mockery masked in politeness and the like.

Woody Allen parodies films in *Bananas* and film styles and genres in *Take the Money and Run*. His *Play It Again, Sam* is a pleasant burlesque of *Casablanca,* especially at the end. Chaplin's *Modern Times* burlesques the factory production line. Gene Wilder's *The World's Greatest Lover* satirizes the Rudolph Valentino craze. Mel Brooks' *High Anxiety* is a takeoff on Hitchcock suspense films, with references to *Psycho, Vertigo, North by Northwest, Spellbound* and *The Birds*. *Young Frankenstein* parodies the Frankenstein genre. A number of Abbott and Costello films, such as *Abbott and Costello Meet Frankenstein,* parody horror films. Billy Wilder's *Some Like it Hot* was a parody of gangster films and of sexual love and romance.

The Last Remake of Beau Geste, besides being a parody of that classic, also parodies two traditional film transition devices. A spinning newspaper headline never stands still long enough to be read and the pages of a calendar fly off to show time passing and accumulate knee-deep on the floor.

The Apartment satirizes American business values of dedicated work, initiative and integrity by showing how an insurance clerk rises in the organization by loaning his apartment key to his superiors for their assignations. He is promoted rapidly until—ironically—he finally attains a key to the executive washroom.

Bob and Carol and Ted and Alice was a takeoff on open marriage and the authenticity fad. It is ironic that the only word spoken in *Silent Movie* is said by a mime. *Dr. Strangelove* is a fine satire on cold war antagonism.

Monty Python uses frequent parodies and spoofs of BBC announcers and programs, the army, politicians, the courts, royalty—just about anything and anybody. One of their parodies of TV sports features an Olympic-type coverage for the finals of men's hide-and-seek of which the previous record was some eleven-plus years. An army training session teaches the troops how to protect themselves against attackers armed with fruit. An army drill team includes swishy manuevers to the command, "Camp it up." Pseudoserious documentary treatment is given to the discovery of the Killer Joke and joke warfare.

Saturday Night Live does a number of parodies. Their Weekend Update is a takeoff on television news. They did a sketch about a child psychologist who was, herself, a young child. She was remarkably effective in her treatment but had to cut it short when she urgently had to go to the bathroom. An American car manufacturer had a commercial that featured a diamond being cut in the back seat of a car while it rides over difficult roads; they were making the point that it is a smooth ride. The *Saturday Night Live* parody featured a circumcision being performed as the car drove along; the car swayed, jolted around corners and braked suddenly for a bouncing ball that rolled out into the street.

The Suggestive: Sexual Innuendos and Double Entendres

Sexual innuendos and double entendres are, unfortunately, all too common on television. Done well, they can be quite fun, for we tend to take sex too seriously and a bit of humor with it can be refreshing. Regrettably, too much of it is at the snickering, adolescent level.

On an *Agnes* television show, a scene ends when an angry person picks up two candles and aggressively asks, "Where do you want me to stick these?"

Here are two from the BBC comedy show the *Two Ronnies*. In a newscaster sketch, it's announced that detectives are investigating the robbery of all the toilets in the police station. About the crime, "police say they have absolutely nothing to go on." In a mock documentary report, it was stated that "for centuries women have been beneath men—in the home, as well as in the office."

The Insult, Cut and Put-down

Verbal comedy can be as cruel as visual comedy. The joke at the expense of another, or of oneself, is common. Don Rickles is well-known as a comedian of the insult. Put-downs and cuts are usual on the "angry" sit coms of Norman Lear and often feature Archie vs. Mike, J.J. vs. Thelma, Maude vs. Walter and Fred Sanford vs. everybody. Fred can get in a dig when he promises to be kind to someone by saying "it's be kind to buzzards week." To a dentist whom he distrusts, he says, "Did you go to school? Or take a correspondence course?" Aunt Esther is one of his favorite targets, as when he calls her "old gorilla face."

Archie seems to thrive on putting down Mike—"Meathead." Once, when Mike says he doesn't notice anything unusual about Edith, Archie replies, "You wouldn't notice nothin' unless it was covered with food!" Talking about the depersonalization of modern life, Mike asks Archie if he wouldn't rather talk to a human being than to a computer, to which Archie replies, "Sure I would, but all I got is you." Once, when Mike makes a comment after being quiet for a while, Archie feigns surprise and says, "It talks! I thought that was a dummy outta the Wax Museum!" When Mike is contemplating an appendix operation, Archie comments, "Them doctors open him up, they might find themselves routin' around in a bottomless pit."

The *Laverne and Shirley* television show frequently gives the two male comic characters—Lenny and Squiggy—an initial comic entrance. They usually come in as if in answer to a previous uncomplimentary comment. In one program, the two women had made a great Christmas scene decoration. One comments, "All we're missing are the furry beasts." Then Lenny and Squiggy burst in.

Deflating the Pompous and Pretentious

We enjoy seeing the pompous deflated, the haughty brought low, rigid officiousness punctured. Comedy is often a threat to dignity, especially if the dignity is pretentious. Chaplin did this often. So did the Marx Brothers. In *A Night in Casablanca,* Harpo is leaning against a building when a sarcastic policeman comes by asking him if he's holding it up. Harpo affirms that he is. The outraged policeman yanks him away and the building collapses. There's a bit of the pompous about Oliver Hardy, and this overgrown child frequently gets his pretentions to maturity and sophistication punctured.

Often our pleasure comes from seeing someone get what they justly deserve. This can happen when Edith stands up to an egotistic Archie or when someone shows up the fatuous pseudo-conceit of Ted Baxter. It's also some of the enjoyment we get from seeing the proud and overconfident get theirs, as when the arrogant guardsmen of the Cardinal are defeated in duels with D'Artagnan and the Musketeers in Lester's *The Three Musketeers*.

The Pink Panther

We will analyze the comedy of three films. The first is Blake Edward's *The Pink Panther* (with Peter Sellers as Inspector Clouseau and David Niven as Charles).

The dominant storyline is the attempt of Sir Charles, really the famous jewel thief known as the Phantom, to steal the fabulous Pink Panther diamond. Another storyline is Inspector Clouseau's attempt to catch the Phantom, with a related implicit internal storyline of Clouseau's attempt to succeed in life as a well-meaning (though he is bumbling and ineffective) detective. There is a strong interpersonal storyline between Clouseau and his wife: he repeatedly tries to make love to her while she resolutely refuses to make love to him, since she is really the accomplice and lover of Sir Charles. There is a slight hint of romance developing between Charles and the Princess who owns the diamond, but his intentions are all business and stop short of actual seduction. A complication is caused by young George, the nephew of Charles, who comes to find his uncle while fleeing a bad debt, tries to seduce Clouseau's wife and later tries to steal the diamond himself.

The story develops this way. At a ski-resort hotel, Charles charms the Princess with the intention of stealing the diamond. He stages the kidnapping of her pet dog so that he can later rescue it and win her gratitude. Also at the hotel is Inspector Clouseau. Keeping an eye on him is his wife, who is really Charles's lover and accomplice. Charles romances the Princess but stops short of seduction; she gets drunk and passes out. Later she plans to leave the hotel, but Charles stages the rescue of her dog so that she will stay a while longer. Nephew George complicates things by trying to seduce Clouseau's wife and by discovering that Charles is the Phantom. He then sets out to steal the jewel for himself. But neither one gets the gem; it is already stolen, they discover. Clouseau gets a tip that leads him to Charles and finally arrests him and George after a number of bumbling attempts. But they are freed when, at the trial, Clouseau, the diamond being planted on him, is blamed for the Phantom's previous thefts. (It seems that the Princess, for her own reasons, had stolen her own diamond. Out of consideration for Charles, she permits the plant on Clouseau.) Charles, George and the wife all leave together. They have not stolen the diamond, but they are at least free for further adventures.

Clouseau really does little to catch the Phantom until near the film's end, when a tip puts him onto Charles. The surprise twist at the end promises Clouseau the success he seeks. For, while he will serve a short prison sentence—two or three years—he will then come out to be met by a horde of adoring females who believe he is the dashing and debonair Phantom.

The secondary storyline is developed over a series of bedroom scenes placed throughout the film in which Clouseau almost gets into bed to romance his wife, but is always blocked before he can successfully do so.

Here is how the film's comedy develops. The comic climate is established in the charming titles, which feature the cartoon character the Pink Panther. In the first few scenes, we learn of the wife's hidden identity and thus see the irony as Clouseau tells of his intention to search for the Phantom's female accomplice, whom we know to be his wife. A physical joke in the scene has him slip on the world globe in his office.

When Charles first plans the kidnapping, we are led to believe it will be of the Princess, then are surprised to see that it is only her dog that is taken.

There is some physical comedy as Clouseau and his wife arrive at their room in the hotel. He kisses her—and they both lose their balance and fall into the closet. He trips on the wastebasket. As he leaves to see the manager, his wife runs to Charles. So Clouseau is the victim of a variation on the old cuckold theme. This scene introduces two running bits in the film. One is the sickly sweet and solicitous way in which Clouseau and his wife speak to each other—with words such as: "Yes, my darling, my precious." "Thank you, my angel." "Thank *you,* my angel." All this provides added irony, for we know that she means none of it. Another running gag is that Clouseau is constantly suspicious that someone is spying on him and so he jerks open the door to catch whoever is there—and, of course, no one ever is. This occurs a number of times in the film and, as intended, he looks ridiculous doing it.

Later, as Clouseau starts to join his wife in bed, he has trouble undressing. She sends him down to get a glass of milk for her and, after he leaves, runs off to find Charles. Pajama-clad, Clouseau sneaks around every turn in the hotel corridors, expecting suspicious characters and spilling milk in the process.

When he's back in the bedroom, there's a sexual innuendo as she demurs that she's tense, and he swears he'll "do it gently, softly." We think sex. It turns out to be playing the violin in an attempt to relax her. Naturally, he plays badly. Sent to fetch her a sleeping pill, we hear him (offscreen) spill the pills on the bathroom floor. Coming back after putting out the light, he steps on and crunches his violin, commenting: who would care about a Stradivarius.

There's a romantic scene played between Charles and the Princess; it takes place in his room, complete with soft lights, music, a tiger rug, a fireplace and champagne. She seems vulnerable to seduction, but he gallantly holds off. She gets drunk and passes out. It is rather comic when he has to drag her body out.

George tries to kiss Clouseau's wife while she's giving him a skiing lesson. He loses his balance and tears helplessly down the steep mountain slope on his skis. This is funny, but it is also setting up a comic delay. In the next scene, Charles says goodbye to the Princess, who is about to leave on the train. Then he sees the man who stole her dog. He gives chase, catches the man (really his accomplice) and they stage a fight. Charles is about to return the dog when George comes down the slope and crashes into him.

In the hotel bar, Clouseau's hand is caught in a beer glass. Back in the room, he is about to join his wife in bed when he gets an anonymous phone call (from George, who is holding his nose) summoning him out of town to check a clue about the Phantom. (George is trying to remove Clouseau so that he can seduce his wife.) Clouseau does the jerk-open-the-door bit as he leaves.

The next scene is a classic "hiding characters" ploy. The wife summons Charles and they embrace, but then George arrives and Charles hides under the bed. George brings her flowers and tries to seduce her, but Clouseau returns and George hides in the bathroom. Clouseau had discovered the call was a ruse. He becomes more suspicious when he trips over the flowers, spilling them. While Clouseau readies for bed and a bellhop returns the repaired violin and a maid wipes up the spilled flowers, the two hiding characters move from one spot to another until each finally gets away. Clouseau becomes further suspicious when he sees wet footprints on the floor leading out of the bathroom (George hid in the shower), but the wife distracts him with an amorous embrace. Just when it appears that Clouseau will achieve his goal with her, there is an explosion from inside the bed covers; the champagne bottle one of her visitors brought blows its cork.

From the balcony, Charles watches George discover his burglary tools and the white glove that is the trademark of the Phantom. Then he falls off the balcony into the snow—to the surprise of passing hotel guests.

We are now nearing the end of the film, and some big scenes are in order. There is a masquerade party during which Charles and George separately plan to steal the diamond. They each happen to dress in gorilla costumes. Clouseau has received a tip about this but mistakenly arrests a dignified English Lord who is also in a gorilla costume. Clouseau is in a suit of armor, which makes for awkward movements. At one point, when the lights go out, he mistakes fireworks for a candle and prematurely ignites the entire fireworks display. George and Charles, in costume, each try to rob the safe, with comedy built around "who's-that-other-gorilla." They admit neither has stolen the gem and then join forces.

A wild chase scene played on the quiet night streets of the resort follows.

Charles and George escape in different open sports cars, each still in complete gorilla costume. They are pursued by police in a jeep and a car and by two people in a zebra costume. This is humorously presented from the point of view of a perplexed laborer who happens to be out on the street. Cars pass him in all directions, honking as they drive by. George and Charles stop and talk to each other, with the laborer standing between the two cars watching the two gorillas converse. (They completely ignore him.) The scene ends with the camera holding on the laborer while we hear an offscreen crash and horn noises; we see him slowly walk to where the cars are all piled high.

Charles and George are in jail. At the trial, Clouseau testifies that Charles was present in the area of all sixteen Phantom thefts. But the cross-examining attorney points out that someone else was too—Clouseau himself. And what of the fortune his wife recently spent on clothes (of which he knows nothing, of course). A nervous Clouseau pulls a handkerchief from his pocket to wipe his brow and out drops the Pink Panther diamond. Clouseau faints.

Outside the courtroom, as Charles, George and Clouseau's wife drive off, Clouseau is mobbed by a crowd of women who believe he is the romantic Phantom. The last scene shows him in the police car while the two policemen (one of whom's wife tried to rip off Clouseau's clothes) discuss what a fantastic future he will have when he is out of jail two or three years hence. Thus, through an ironic twist, Clouseau can contemplate a future paradise.

The Three Musketeers

Richard Lester's *The Three Musketeers,* purportedly the twelfth film version of Dumas's classic, is a parody of the romantic genre and of Dumas's work. The challenge was how to take this classic work and make it into a comedy.

Part of the solution was to give it a broad, farcical treatment in which sight gags abound. Comic characters also help. A comic touch is given by exaggerating some characters. The foppish king appears on a horse accoutered with a pair of large, silly-looking wings. In another scene, he is playing chess where the large board is laid out on the ground and the pieces are dressed-up dogs. One dog has an outfitted monkey sitting on its back. In a ball scene, the king mistakenly lines up on the wrong side of the queen and has to switch in order to proceed with the dance. He is a fool.

There is the old, stupid innkeeper with a beautiful young wife who cuckolds him and ends up with D'Artagnan. The innkeeper is tricked under a presumed threat of torture to help the Cardinal. As he is released, he accidentally sits on a hot potato heated by the torturers along with their torture instruments. The sexy wife enjoys being seduced by D'Artagnan. She provides the final visual joke of the film when a jousting dummy swings around and knocks her, face forward, into a pratfall.

Servants are incompetent. The Cardinal's guards are properly villainous. A protean beggar soliciting alms pretends to be a blind man, a cripple, an orphan and war veteran—in the same scene.

D'Artagnan's servant is a bumbling comic, a buffoon given to misfortune and put-downs. He is frequently used to supply a comic reaction. On shipboard he is hanging over the rail being sick. He falls off his horse. In a duel, he barely escapes being stabbed a number of times, then concludes the duel by a massive intervention with a huge wooden beam. When he is slapped by D'Artagnan for commenting that a woman is charming, he flatly replies, "Thank you."

Of course, there are also serious characters to develop the serious plot: the Cardinal, the Queen and Lord Buckingham, the Queen's lover.

Duel scenes are expected in the film. They are handled comically as clashes between brawlers and ruffians, as roughhouse free-for-alls rather than classic, formal duels. They develop with hat-stealing, various clever tricks, acrobatics (somersaults, pole vaults, swings on ropes), kicking behinds, comic hits and falls, flips into water, a dashing swing on a swing that fails and leads to a fall and the disconcerting presence of a chicken in one duel scene. In an early scene, D'Artagnan confidently challenges a nobleman to a duel only to have blows from a servant's shovel break his sword and smash his head. Once he tries to dramatically put a candle out with his sword's point only to fail and have to use his fingers (a parody of the romantic tradition). Another time he tries the old "jerk-up-the-rug-on-which-your-adversaries-are-standing-and-flip-them" trick and the rug tears apart in his hands. A dueling musketeer gets hooked from behind by a turning mill wheel and is hoisted up into the air.

There are the expected seduction scenes. One is filled with seductive subtext as D'Artagnan and the woman maneuver themselves into an embrace. Later, when embracing, she gets her foot stuck in a pot on the floor.

There are many physical comic bits. While chasing after a woman and trying to put his boot on at the same time, D'Artagnan has to fend off a dog who tugs persistently on his clothes. A man leaps onto his horse—only to miss and go flying offscreen. D'Artagnan swings on a rope to intercept a horseman and misses him. When the heroes ride under a tree, some dozen men jump from ambush in the tree to fall on them—but all of the men miss. When D'Artagnan throws the missing jewels up to the Queen's maid, he throws them into the wrong room.

D'Artagnan and his woman hide in a free-standing wardrobe and overhear that they are to be arrested. The scene concludes as the wardrobe falls over with them inside.

There occurs the previously described delay and fall when the man with the huge basket of eggs escapes being knocked over by a rolling barrel which just touches his leg. A moment later he trips and falls into the eggs.

There is one sequence in the film which is purely a comic break. In an inn, two musketeers pretend to quarrel and duel in order to distract the patrons while the others steal food from the unsuspecting diners. The servant uses bellows to suck wine from a glass being held by someone watching the fight. The innkeeper seems to notice what's going on, so they pay him for the inconvenience by throwing him a money bag—which turns out to be filled with sand or salt.

There is also social commentary in the film. It shows the pomposity of the rich nobles and the demeaning treatment given servants. Human life is taken lightly. "If anyone should follow me, would you be good enough to kill him." The contrasts between the rich and the poor are striking. In one scene, D'Artagnan and his servant are going to England. In order to be able to leave, D'Artagnan steals a pass from a Cardinal's man. The pass is for one, and there are two of them. The ship's captain says, "—only for one." D'Artagnan replies, "I am only one person. That is a servant." The captain avers, "All right."

The film is an enjoyable comic parody adapted from a classic romantic adventure tale.

The Out-of-Towners

The Out-of-Towners (directed by Arthur Hiller, screenplay by Neil Simon) is a more realistic comedy with believable people and plausible, though exaggerated, happenings. Its humor comes less from clowns and slapstick than from the frustrations of a couple who find everything going against them. Their adversary in this conflict is none other than New York City and the strange and intimidating things that can happen there to a couple from Ohio.

The man (Jack Lemmon) and his wife (Sandy Dennis) have come from Ohio so that he can have an important job interview which could mean a promotion to join the corporate offices in New York City. This is something he wants very badly, but she's uncertain, doubting that she can adjust to the pace and stress of the city. A transportation strike is paralyzing New York, so they couldn't fly in but had to take the packed train and stand all the way. In the city, they get mugged and robbed, and then kidnapped by some armed guys joyriding in a police car. At the point at which we'll pick them up—around the middle of the film—they are stranded in Central Park late at night with no money and no available transportation. His objective is at all costs to get to the interview the next morning looking as well-groomed and presentable as possible. Both of them perceive the city of New York and its lifestyle as an adversary trying to defeat them—and trying to keep him from realizing his objective. There is also an interpersonal storyline, for, as frustrations mount, they increasingly argue and bicker and their relationship is moderately threatened. What follows is an escalating series of misadventures as the story develops.

Thrown from the stolen police car, they try to walk out of Central Park but discover that she has broken a heel and cut her foot. He tries to carry her but can only get so far, so he decides they must spend the night sleeping in Central Park and hope for the best in the morning. He no sooner falls asleep when a man in a cape appears and she says her dry "Oh, my God . . . ," which is both a tag for her and a running gag in the film—she says it in a flat and resigned here-we-go-again way whenever she's aware of another problem.

The next morning, hungry and broke, they find a box of crackerjacks only to have it stolen by a dog. When they finally recover part of the box, he breaks his tooth biting on the prize; it makes him sibilantly whistle as he speaks. This increases his frustration, as it means he'll make an even worse impression in the promotion interview. He gets the dog's collar and writes down the owner's name, swearing to get even. (This is a running gag in the film as well as a bit of characterization. Any time someone crosses him—and this seems to happen continually—he writes down their name or badge number and threatens legal action—"My lawyer will get in touch with your boss.")

His wife informs him (exposition) that she gave his watch to the caped man in the park, who must surely have had a knife. Now he won't know the time and might miss his appointment.

They find a kid who only speaks Spanish sitting on a bench crying. The man wants to get a dime from the boy so he can call Traveler's Aid and get help. His wife cautions him not to try to do this where he might be seen, so he takes the boy off into the bushes. The camera remains on her as we hear his offscreen voice stumblingly apologizing to a deep-voiced, angry woman. He rushes out, grabs his wife's hand, and they run across a field in the park, pursued by a policeman on horseback. They manage to outrun him and hide. Why? the wife asks. How, he asks, could he explain why he had his hands in the boy's pockets in the bushes?!

Then she loses her wedding ring and refuses to leave the park until they search for it. He argues with her; he must be on time to the appointment or lose the job. As they are arguing, two joggers approach and punch him out, because they think he is attacking her. They find the ring.

Later, out of the park, he says that they were kicked off a bus for having no money—but he got the bus driver's number and will make him pay. (This is exposition of a scene that happened offscreen and outside of screen time. The exposition delivery is covered by his usual mumbling of vengeance against the bus driver.)

She feels beaten and stops and refuses to go any further. As they argue, we hear an ominous rumbling; he just steps off a gas main cover as it explodes, shoots into the air and crashes beside him with a resounding clang that leaves him temporarily deafened with ringing in his ears.

Desperate, they enter a church to pray but are told they can't do so because network television is setting up for a production there and the church won't be available for praying until that afternoon. He threatens that his lawyer will get off a letter to the network about that.

She is ready to give up and say that New York has beaten them. He isn't. In the early morning light, he steps into the middle of an intersection and shouts out to the city that he's not beaten—"I've got your names and addresses . . ."

They flag down a car to get a lift to their hotel, but it turns out to be the

Cuban delegate to the United Nations; they then get involved with angry protestors who rock the car—even though he keeps saying "Americanos" and she keeps adding "from Ohio." Police arrive and get them away safely but not before the news coverage of the protest, which shows him in the Cuban delegate's car. Now he feels he'll surely be turned down for the job.

At the hotel, he discovers that the key to his break-in-proof suitcase was in his stolen billfold, so he can't even change his clothes. He can't get any hot food. He's a mess. But he still goes to his interview.

In a music-over, MOS scene, he walks to his promotion interview and we see the company official greet him in a surprisingly warm and cordial fashion.

Back at the hotel, he informs his wife he was offered the position. She tells him she had hoped he wouldn't accept it. She enumerates all they've been through in the city, and says she wishes he had told both this to the executive and that he wanted to stay in Ohio. That's exactly what he said, he replies, word for word. (Both storylines are now resolved—his job interview and their interpersonal line of being happy together.)

The comedy then ends with a topper. They are on a plane returning to Ohio when the plane is hijacked to Havana. The last line is her: "Oh, my God. . . ."

REFERENCES

1. Groucho and Chico Marx in *Duck Soup*.
2. Walter Kerr, *Tragedy and Comedy* (New York: Simon and Schuster, 1967).
3. Jack C. Horn, ed., "Newsline. Humor: Sigmund, Here's a Joke on You" (a report of two psychological studies), *Psychology Today* 10 (April 1977): 30, 34.
4. My source for this as well as many of the other comic examples from the Silents is the fine book by Walter Kerr, *The Silent Clowns* (New York: Alfred A. Knopf, 1975).

Also:

Durgnat, Raymond. *The Crazy Mirror*. New York: Horizon Press, 1969.

Mast, Gerald. *The Comic Mind*. Indianapolis/New York: Bobbs-Merrill, 1973.

11

Adaptation

> Look, you can't be faithful to the book. Or, if you're faithful to the book, it's only where it's coincidental. You've got to be faithful to the audience.[1]
>
> —Nunnally Johnson

A BEGINNING WRITER is best advised to write an original screenplay which demonstrates his own imaginative ideas. However, at some point in his writing career, he will probably do some adaptations. Adaptations are prevalent in film. Some of the films and television programs that have been adapted from novels, short stories and theatrical plays are: *The African Queen, Catch-22, David Copperfield, Dr. Jekyll and Mr. Hyde, The Exorcist, Frankenstein, From Here to Eternity, The Godfather, Gone With the Wind, The Graduate, The Grapes of Wrath, Greed, The Informer, Jaws, Love Story, The Maltese Falcon, Of Mice and Men, One Flew Over the Cuckoo's Nest, The Poseidon Adventure, Psycho, Rashomon, Roots, Slaughterhouse Five, The Third Man, Tom Jones, Ulysses,* and *War and Peace.*

It has been estimated that for most years the proportion of American films based on novels is around 30 percent. Approximately 80 percent of the best-selling novels for each year are made into films. Some sixteen of the top twenty money-making films as of 1977 were adaptations. More than three-fourths of the Academy Awards "best-picture" awards have gone to adaptations, with about three-fourths of these based on novels or short stories. Some two-thirds of the New York Film Critics Awards for best motion picture have been for adaptations.[2]

The popularity of adaptations is understandable. Many properties used for adaptation have demonstrated audience appeal and critical response. They are, in effect, presold; audiences are attracted to the movie because of the success of the novel or play.

This prior recognition has been so important that until recently, a beginning writer who wrote a good original screenplay was well-advised to write his screenplay into the form of a novel and have it published somewhere—holding his script in reserve ready to submit if a producer showed interest in the book. This situation has changed so that today more producers are ready to examine original scripts. (Still, the novel route is a consideration if there is no immediate market for the script. Major studio story departments review novels—often in the galley-proof stage—ready to option any promising property.)

One consideration in making an adaptation is how closely the film should follow the original work. There is no proscribed answer. Some adaptations stay very close to the original material (as with the novel *The Maltese Falcon* and the play *Who's Afraid of Virginia Woolf*). Others are less similar and may be described as "freely adapted" or "based on" the original (*2001* and *Blow-Up*).

The film *Blow-Up* was little more than suggested by a short story, "Las Babas Del Diablo" ("The Devil's Drool;" i.e., "a close shave") by Julio Cortázar. A brief comparison of the film with the original shows some obvious differences.

The short story takes place in Paris, a very different setting from the mod London of the film. The story mentions jazz, while rock music is used in the film. In the short story, there is no murder; neither is there a studio visit to attempt to obtain the films nor a theft of the films. Michel, the photographer in the story, is also a writer, unlike Thomas. The photographs are taken in a Paris square, not in a park. The couple photographed are a young man and a somewhat older woman; in the film it is the other way around. The young man leaves the scene just after the photographs are taken. The woman and the photographer begin arguing and are soon joined by an accomplice of the woman—a man who was seated in a nearby parked car. In the story, it was an attempted homosexual pickup; the woman was trying to recruit the young man for the older man in the car. By taking his pictures, the photographer saved the young man from this.

What is common to both story and film is the build toward the moment of discovery. The photographers gradually discover the meaning of the blow-ups. We share with them this developing experience of discovery. But there is an interesting difference. In the short story, only one still picture is enlarged. In the film, the discovery comes from examining a series of blow-ups in a definite sequence—an arrangement that is significantly more "filmic."[3]

A successful film adaptation will be more of a paraphrase than a translation, since each medium has its own characteristics which militate against a direct translation. What is important is that the writer doing the adaptation retain the key elements from the original and catch its flavor—the "personality" or feeling-tone of the original.

The popularity of the original material affects how much one would want to change in an adaptation. With famous or best-selling novels such as *From Here to Eternity* or *War and Peace*, it would be inadvisable to eliminate major characters or events that the audience would expect in the film. Commercial considerations would suggest staying close to the novel to capitalize on the popularity and familiarity of the original.

Deep structure elements—story, characters, theme—may adapt to the film, but the aesthetic surface structure can be more elusive. So often it is the style of a work—the use of words and syntax which in accumulation create the total effect—that does not adapt well. Consider these two adaptations:

Slaughterhouse Five was a successful adaptation, perhaps actually improving on the novel in some respects by presenting the significance of the novel in a more striking and accessible form. The film is more personal and subjective for the central character Billy Pilgrim. Billy's dog plays a minor role in the book but is an important element in the film as a concrete object of Billy's affection. The film makes Lazzaro's threats against Billy more personal than does the novel. The events in the film develop more suspensefully. The film has a more positive ending, with Billy, Montana Wildhack and their baby happily settled on the planet Tralfamadore; the book ends back at the destruction of Dresden.

Catch-22 works less well as a film. The book is absurdly funny, the film less so. Incidents and characters that come to life in the reader's imagination translate less effectively to the concrete world of the film. In the specific, realistic film context, many of the characters and events of the novel seem rather stupid and not as funny as in the book. There is an absurd, almost surreal tone to the novel, which is needed in the film. Because a photograph is so literal, presenting the surface of reality, it is difficult to capture this absurd tone if the material is treated in a realistic manner as is done in the film.

There are problems adapting a novel to the screen. The novelist can do many things not so readily available to the filmmaker. A novelist can go into the thoughts and feelings of a character and describe what the character is wondering about or wishing for. Film can use voice-over technique or suggestive editing, but the effect is not as smooth. A novelist can directly point out the significance and meaning of an action or event, a gesture, a hesitation. Or the novelist can comment on an activity or condition, as when he writes, "John was not a natural listener." A novelist can mention contingencies not present in the scene by pointing out what a character *didn't* say or do or what a character might have or should have said or done. A novelist can casually mention the changing of events over time: "Harold made no friends of his own," or "Over the weeks, Ann became increasingly insulated and depressed." These can be expressed filmically, but not nearly as conveniently. A novel can also build its effect by easy references to absent actions and events: "He picked up the file at the Ministry yesterday through a minor subterfuge." A film writer has to forgo this ease and the effect of such references. He would have to either show the incident—which is probably too slight for such emphasis—or mention it in dialogue—which might be inappropriate to the character and circumstances.

Doing an Adaptation

Here are some suggestions as to how to proceed with doing an adaptation. The first thing is to become familiar with the original work. The first reading will give a general sense of the work. Subsequent readings will bring forth more specific details. Some writers might prefer to set the original aside awhile after the first reading to allow their unconscious time to cook over the material. Perhaps they'll jot down some subjective impressions if something comes. Then they go back for a more detailed analysis.

Since with a very loose adaptation there is little attempt to remain faithful to the original, the writer may merely identify those elements in the work that excite him and build from these. Or he may pick out only an essential element from the work—an unusual premise, intriguing situation or character—and write his own story from this. For example, Jerry Lewis' *The Nutty Professor* is a very free, comic variant of *Dr. Jekyll and Mr. Hyde*. It presents an awkward, unattractive chemistry professor who, by taking a secret potion, turns into the hip, aggressive, swinging Buddy Love.

If the adaptation is to be closer to the original work, it should be analyzed down to its basic elements—its deep structure—then built up from these as any film story would be, the writer, at the same time, trying to retain the flavor, the feeling-tone, of the original.

When analyzing the original, break it down to its basic storyline structure, including all complex storylines. Identify conflicts, problems and character objectives. List the major characters, their role in the story and their objectives and motivations. Map out character relationships. How do their relationships grow and change? How do they feel about each other? What do they want from each other? How do the characters grow and change over the script? Whose story is it? Then, outline the original work, sequence by sequence, briefly describing the function of each sequence in the story, the action in each sequence and its internal development. Finally, reassemble these elements—changing them, combining them, adding new elements as needed—to develop the script.

In keeping with the visual impact of film, try to show actions and events that are described in the original rather than have characters talk about them. It may be necessary to combine some characters into a single character, to eliminate other characters or to add new characters. Events and sequences may have to be eliminated or combined; new ones may have to be added. Some may be shortened, others extended.

A narrator might help overcome problems and make the adaptation work, as might flashbacks to show past events or to establish a structural unity (as in *Dr. Zhivago, Little Big Man* and *Serpico*).

A novel will usually have to be condensed in many ways, with some subplots and events and perhaps some characters eliminated. Where a novel is introspective, the script will have to find ways to externalize this with behavioral detail or filmic metaphor. Adapting a theatrical play often requires expansion—enlarging its scope by including locations and actions only alluded to in the play or adding others not mentioned. Try to present as much as you can visually, cutting down on some of the dialogue of the play so that the film won't seem too talky.

REFERENCES

1. Nunnally Johnson as quoted in William Froug, *The Screenwriter Looks at the Screenwriter* (New York: Dell Publishing Co., 1972), p. 246.
2. Morris Beja, *Film & Literature* (New York: Longman Inc., 1979).
3. Roy Huss, ed., *Focus on* Blow-Up (Englewood Cliffs, New Jersey: Prentice-Hall, 1971).

Also:

Bluestone, George. *Novels into Film*. Baltimore: Johns Hopkins University Press, 1957.

Harrington, John. *Film and/as Literature*. Englewood Cliffs, New Jersey: Prentice-Hall, 1977.

12

Documentary, Non-fiction, Fact Films

> A film of my father would be for me an exploration into a man I know little but love deeply. This exploration, and others like it, are a route to an understanding, man to man. And if we as humans can operate with compassion and truth, this type of film can become a base for wider understanding of ourselves.[1]
>
> —George Semsel

THIS WILL BE a brief introduction to the non-fiction film, whose intent is more communication and information than entertainment and aesthetic appreciation. The field of the non-fiction film is so broad that it would be difficult to attempt to cover even a portion of it in a single chapter. It includes such film types as ethnographic (*Nanook of the North, Circle of the Sun*), natural history (Disney's *The Living Desert* and *The Vanishing Prairie,* PBS *Nova*'s "Still Waters"), historical (*City of Gold, Czechoslovakia, 1968*), cultural, religious, personal, travel, informational, instructional, promotional, training, sales, public service, commercials, news, propaganda, industrial (including scientific and medical), scientific for the general public (as much of *Nova*), art films and many others.

Of all non-fiction film types, the documentary lays most claim to artistic excellence and in this is closest to the fiction film. The documentary has been defined as the creative interpretation of reality. It is more a personal expression of the filmmaker—in its classic type—than the dictation of client or sponsor. The television journalistic documentary is somewhat different, being an in-depth examination of an important news issue or social development.

There are many opportunities for writers in the non-fiction film field but few in documentaries, since the two major sources for documentaries today are television networks, which have a rather firm policy of developing their own journalistic documentaries and not accepting outside scripts, and the New Documentary filmmakers, who make their own films with usually little pre-scripting.

The classic period for documentaries was from the 1930s through the Second World War. This was the period of the British documentaries of Basil Wright, Harry Watt, John Grierson and others of the General Post Office film unit, of titles such as *Night Mail, Target for Tonight, Song of Ceylon, Fires Were Started, Listen to Britain* and *A Diary for Timothy*. In the United States, with only limited government support, documentaries were made by isolated filmmakers including Pare Lorentz, Willard van Dyke and Robert Flaherty, with such films as *The River, The Plow that Broke the Plains, Nanook of the North* and *Moana* (both made earlier), *The Battle of San Pietro,* the *Why We Fight* series and, with showings on early television, *Victory at Sea*.

Through most of the 1950s, the most noted television documentary series was Edward R. Murrow's and Fred Friendly's *See It Now*. In 1959–1960, the TV networks each started a major documentary series: *CBS Reports, NBC White Paper* and *ABC Close-Up;* thereafter, television became the major source for documentaries. These series have given us some notable programs: *Harvest of Shame, Sixteen in Webster Groves, The Selling of the Pentagon, Pensions: The Broken Promise, Fire!* and *The Business of Heroin*. Public television is now a promising outlet for documentary and non-fiction material. It has given us *Nova, The Ascent of Man, The Mind of Man* and the work of some New Documentarists.

There was a major change in the documentary around 1960 with the advent of Direct Cinema (cinéma vérité). It was brought about in part by technical innovation: lightweight film equipment, crystal sync, quality ¼-inch audio recorders and faster film stocks permitted more portable, flexible filmmaking. The New Documentary is characterized by a more committed, personal point of view on the part of the filmmaker. Little pre-scripting is done; a filming team often shoots from an outline—or from simply an idea—expecting to assemble the finished product in the editing room. (Allen King shot seventy hours of film—140,000 feet—to get a completed hour-and-a-half film, *A Married Couple*.)

There is a danger in filming this way. The "privileged moment," which the filmmaker hopes to capture, may never happen. Would *Warrendale* have worked without the death of the Black cook? Or *Salesman* without the disintegration of Paul to provide its required focus? Lacking a strong structure, the New Documentaries risk lagging audience interest. This happens with the Maysles's *Grey Gardens* (1976), which is interesting up to a point, but then repetitious and tiring.

Still, there is an excitement in these looser and bolder forms, in their approaching the subject matter of a film with few preconceptions, preferring to discover what's there and to respond to the material and action as it happens.

The New Documentary has given us Frederick Wiseman's *High School, Primate, Welfare, Titicut Follies* and *Hospital,* and the Maysles's *Salesman* and *Grey Gardens.* Marcel Ophuls has made the powerful *The Memory of Justice* and *The Sorrow and the Pity.* Barbara Kopple's *Harlan County, U.S.A.* was made without any narration. The PBS series *An American Family* gave us an intimate account of the joys and tribulations of the Loud family.

One of the most promising future developments, as yet largely unfulfilled, is with video. As color video equipment becomes more portable, dependable and inexpensive, and as home video players and video discs become more widely marketed, we could enter an intriguing and exciting media future.

An interesting variant of the non-fiction documentary is the fictionalized documentary or the docudrama. It is a semi-fictionalized presentation of actual incidents. Peter Watkins did something like this in his *Culloden,* in which this historic battle between the English and the Scots was treated as if it were being covered by live television. Feature films are often based on historical events and in some cases (as the British *Sink the Bismarck* and *The Pursuit of the Graf Spee* and the French *The Battle of Algiers*) can be rather authentic. But television is the real province of the docudrama. Some of its programs have been outstanding, illuminating the history they present: *21 Hours at Munich, The Missiles of October, The Pueblo Incident, Judge Horton and the Scottsboro Boys, Raid on Entebbe* and *Victory at Entebbe. Miss Jane Pittman* and *Roots* are similar to the type. *Washington: Behind Closed Doors* and *The Trial of Lee Harvey Oswald* are more doubtful in their authenticity.

The personal film is another development in non-fiction filmmaking. Filmmakers are turning the camera on themselves and on those with whom they are intimately involved. They are spontaneously revealing themselves and others on film or videotape in ways which at times seem more reminiscent of sensitivity group encounters or intimate family moments than traditional filmmaking. The results are more in the nature of explorations than predetermined works. Film becomes the medium to facilitate interaction and revelation.

The documentary of social issues has also taken a more personal turn in some films. In 1967, the National Film Board of Canada shot twenty hours of film on the economically depressed Fogo Island. The films were shot with the guidance and cooperation of the people of the island. A communion developed between the filmmakers and the people, and among the people themselves. The films were a catalyst to facilitate communication among individuals and communities. The Fogo Islanders selected the topics to be discussed and made editorial decisions; they decided whether and where the films were to be distributed. This is truly film for social change.

Writing the Non-Fiction Film

Writing the non-fiction film is analogous in many ways to writing the fiction film, but instead of a story, the subject will be an issue, idea, process or event.

Most non-fiction films are shorter than feature-length films and have to consider production exigencies, since they usually are made under low-budget restrictions. Before planning the film, there are a number of things the writer should know. You will want to know the length of the film, the general purpose of the film (e.g., public relations, training, instruction) and the specific purpose of the film (e.g., to inform, persuade, convince, reinforce, actuate, impress, promote, inspire, entertain, sell). Why make the film? What does the client or sponsor want the film to do?

You will need to know the budget for the film and any other exigencies of production, such as whether it will be shot on location or on a soundstage and if there will be sync sound or just a voice-over narration. You will need to know the intended audience for the film. You will want to determine any expectations of the sponsor.

Before you begin writing, you will need to thoroughly know the subject matter. Research is crucial in preparing the non-fiction film; know what you are writing about. If it is a journalistic issue, be familiar with all aspects of the issue. You may have a technical consultant from whom to get help, but this doesn't negate your responsibility to thoroughly know the subject, whether it be nuclear power plants, gun control, the use of Peyote in Indian rituals or the processing of sausage. Your research will include reading, field observation and interviewing. Jack Willis, who made *Hard Times in the Country,* a documentary on the abuses of the American food industry that was broadcast on public television in 1970, spent six months researching the film—studying reports and talking with farmers, congressmen, anyone who could provide information on the topic.

Just as a fiction film starts with a basic story, a scripted non-fiction film starts with a central concept—a basic premise, a core statement of what the film is about. This should be phrased in one or two sentences. It will serve as the unifying concept of the film. It clarifies your approach to the problem. It is expressed as concisely and precisely as possible and states what the audience should carry away with them after viewing the film.

In the documentary *Harvest of Shame,* Edward R. Murrow voices what might well be the premise of that film. His words, in effect, ask if the richest nation in the world wants to endure the plight of thousands of migrant workers who are ill-fed, ill-clad, continually degraded and living at a miserable bare-subsistence level. It is a harsh challenge—and that's what the film is about.

The basic concept should incorporate the focus of the film as much as possible, answering the question: what does the film say about its subject? Since this central concept is the focal point guiding the writing of the script, how it is phrased is important. Don't phrase your statement casually. It should include the particular stress and point of view of the film. Consider the different emphasis and focus in each of the following three premises for a film on college sororities.

> Although sororities have come under criticism recently, the experience a woman gets in a college sorority can be very meaningful to her.
>
> Sororities have come in for much recent criticism, yet an honest look at what happens in a sorority reveals that they are meaningful and valuable organizations.
>
> A sorority is more than a campus social organization; it makes a valuable contribution to the university and to the community as well as to the growth of its members.

The first approach is very personal and might well center on the experience of one woman in the sorority. The second could show a week with a sorority, giving the audience a feel for what happens in the organization. Both these approaches would point out the criticisms sororities have received. The third idea would stress sorority activities to the school and the community. Each has a different focus, which is expressed in the basic assertion of what the film is about.

Much of your initial work with a client will be to determine this focus. The client may know that he wants a film about, say, his museum's summer program for children. You would need to explore this further with the client in order to answer the question: What is it that you want to say about your museum's program?

A scripted non-fiction film will have some sort of logically organized pattern through which to present the subject matter. Such patterns include the chronological, the spatial (organized around locations and moving from one to another), cause to effect, problem to solution, simple to complex, familiar to unfamiliar, specific to general, general to specific, personal experience (concentrating on the experience of a person or group) or any other pattern suggested by the subject matter.

With your knowledge of the subject matter and purposes of the film, with your formulated central concept and an idea of the pattern to be used, you can now prepare an outline of the film. This is typically a succinct, present-tense, third-person summary of the film (analogous to a fiction film narrative story outline). Usually the briefer it is the better; this will help insure a unity to the film. You may then expand the summary into a more lengthy description or sequence outline. The outline should be reworked until satisfactory. Check it for sequence balance and pacing. Determine if the major points are made and if they are given adequate support and development.

To hold audience interest, try to incorporate conflict, the challenge of problems or of difficult choices. Some issues are intrinsically controversial, such as the pros and cons of gun control. It is natural to develop conflict through the presentation of opposing arguments.

There is conflict when you challenge or reveal an existing problem in society: *The Selling of the Pentagon* shows the questionable practices of Pentagon public relations activities, *Hard Times in the Country* exposes the manipulation and control of the American food industry. *Sixteen in Webster Groves* says to us, in effect: these are your children, the children of the American dream. Look at them as perhaps you've never really seen them before. Is this what you want them to be?

A non-fiction film, too, has its beginning, middle and end. The *beginning* captures the audience's attention, whetting their interest in the film. Most often the beginning lets the audience know what it will be seeing, what it can expect. This usually means presenting, in some form, the basic assertion of the film. The latter may be the major point to be supported and developed during the rest of the film; it may be the controversy the film examines; it may be the question the film explores; it may be a general introduction to the technique the audience is to learn from the film. In some way, the beginning usually cues the audience as to what they can expect from the rest of the film; it tells the audience why they should watch the film or why they should care about the subject matter of the film.

The *middle* develops the key assertion of the film, explores issues, makes points, presents arguments and controversy and otherwise develops the central concept. Points and arguments are often presented in ascending order, building to the most important, most interesting or most dramatic. If there is conflict and controversy, it is fully explored in the middle section. The middle should prove your point.

The *end* presents some sort of climax payoff. You draw your conclusions and give a summary of what has been presented—often in a key phrase or question or in a restatement of your basic premise. The end should leave your audience with what you would like to have them take away.

Many non-fiction films use narration. Keep your narration clear and understandable. Avoid heavy use of statistics, lists and confusing specialized terminology. Be economic with your narration; don't overcrowd it and make the film too talky. Integrate the visual and the narration, but avoid the "illustrated lecture" that results from first preparing a detailed narration and then matching visuals to it. Think visuals first! Avoid the "guided tour" approach of constantly describing what the camera is doing (e.g., "We are now entering the main salon dining room . . .")—we can see what it is doing. Consider using a personal second person ("you") and active voice to help involve the viewer. If the narration is pre-scripted, expect that changes will have to be made in it after editing. If using a live on-camera narrator, don't keep him alone on camera for such long stretches that it becomes tedious.

Remember that film writing is lean and economical. Keep your writing vivid, imaginative, clear and understandable. Keep the script moving; don't let it drag. Don't crowd the script by giving the audience a greater information density than they can reasonably process. Introduce emotional values to involve the audience and confict to keep interest going. Develop the habit of translating generalities into specific, meaningful images. "Military power" is expressed by visuals of planes, rockets, tanks; "widespread poverty" by tar-paper shacks, hungry-eyed children and scrawny dogs scavenging in garbage cans.

Let the visual carry as much of the message as possible. If you make an important point on the sound track, don't let the visual fight it with a distracting, off-point image (and conversely). Avoid unplanned conflict between visual and sound. Be sure your sequences always make a point. Personalize your film when you can. Show us people with whom we can identify; express points through people. The individual, the human face, is one of the most involving film images and encourages audience participation. (A striking sequence in *Harvest of Shame* occurs when Murrow talks with a young migrant child, about the age of eight or nine, living in a shack, who is taking care of her even younger brother. She artlessly underscores the message of the film as she describes the miserable poverty that is her everyday existence.)

In your outline, give special attention to the transitions between points. Write for implicit meaning as well as for explicit. Adopt a mood and tone appropriate to the subject matter, premise and purpose of the film.

Remember that much of what has been discussed for the fiction film will be applicable, in principle, to the non-fiction film.

Script format for the non-fiction film is often the split-page, two-column format used for television commercials. This format is presented in the Appendix. Films to be shot on location which can't be scripted in detail (as cinéma vérité and travel films) are often written in shot-list format. This is merely a list of sequences and scenes you expect to shoot, a guide for the actual location activity. Sometimes this is accompanied by a rough narration, sometimes it is not.

REFERENCES

1. George S. Semsel, "Toward a Personal Documentary," *Filmmakers Newsletter* 4 (July–August 1971): 56.

Also:

Jacobs, Lewis, ed., *The Documentary Tradition*. New York: Hopkinson and Blake, 1971.

Rosenthal, Alan. *The New Documentary in Action*. Berkeley: University of California Press, 1971.

Swain, Dwight. *Film Scriptwriting*. New York: Hastings House, 1976.

APPENDIX I

Marketing Your Script

IT IS DIFFICULT to market a script or script idea without an agent. Rarely will a studio or production company look at a submission from an unknown writer. Sometimes this is done if the writer first obtains a release form to include with his material in order to protect the studio from possible legal action; such forms are available from the studio or production company. However, the writer will usually find that this doesn't work. You can expect that you'll need an agent. A beginning writer should prepare some original material—scripts, series presentations—and try to find an agent who will look at them. A list of agents who are willing to look at the work of a new writer—sometimes for a fee—is available from the Writers Guild of America West, 8955 Beverly Boulevard, Los Angeles, CA 90048 (213–550–1000). A writer can have reasonable confidence in any agent recommended by the Guild.

There are some other long-shot possibilities. A feature film script can be rewritten as a novel and submitted for literary publication. It's a long route but a possible one. An easier possibility is to submit your script to a script contest, such as those sponsored by various film festivals or studios. University film departments and film schools will have announcements of these contests. An award-winning entry is usually given some follow-up studio exposure or is read by a producer. However, finding an agent is still your best bet.

A writer can protect any of his material—a script, a treatment or a series idea proposal—by registering it with the Writers Guild. The Guild offers this protection for a small fee ($10.00 as of this writing). It is available for members and non-members alike. Information can be obtained from the Writers Guild at the above address.

APPENDIX II

Script Formats

Motion Picture Script Format

The motion picture script format is a standardized method for composing the script on the page. One advantage of the format is that it times out to approximately one minute per page, which helps in estimating the timing of the script and its scenes. It is written in modified master scene form with a designation given for each scene. Usually the shots within each scene are given only a rough description (e.g., ANGLE or EMPHASIZING JOHN), since detailed shot choice is generally left to the director. However, variations on the basic format and the amount of detail described will depend on the individual writer, his market and his vision of the film.

It is standard to use a typewriter with pica type. With this size type, spacing for the script format is as follows.

Pages are usually numbered in the upper right-hand corner, two spaces from the top of the paper. Sometimes, instead, page numbers are centered in the upper middle of the paper. Either is appropriate.

The bottom line on the page shouldn't go lower than six lines from the bottom of the paper. Triple space between any two scenes. Double space between the scene or shot heading and anything else below it.

For horizontal spacing, set the paper edge at zero. Camera shots are numbered along both sides of each page. The horizontal spacing is then as follows:

15 Scene or shot number.

20 Camera directions and scene sluglines (typed in CAPITALS opposite scene or camera shot number) and general scene descriptions.

30–60 Dialogue. Dialogue is spaced in an approximately three-inch-wide column down the middle of the page.

35 Business. Business appears in parentheses and describes how a character should speak his lines. It should be used sparingly.

40 Character name—in CAPITALS.

60 Transitions, such as CUT TO, DISSOLVE TO, FADE OUT. CUT TO is usually implied and need not be written in each time you go to a new scene or shot.

75 Scene or shot number. Also page number if in upper right-hand corner.

If a scene continues to another page, write CONTINUED in the bottom right-hand corner at 60 spaces.

If a dialogue speech continues to the next page, write (MORE) at the bottom of the page and on the following page write the character's name, in capitals, followed by (Cont'd).

Scene or shot sluglines appear in all capitals, beginning with INTERIOR or EXTERIOR (often abbreviated as INT. or EXT.), then the subject of the camera shot, then DAY or NIGHT.

Capitalize within each scene/shot description the names of characters when they first appear in the script (and not after that), all camera cues, sound effects of any kind, including music, and any credits, titles or subtitles.

Use three dots (. . .) for a pause within a speech.

Use four dots (. . . .) if the speech trails off and concludes without formally ending the sentence.

Use a dash (—) for a break in thought or an interruption.

The telephone effect (filter), or voice over (VO) or offscreen dialogue (O.S.) may appear as parenthetical business, or opposite the character's name, as STEVE (O.S.).

A sample page of a script appears below. It is set up as though this is Shade's first appearance in the script, hence her name is capitalized.

Written in motion picture script format, a screenplay times out at approximately a minute a page. A half-hour teleplay runs from 30 to 40 pages, an hour teleplay from 55 to 70 pages, an hour-and-a-half teleplay from 90 to 110 pages, and a film script anywhere from 130 pages up.

15 INT. RESTAURANT - NIGHT 15

Peter and Curry are continuing their conversation. SHADE, a young woman in her mid 20s, enters. Curry can see her, but Peter can't as his back is to her.

CURRY
Are you sure?
You look like you make dirty movies.

PETER
I don't make dirty movies!

16 ANGLE - SHADE 16

SHADE
--But you'd love to, wouldn't you?!

17 MS - SHADE, PETER 17

PETER
(abashed)
Uh, hello, Shade.
I bet you didn't expect to see me.

SHADE
I bet you don't expect me to talk to you!
(to Curry)
This is him! The X-rated producer I told you about.

18 MS - CURRY 18

CURRY
(mock shock)
No! Well, well . . . .

DISSOLVE TO:

19 INT. RESTAURANT - LATER THAT NIGHT 19

Curry, Shade, Walt and Brad are relaxing at this late hour. Curry is stretched out on the bar. Shade and Brad are playing gin rummy. Liz comes sailing in full of her usual vigor.

CONTINUED

Three-camera Live Television Script Format

The format for a live television series script is a much looser form. There are very few separate scenes. Shots are not indicated. Dialogue is written in lower case type, all other material appears in capitals. New scene locations, visual instructions such as fade in or dissolve to, and sound effects are underlined as well as capitalized, for example: FADE IN, DISSOLVE TO:, INT. HALLWAY, INT. BUNKER HOUSE – MORNING. Dialogue is double spaced, descriptions and other material is single spaced. An example of this format appears on the following page.

ACT TWO

FADE IN

INT. RESTAURANT - LATER THAT NIGHT

(THE LAST FEW PATRONS LEAVE AND CURRY CLEARS AWAY THE LAST GLASSES. HE SITS AT THE BAR, HIS HEAD IN HIS HANDS. PETER ENTERS. CURRY DOESN'T NOTICE HIM AT FIRST.)

PETER

Hello. May I come in?

CURRY

Sure.

PETER

I came to see Ms. Altman--

CURRY

(POURING HIMSELF COFFEE)

--Shade?

PETER

Right, Shade. I tried her apartment upstairs, but there's no answer. Do you know--

SOUND: CLOCK STRIKING TWELVE

(CURRY STUDIES PETER QUIZICALLY WHILE THE CLOCK SOUNDS)

PETER

(HESITANTLY RESUMING)

Do you know if she'll be-- I mean-- it's rather important that I see her and

(MORE)

The Split-Page Format

The two-column, split-page format is used in local-station live television production, in many non-fiction films and in television commercials. The visual appears on the left side of the page, the audio on the right. The split-page format is less standardized than film format and may vary widely from one station or company to another. The example presented here is used for local-station live studio production. The visual descriptions are not scene descriptions, but rather camera movements and shots. Which cameras are used will be added in by the director during run-throughs. All material in lower case type is spoken on the air. Lines are often numbered, with the numbers running consecutively starting from one at the top of each new page (they are not so shown on this example). All sound cues are underlined and written in capitals. Talent cues are in capitals and parentheses. Visuals are in capitals and single-spaced, audio is double-spaced. There should be no hyphenated words at the ends of lines, and no sentences carried to the next page.

FADE IN: GRAPHIC TITLE (HOBBY HOUSE)	<u>THEME FULL . . . UNDER</u> ANNCR (VO): Hobby House--your weekly five-minute hobby program, giving you valuable hobby tips. Today in Hobby
DISS MS DOOR TO ROOM	House, we visit the photography room--and greeting us is the host of Hobby House, Larry Mitchell.
DOLLY THRU DOOR TO MLS MITCHELL	(DOOR SWINGS OPEN) <u>MUSIC OUT</u> MITCHELL: Hi again. Today I'm going to pass along some tips on how you can get first-class photographs of this glorious, warm-weather
FOLLOW MITCHELL TO DESK	scenery. (CROSSES TO DESK) I'll be talking about lighting and picture composition. And toward the end of the program, I'll show you some important tricks of the trade.
MS MITCHELL	But first things first. Many of you have written in wanting to know the best type of camera for general use. Chances are you'll want to stick with the smaller, lightweight cameras.

APPENDIX III

Glossary of Common Script Format Terms and Abbreviations

Shots

ANGLE: Used to refer to a new angle in the scene without the writer trying to specify just what the shot should be. Can sometimes be seen as: ANGLE ON HAROLD, ANGLE — INCLUDING GEORGE, ANGLE — VIC, ANOTHER ANGLE, ANGLE WIDENS, NEW ANGLE, REVERSE ANGLE.

BACK TO SCENE, SCENE: A shot description which might be used after an insert, signifying returning to the scene as it was previously shown.

CLOSE, CLOSER: A general designation to move the camera closer, as, CLOSE ON MONITOR, CLOSER ON HILDA, CLOSER ANGLE.

CU: Close-Up, as from shoulders up.

ECU: Extreme Close-Up, as of the eyes.

ELS: Extreme Long Shot. A very long shot as of a village, or of characters who are very small in the distance. Even wider is a *panoramic shot,* which covers the horizon.

FAVOR: To compose the shot so that it favors, say, one person over others in the shot, as, FAVOR MEREDITH.

INCLUDE: To include in the shot someone who was previously not there, as, INCLUDE MARION, INCLUDE GUESTS.

INSERT: A close shot of some object in the scene, usually inserted into shots of characters, as, INSERT—PRESCRIPTION BOTTLE.

INTERCUTS: To intercut back and forth between elements, as, INTERCUT: GEORGE-GLORIA.

LS: Long Shot, as a shot of two or three persons showing the complete person. Sometimes called a *full shot*.

MCU: Medium Close-Up, tighter.

MLS: Medium Long Shot, tighter in.

MS: Medium Shot, as from waist up.

OS: Over-Shoulder, a shot of someone over the shoulder of someone else, as, OS — JEAN.

POV: Point of View. A shot taken as a character would see something, as, JOHN'S POV.

RESUME-SHOT: A return to a shot after cutting away for an insert or point of view, as, RESUME-JOHN.

TCU: Tight Close-Up, as face.

TWO-SHOT: Two persons, usually in medium shot.

VLS: Very Long Shot, as of a crowd.

Transitions

CUT, CUT TO: An abrupt shot transition. Since it is used so frequently, it is often not typed in the script but assumed to be there if no other transition is given.

DISSOLVE, DISSOLVE TO: A transition from one shot or scene to another, involving an overlap during the transition.

FADE IN, FADE OUT: To come up on a picture from a blank screen, or to go to a blank screen. Used to begin and end a film, and for some internal transitions, usually those involving a large change of time and space.

Other less popular transitions include the WIPE, SPIRAL, DEFOCUS—FOCUS, SWISH PAN or WHIP, BLUR, PAN TO. Generally, avoid gimmicky transitions unless you have a good reason to use one.

Camera Movements

ARC: A combined dolly and truck, almost always with the camera moving in as it moves right or left. Can be used to maintain constant subject distance as camera moves sideways. Often used in live television.

CRANE SHOT: The camera moves up and away. Sometimes used to end films.

DOLLY IN, DOLLY OUT, DOLLY BACK: Camera moves toward or away from the subject. Sometimes seen as *pull back* or *move in*.

PAN: Left or right movement from a stationary camera.

TILT: Up or down movement from a stationary camera.

TRAVELING: A general term meaning the camera moves. Useful when following action. Also FOLLOW.

TRUCK: Right or left movement of the camera.

ZI, ZO, ZOOM IN, ZOOM OUT: In or out movement of the zoom lens of the camera.

Other Abbreviations and Terms

EXT: Exterior location.

FREEZE FRAME: A frame of the film is frozen as a still picture.

INT: Interior.

MONTAGE: A series of short shots combined for their total effect.

MOS: "Mit Out Sound," as when the scene is shot without any recorded sound, or is played without sound originating in the scene.

O.S.: Offscreen. Describing an action or sound happening offscreen.

RP: Rear Projection, as of a city skyline outside an apartment window on a studio soundstage set.

SPLIT SCREEN: Dividing the screen—usually into two halves—with different action in each half, as in showing two characters talking on the phone to each other with both on the screen.

SUPER, SUPERIMPOSITION: The superimposition of one image on top of another for a double-image effect.

VO: Voice Over, as a narrator's voice laid over the visual image.

APPENDIX IV

Television Series Idea Proposal

THERE IS A large market for television series ideas. An imaginative writer might prefer to come up with an idea for a series rather than work on a longer script. He can then propose this idea to the appropriate studio or production company either by submitting through an agent or by obtaining a release form and permission to submit directly. The idea should first be registered with the Writers Guild.

An effective series proposal will run about eight to ten pages. The first page will be the title page and include the title, the length and film or live nature of the show (such as, "A Half-Hour Situation Comedy to be Taped Before a Live Audience"). It will include the name of the series creator, his agent if he has one and a statement of Guild registration if it is registered.

The second page will contain a single paragraph description of the series and what makes it unique and special.

The third page will give a more detailed description of the series, the situation of the series, the setting and so on.

The next three or four pages will be character descriptions, with one paragraph describing each character.

The last few pages will present approximately four ideas for individual shows in the series—typical story ideas. These will be around one per page.

APPENDIX V

The Narrative Scene Schema of Christian Metz

HERE IS THE narrative scene schema of Christian Metz as presented in his *Film Language: A Semiotics of the Cinema,* translated by M. Taylor (New York: Oxford University Press, 1964). Metz describes eight narrative scenic elements embedded one within the other; I have tried to retain an indication of that pattern. I have somewhat modified his descriptions in order to make his outline more accessible.

1. *The autonomous single shot*

   This includes the "sequence shot," i.e., when an entire scene is treated in a single shot. (Godard has some examples of this in his films, some are also featured in *Annie Hall.*)

   This also includes *inserts.*

   An *explanatory insert* in enlarged detail, such as a close-up of a letter or visiting card.

   Displaced insert—a "real" image displaced from its normal filmic position and purposely intruded into another sequence, such as in a sequence showing pursuers, inserting a single shot of the pursued.

   Subjective insert—an image conveying an absent moment experienced by the film character, such as images of memory, dream, fear, premonition, and so on.

External insert—showing an object which is external to the action of the film, thus having a purely comparative function, as Eisenstein's inserted peacock as Kerensky climbs the stairs.

Non-chronological sequences (2 and 3)

2. *Parallel sequences*
   A systematic alternating of images in interwoven series, as scenes of the life of the rich interwoven with those of the poor, images of tranquility alternating with images of disturbance.

3. *Bracket sequences*
   A series of very brief scenes emphasizing their relationship, but this relationship is not chronological, such as the first erotic images of Godard's *A Married Woman* presenting a picture of "modern love" or the opening of Wurtmuller's *Seven Beauties* featuring varied images of destructive warfare.

Chronological sequences (4 through 8)

4. *Descriptive sequences*
   Spatial rather than temporal relations. Establishing sequences often do this, as showing a hill, a stream, a tree or such. Or, prisoners being marched, shots of prisoners, the guards, the commander. Such sequences are not read by the viewer as developing consecutively.

Narrative sequences (5 through 8)

5. *Alternate narrative sequences*
   As in a chase scene when cutting back and forth between pursuers and pursued, giving a feeling of simultaneity. Within each alternating series, the time sequencing is read as consecutive, but for the series as a whole it is taken as happening simultaneously.

Linear narrative sequences (6 through 8)—in which a single succession links together all the action seen in the images.

6. *Scene*
   The succession of events is a continuous linear narrative. The impression is of a unified and continuous segment with spatio-temporal integrality, existing in a place, for a period of time, with specific action (such as a dialogue scene).

Proper sequences (7 and 8)—the temporal quality is broken up; linear, narrative, chronological, but discontinuous.

7. *Episodic sequence*
   Organized discontinuity. A series of very brief scenes succeeding each other in chronological order and forming a meaningful and autonomous whole segment. (For example, the breakfast table sequence in *Citizen Kane,* which presents the progressive deterioration of Kane's marriage through a series of scenes at the breakfast table. Each scene takes place at a different time, but all form a unified, organized sequence.)

8. *Ordinary sequence* (the most common in film)
   The temporal discontinuity is unorganized. This is the common sequence made up of different scenes, from different locations, presenting the events which have meaningful relevance to the story.

References

(See individual chapters for other references.)

Blum, Richard A. *Television Writing: From Concept to Contract*. New York: Hastings House, 1980.

Brady, Ben. *The Keys to Writing for Television and Film*, 3rd ed. Dubuque, Iowa: Kendall/Hunt Publishing Company, 1978.

Brande, Dorothea. *Becoming a Writer*. New York: Harcourt, Brace and Company, 1934.

Braudy, Leo. *The World in a Frame*. Garden City, New York: Anchor Press/Doubleday, 1977.

Casebier, Allan. *Film Appreciation*. New York: Harcourt, Brace, Jovanovich, 1976.

Corliss, Richard, ed. *The Hollywood Screenwriters*. New York: Avon, 1972.

Corliss, Richard. *Talking Pictures*. New York: Penguin Books, 1974.

Cousin, Michelle. *Writing a Television Play*. Boston: The Writer, Inc., 1975.

Egri, Lajos. *The Art of Dramatic Writing*. New York: Simon and Schuster, 1946; revised and reprinted 1960.

Fell, John L. *Film: An Introduction*. New York: Praeger, 1975.

Froug, William. *The Screenwriter Looks at the Screenwriter*. New York: Delta/Dell, 1972.

Gessner, Robert. *The Moving Image*. New York: E. P. Dutton, 1970.

Giannetti, Louis D. *Understanding Movies* (2nd ed.). Englewood Cliffs, New Jersey: Prentice-Hall, 1976.

Herman, Lewis. *A Practical Manual of Screen Playwriting for Theater and Television Films*. New York: Meridian/New American Library, 1952.

Johnson, Ron, and Jan Bone. *Understanding the Film*. Stokie, Illinois: National Textbook Co., 1976.

Monaco, James. *How to Read a Film*. New York: Oxford University Press, 1977.

Nichols, Bill, ed. *Movies and Methods*. Berkeley: University of California Press, 1976.

Rilla, Wolf. *The Writer and the Screen*. New York: W. H. Allen, 1973.

Smiley, Sam. *Playwriting: The Structure of Action*. Englewood Cliffs, New Jersey: Prentice-Hall, 1971.

Swain, Dwight V. *Film Scriptwriting*. New York: Hastings House, 1976.

Trapnell, Coles. *Teleplay*. San Francisco: Chandler, 1966.

Vale, Eugene. *The Technique of Screenplay Writing*. New York: Grosset and Dunlap, 1944, revised and reprinted 1972.

Willis, Edgar W. *Writing Television and Radio Programs*. New York: Holt, Rinehart and Winston, 1967.

Filmography

(Following the film title is the name of the director, then the screenwriter(s) of record. A single name appears if the film is a documentary and considered the work of this one filmmaker.)

Abbott and Costello Meet Frankenstein. Barton; Lees, Rinaldo, Grant, 1948.
Admirable Crichton, The. Gilbert; Harris, 1957.
African Queen, The. Huston; Agee, Huston, 1951.
Airport. Seaton; Seaton, 1970.
Alfie. Gilbert; Naughton, 1966.
Alien. Scott; O'Bannon, Shusett, 1979.
All About Eve. Mankiewicz; Mankiewicz, 1950.
All Quiet on the Western Front. Milestone; Andrews, Anderson, Abbott, 1930.
All the President's Men. Pakula; Goldman, 1976.
Amarcord. Fellini; Fellini, Guerra, 1974.
American Graffiti. Lucas; Lucas, Katz, Huyck, 1973.
Animal Crackers. Heerman; Ryskind, Collings, 1930.
Annie Hall. Allen; Allen, Brickman, 1977.
Apartment, The. Wilder; Wilder, Diamond, 1960.
Auntie Mame. DaCosta; Comden, Green, 1958.

Bad Day at Black Rock. Sturges; Kaufman, 1954.
Bananas. Allen; Allen, Rose, 1971.

Barry Lyndon. Kubrick; Kubrick, 1975.
Battle of Algiers, The. Pontecorvo; Solinas, Pontecorvo, 1966.
Battle of San Pietro, The. Huston, 1945.
Battleship Potemkin, The. Eisenstein; Eisenstein, 1925.
Belle de Jour. Buñuel; Buñuel, 1966.
Billy Jack. Frank; Christina, Frank, 1971.
Birds, The. Hitchcock; Hunter, 1963.
Birth of a Nation. Griffith; Griffith, Woods, Dixon, 1915.
Blazing Saddles. Brooks; Brooks, Steinberg, Bergman, Pryor, Uger, 1974.
Blow-Up. Antonioni; Antonioni, Guerra, 1966.
Bob and Carol and Ted and Alice. Mazursky; Mazursky, Tucker, 1969.
Bonnie and Clyde. Penn; Newman, Benton, 1967.
Breathless. Godard; Godard, 1961.
Bridge on the River Kwai, The. Lean; Boulle, 1957.
Brief Encounter. Lean; Coward, 1946.
Butch Cassidy and the Sundance Kid. Hill; Goldman, 1969.

Cabaret. Fosse; Allen, 1972.
Caine Mutiny, The. Dmytryk; Roberts, 1954.
Carnal Knowledge. Nichols; Feiffer, 1971.
Carrie. DePalma; Cohen, 1976.
Casablanca. Curtiz; Epstein, Epstein, Koch, 1944.
Cat People. Tourneur; Bodeen, 1942.
Catch-22. Nichols; Henry, 1970.
China Syndrome, The. Bridges; Gray, Cook, Bridges, 1979.
Chinatown. Polanski; Towne, 1974.
Circle of the Sun. Low, 1961.
Citizen Kane. Welles; Mankiewicz, Welles, 1941.
City of Gold. Low, 1957.
Clockwork Orange, A. Kubrick; Kubrick, 1971.
Close Encounters of the Third Kind. Spielberg; Spielberg, 1977.
Cocoanuts, The. Santley; Ryskind, 1929.
Coming Home. Ashby; Dowd, Salt, Jones, 1978.
Conformist, The. Bertolucci; Bertolucci, 1971.
Conversation, The. Coppola; Coppola, 1974.
Cool Hand Luke. Rosenberg; Pearce, Pierson, 1967.
Cooley High. Schultz; Monte, 1975.
Cousin, Cousine. Tacchella; Tacchella, 1975.
Cria. Saura; Saura, 1977.
Cries and Whispers. Bergman; Bergman, 1972.
Culloden. Watkins; Watkins, 1967.
Czechoslovakia, 1968. USIA, 1970.

Dark Passage. Daves; Daves, 1947.
David Copperfield. Cukor; Estabrook, 1935.
Day for Night. Truffaut; Truffaut, Schiffman, Richard, 1973.
Day of the Jackal, The. Zinnemann; Ross, 1973.
Death of a Bureaucrat. Alea; Del Cueto, Suarez, Alea, 1966.
Deliverance. Boorman; Dickey, 1972.

Diary for Timothy, A. Jennings; Forster, 1945.
Diary of a Country Priest. Bresson; Bresson, 1950.
Dirty Harry. Siegel; Fink, Fink, Riesner, 1971.
Disorderly Orderly, The. Tashlin; Tashlin, 1964.
Discreet Charm of the Bourgeoisie, The. Buñuel; Buñuel, Carriere, 1972.
Dr. Jekyll and Mr. Hyde. Mamoulian; Hoffenstein, Heath, 1932.
Dr. Jekyll and Mr. Hyde. Fleming; Mahin, 1941.
Dr. Strangelove. Kubrick; Kubrick, Southern, George, 1964.
Dr. Zhivago. Lean; Bolt, 1965.
Dodes'ka'den. Kurosawa; Kurosawa, Oguni, Hashimoto, 1970.
Don't Go Near the Water. Walters; Kingsley, Wells, 1957.
Doubletalk. Beattie; Beattie, 1975.
Duck Soup. McCarey; Kalmar, Ruby, 1933.
Duel. Spielberg; Matheson, 1971.

Earthquake. Robson; Fox, Puzo, 1974.
Easy Rider. Hopper; Fonda, Hopper, Southern, 1969.
8½. Fellini; Fellini, Flaiano, Pinelli, Rondi, 1963.
El Topo. Jodorowsky; Jodorowsky, 1970.
Exorcist, The. Friedkin; Blatty, 1973.

Fail-Safe. Lumet; Bernstein, 1964.
Fingers. Toback; Toback, 1978.
Fires Were Started. Jennings; Jennings, 1943.
Five Easy Pieces. Rafelson; Eastman, 1970.
Fort Apache. Ford; Nugent, 1948.
Four Feathers. Korda; Garrett, 1939.
Frankenstein. Whale; Fort, Faragoh, 1931.
French Connection, The. Friedkin; Tidyman, 1971.
Freshman, The. Taylor & Newmeyer; Taylor, Grey, Wilde, Whelan, 1925.
From Here to Eternity. Zinnemann; Taradash, 1953.

Geisha Boy, The. Tashlin; Tashlin, 1958.
General, The. Keaton; Boasberg, Smith, 1927.
Giant. Stevens; Guiol, Moffat, 1956.
Godfather, The. Coppola; Puzo, Coppola, 1972.
Gold Rush, The. Chaplin; Chaplin, 1925.
Golem, The. Wegener; Wegener, Galeen, 1920.
Gone With the Wind. Fleming; Howard, 1939.
Good, the Bad, and the Ugly, The. Leone; Vincenzoni, Leone, 1968.
Goodbye Columbus. Peerce; Schulman, 1969.
Goodbye Girl, The. Ross; Simon, 1977.
Graduate, The. Nichols; Willingham, Henry, 1967.
Grapes of Wrath, The. Ford; Johnson, 1940.
Greed. Von Stroheim; Von Stroheim, 1924.
Grey Gardens. Maysles, 1976.

Halloween. Carpenter; Carpenter, Hill, 1978.
Hard Times in the Country. Willis; Willis, 1970.
Harlan County, U.S.A. Kopple, 1977.

Harold and Maude. Ashby; Higgins, 1972.
Harp of Burma, The. Ichikawa; Wada, 1956.
Harry and Tonto. Mazursky; Mazursky, Greenfield, 1974.
Haunting, The. Wise; Gidding, 1963.
Hellzapoppin. Potter; Perrin, Wilson, 1941.
High Anxiety. Brooks; Brooks, Clark, DeLuca, Levinson, 1977.
High Noon. Zinnemann; Foreman, 1952.
High Plains Drifter. Eastwood; Tidyman, 1973.
High School. Wiseman, 1968.
Hiroshima, Mon Amour. Resnais; Duras, 1960.
Hospital. Wiseman, 1970.
Hospital, The. Hiller; Chayefsky, 1971.
Hotel. Quine; Mayes, 1967.
Hour of the Wolf. Bergman; Bergman, 1968.
How Tasty Was My Little Frenchman. Dos Santos; Dos Santos, 1971.
Husbands. Cassavetes; Cassavetes, 1970.

I Am a Camera. Cornelius; Collier, 1955.
If. . . . Anderson; Sherwin, 1969.
Ikiru. Kurosawa; Hashimoto, Oguni, Kurosawa, 1952.
Informer, The. Ford; Nichols, 1935.
Intolerance. Griffith; Griffith, 1916.
It's a Wonderful Life. Capra; Goodrich, Hackett, Capra, 1946.

Jaws. Spielberg; Benchley, Gottlieb, 1975.
Joseph Andrews. Richardson; Scott, Bryant, 1977.
Jules and Jim. Truffaut; Truffaut, Gruault, 1961.
Juliet of the Spirits. Fellini; Fellini, Flaiano, Pinelli, Rondi, 1965.

Kelly's Heroes. Hutton; Martin, 1970.
Knife in the Water. Polanski; Polanski, Skolimowski, Goldberg, 1963.
Knock on Wood. Panama; Panama, Frank, 1954.
Kwaidan. Kobayashi; Mizuki, 1965.

La Chinoise. Godard; Godard, 1967.
La Dolce Vita. Fellini; Fellini, Flaiano, Pinelli, Rondi, 1961.
La Grande Illusion. Renoir; Spaak, Renoir, 1937.
La Strada. Fellini; Fellini, Pinelli, Flaiano, 1954.
Lady from Shanghai, The. Welles; Welles, 1948.
Lady in the Lake. Montgomery; Fisher, 1946.
Lancelot du Lac. Bresson; Bresson, 1974.
Last Picture Show, The. Bogdanovich; McMurty, Bogdanovich, 1971.
Last Remake of Beau Geste, The. Feldman; Feldman, Allen, 1977.
Last Tango in Paris. Bertolucci; Bertolucci, Arcalli, 1973.
Last Year at Marienbad. Resnais; Robbe-Grillet, 1962.
Laura. Preminger; Dratler, Hoffenstein, Reinhardt, 1944.
L'Avventura. Antonioni; Antonioni, Bartolini, Guerra, 1960.
Lawrence of Arabia. Lean; Bolt, 1962.
Les Ordres. Brault; Brault, 1974.
Lifeboat. Hitchcock; Swerling, 1944.

Listen to Britain. Jennings, 1941.
Little Big Man. Penn; Willingham, 1970.
Living Desert, The. Algar; Algar, Hibler, Sears, Moffitt, 1953.
Looking for Mr. Goodbar. Brooks; Brooks, 1977.
Love and Death. Allen; Allen, 1975.
Love Story. Hiller; Segal, 1970.

M. Lang; Von Harbou, 1931.
Magnificent Ambersons, The. Welles; Welles, 1942.
Maltese Falcon, The. Huston; Huston, 1941.
Man for All Seasons, A. Zinnemann; Bolt, 1966.
Manhattan. Allen; Allen, Brickman, 1979.
Married Couple, A. King, 1969.
Marty. Mann; Chayefsky, 1955.
Mary, Queen of Scots. Jarrott; Hale, 1971.
Masculine-Feminine. Godard; Godard, 1966.
*M*A*S*H*. Altman; Lardner, 1970.
Mean Streets. Scorsese; Scorsese, Martin, 1973.
Meet John Doe. Capra; Riskin, 1941.
Memory of Justice, The. Ophuls, 1976.
Mickey One. Penn; Surgal, 1965.
Midnight Cowboy. Schlesinger; Salt, 1969.
Midnight Man, The. Kibbee; Kibbee, Lancaster, 1974.
Missouri Breaks, The. Penn; McGuane, 1976.
Mr. Deeds Goes to Town. Capra; Riskin, 1936.
Mr. Hulot's Holiday. Tati; Tati, Marquet, 1954.
Mr. Klein. Losey; Solinas, 1976.
Mr. Smith Goes to Washington. Capra; Buchman, 1939.
Moana. Flaherty, 1926.
Modern Times. Chaplin; Chaplin, 1936.
Monkey Business. McLeod; Perelman, Johnstone, 1931.
Murder by Decree. Clark; Hopkins, 1979.
My Name Is Nobody. Valerii; Gastaldi, 1974.

Nanook of the North. Flaherty, 1924.
Network. Lumet; Chayefsky, 1976.
Night at the Opera, A. Wood; Kaufman, Ryskind, 1935.
Night Full of Rain, A. Wurtmuller; Wurtmuller, 1978.
Night in Casablanca, A. Mayo; Fields, Kibbee, 1946.
Night Mail. Wright & Watt; Wright, Watt, 1936.
Nine Hours to Rama. Robson; Gidding, 1963.
North by Northwest. Hitchcock; Lehman, 1959.
Nosferatu. Murnau; Galeen, 1922.
Nutty Professor, The. Lewis; Lewis, Richmond, 1963.

O Lucky Man. Anderson; Sherwin, 1973.
Of Mice and Men. Milestone; Solow, 1939.
Omen, The. Donner; Seltzer, 1976.
On the Waterfront. Kazan; Schulberg, 1954.

Once Upon a Time in the West. Leone; Leone, Donati, 1969.
One Flew Over the Cuckoo's Nest. Forman; Blatty, 1975.
Out-of-Towners, The. Hiller; Simon, 1970.

Paper Moon. Bogdanovich; Sargent, 1973.
Parallax View, The. Pakula; Giler, Semple, 1974.
Passenger, The. Antonioni; Peploe, Wollen, Antonioni, 1975.
Paths of Glory. Kubrick; Kubrick, Willingham, Thompson, 1957.
Patton. Schaffner; Cappola, North, 1970.
Pawnbroker, The. Lumet; Friedkin, Fine, 1965.
Persona. Bergman; Bergman, 1966.
Pierrot le Fou. Godard; Godard, 1965.
Pigpen. (*Pigsty*.) Pasolini; Pasolini, 1969.
Pink Panther, The. Edwards; Richlin, Edwards, 1964.
Pink Panther Strikes Again, The. Edwards; Waldman, Edwards, 1976.
Planet of the Apes. Schaffner; Wilson, Serling, 1968.
Play It Again, Sam. Ross; Allen, 1972.
Plow that Broke the Plains, The. Lorentz; Lorentz, 1936.
Poseidon Adventure, The. Neame; Silliphant, Mayes, 1972.
President's Analyst, The. Flicker; Flicker, 1967.
Pretty Baby. Malle; Platt, 1978.
Primate. Wiseman, 1974.
Psycho. Hitchcock; Stefano, 1960.
Public Enemy. Wellman; Thew, 1931.
Pure Hell of St. Trinians, The. Launder; Gilliat, Launder, Valentine, 1961.
Pursuit of the Graf Spee, The. Powell; Powell, Pressburger, 1957.

Rachel, Rachel. Newman; Stern, 1968.
Rashomon. Kurosawa; Kurosawa, Hashimoto, 1951.
Red Balloon, The. Lamorisse; Lamorisse, 1956.
Red Desert. Antonioni; Antonioni, Guerra, 1964.
Return of the Pink Panther, The. Edwards; Waldman, Edwards, 1975.
River, The. Lorentz; Lorentz, 1937.
Rocky. Avildsen; Stallone, 1976.
Roma. Fellini; Fellini, Zapponi, 1972.
Romeo and Juliet. Zeffirelli; Brusati, D'Amico, Zeffirelli, 1966.
Rosemary's Baby. Polanski; Polanski, 1968.

Saboteur. Hitchcock; Viertel, Harrison, Parker, 1942.
Salesman. Maysles, 1969.
Samurai Trilogy, The. Inagaki; Wakao, Inagaki, 1954–1956.
Sanjuro. Kurosawa; Kikushima, Oguni, Kurosawa, 1962.
Satyricon. Fellini; Fellini, Zapponi, 1969.
Serpent's Egg, The. Bergman; Bergman, 1978.
Serpico. Lumet; Wilson, 1973.
Servant, The. Losey; Pinter, 1963.
Seven Beauties. Wertmuller; Wertmuller, 1976.
Seven Samurai. Kurosawa; Kurosawa, Hashimoto, Oguni, 1954.
Seventh Seal, The. Bergman; Bergman, 1956.

Sex and the Single Girl. Quine; Heller, Schwartz, 1964.
Shane. Stevens; Guthrie, 1953.
She Wore a Yellow Ribbon. Ford; Nugent, Stallings, 1949.
Shoot the Piano Player. Truffaut; Moussy, Truffaut, 1962.
Short Eyes. Young; Piñero, 1977.
Silent Movie. Brooks; Brooks, Clark, DeLuca, Levinson, 1976.
Sink the Bismarck. Gilbert; North, 1960.
Slaughterhouse Five. Hill; Geller, 1972.
Sleeper. Allen; Allen, Brickman, 1973.
Small Change. Truffaut; Truffaut, 1976.
Some Like It Hot. Wilder; Wilder, Diamond, 1959.
Song of Ceylon. Wright; Wright, 1934.
Sorrow and the Pity, The. Ophuls, 1972.
Spartacus. Kubrick; Trumbo, 1960.
Spellbound. Hitchcock; Hecht, 1945.
Star Wars. Lucas; Lucas, 1977.
Steamboat Bill, Jr. Reisner; Harbaugh, 1928.
Sting, The. Hill; Ward, 1973.
Straw Dogs. Peckinpah; Peckinpah, Goodman, 1971.
Sullivan's Travels. Sturges; Sturges, 1941.
Sunday, Bloody Sunday. Schlesinger; Gilliatt, 1971.
Sunset Boulevard. Wilder; Brackett, Wilder, Marshman, 1950.
Sweet Movie. Makavejev, 1974 (no screenplay credit).
Swept Away. Wertmuller; Wertmuller, 1975.

Take the Money and Run. Allen; Allen, Rose, 1969.
Target for Tonight. Watt; Watt, 1941.
Taxi Driver. Scorsese; Schrader, 1976.
Third Man, The. Reed; Greene, 1949.
39 Steps, The. Hitchcock; Harvey, 1935.
Three Musketeers, The. Lester; Fraser, 1974.
Through a Glass Darkly. Bergman; Bergman, 1962.
Titicut Follies. Wiseman, 1967.
Tom Jones. Richardson; Osborne, 1963.
Touch of Class, A. Frank; Frank, Rose, 1973.
Tout va Bien. Godard; Godard, Gorin, 1972.
Towering Inferno, The. Guillermin & Allen; Silliphant, 1974.
Track of the Cat. Wellman; Bezzerides, 1954.
Trial of Billy Jack, The. Laughlin; Christina, Christina, 1974.
2001: A Space Odyssey. Kubrick; Kubrick, Clarke, 1968.

Ulysses. Strick; Strick, Haynes, 1967.

Vampyr. Dreyer; Dreyer, Jul, 1932.
Vanishing Prairie, The. Algar; Algar, Hibler, Sears, 1954.
Vertigo. Hitchcock; Coppel, Taylor, 1958.
Viva Zapata! Kazan; Steinbeck, 1952.

Walkabout. Roeg; Bond, 1971.
War and Peace. Vidor; Boland, Westerby, Vidor, Camerini, De Concini, Perilli, 1956.

War and Peace. Bondarchuk; Bondarchuk, Solovyov, 1968.
Warrendale. King, 1967.
Way We Were, The. Pollack; Laurents, 1973.
Wedding, A. Altman; Altman, 1978.
Weekend. Godard; Godard, 1967.
Welfare. Wiseman, 1975.
What's Up, Doc? Bogdanovich; Henry, Newman, Benton, 1972.
What's Up, Tiger Lily? Allen; Allen, Buxton, Maxwell, Lasser, Rose, 1966.
Who's Afraid of Virginia Woolf. Nichols; Lehman, 1966.
Wilby Conspiracy, The. Nelson; Amateau, Nebenzai, 1975.
Wild Bunch, The. Peckinpah; Green, Peckinpah, 1969.
Wild One, The. Benedek; Paxton, 1954.
Wizard of Oz, The. Fleming; Langley, Ryerson, Wolfe, 1939.
Woman in the Dunes, The. Teshigahara; Abe, 1964.
World's Greatest Lover, The. Wilder; Wilder, 1977.

Yojimbo. Kurosawa; Kikushima, Kurosawa, 1961.
Young Frankenstein. Brooks; Wilder, Brooks, 1974.
Young Mr. Lincoln. Ford; Trotti, 1936.

Z. Costa-Gavras; Costa-Gavras, Semprun, 1969.
Zorba the Greek. Cacoyannis; Cacoyannis, 1964.

Index